Among the Tuareg people in the Aïr Mountain region of Niger, women are sometimes possessed by spirits called "the people of solitude." The evening curing rituals of the possessed, featuring drumming and song, take place before an audience of young men and women, who joke and flirt as the ritual unfolds. In her analysis of this tolerated but unofficial cult, Susan Rasmussen analyses symbolism and aesthetic values, provides case studies of possessed women, and reviews what local people think about the meaning of possession.

Cambridge Studies in Social and Cultural Anthropology

94

SPIRIT POSSESSION AND PERSONHOOD AMONG THE KEL EWEY TUAREG

Cambridge Studies in Social and Cultural Anthropology

Editors: Ernest Gellner, Jack Goody, Stephen Gudeman, Michael Herzfeld, Jonathan Parry

Cambridge Studies in Social and Cultural Anthropology publishes analytical ethnographies, comparative works, and contributions to theory. All combine an expert and critical command of ethnography and a sophisticated engagement with current theoretical debates.

A list of books in the series will be found at the end of the volume.

SPIRIT POSSESSION AND PERSONHOOD AMONG THE KEL EWEY TUAREG

SUSAN J. RASMUSSEN
University of Houston

CAMBRIDGE
UNIVERSITY PRESS

Published by the Press Syndicate of the University of Cambridge
The Pitt Building, Trumpington Street, Cambridge CB2 1RP
40 West 20th Street, New York, NY 10011–4211, USA
10 Stamford Road, Oakleigh, Melbourne 3166, Australia

First published 1995

Printed in Great Britain at the University Press, Cambridge

A catalogue record for this book is available from the British Library

Library of Congress cataloguing in publication data
Rasmussen, Susan J., 1949–
    Spirit possession and personhood among the Kel Ewey Tuareg / Susan
J. Rasmussen.
        p.   cm. – (Cambridge studies in social and cultural
anthropology : 94)
    Includes bibliographical references (p.   ) and index.
    ISBN 0 521 47007 2 (hc)
    1. Tuaregs – Religion.   2. Spirit possession – Niger.   3. Women,
Tuareg – Religious life.   I. Title.   II. Series.
BL2480.T82R37   1995
299′.33 – dc20   94–11233   CIP

ISBN 0 521 47007 2 hardback

Contents

Acknowledgments

It would be impossible to mention all the residents of Niger who helped me as informants and as friends, but I owe particular thanks to Mesdames Chabo Dila and Salma Enfa, to Messieurs Mohammed Amouha and Ibrahim Ihossey, and to their families, whose welcome and generous hospitality were indispensable. Azori Falaina, chief of the Kel Igurmaden descent group of the Kel Ewey Tuareg and of the primary village where I resided in 1983/84 and again in 1991, was unfailingly helpful. The director of the local primary nomadic school during my earlier visit, now deceased due to a tragic accident in 1984, graciously assisted me in grasping more precisely the meaning of certain concepts in the Tamacheq language by working with me on transcriptions of possession song texts, folk tales, riddles, popular songs, life crisis rite music, and life histories.

A number of fascinating conversations with many other people, in Agadez, Niamey, and in the Bagzan region of the Aïr Mountains, also helped deepen my knowledge. In addition, I gratefully acknowledge the influences of my teachers outside Niger, who include a number of Africanist scholars as well as social and cultural anthropologists, particularly Ivan Karp, Martha Kendall, Michael Herzfeld, John Johnson, and Charles Bird during my graduate and postgraduate studies. Roy Wagner's early influences, pointing me in the direction of symbolism and systems of thought, and the Africanist perspectives of Johannes Fabian and Robert LeVine are also evident in this study. I also owe a considerable intellectual debt to many other scholars who have contributed to the framework of this book, major portions of which I completed during residence at the Smithsonian Institution on a Postdoctoral Research Fellowship (1989/90). I am grateful for the kind assistance of Mary Jo Arnoldi, Paula Girshick, Chris Mullen Kraemer, William Merrill, Paul Stoller, and Richard

Werbner. Finally, I gratefully acknowledge the valuable editorial suggestions concerning writing, and other assistance on copy-editing matters,
from anonymous readers, from Jessica Kuper at Cambridge University
Press, and Katherine Hagedorn at Pomona College, and encouragement
from my husband, Manuel Heredia.

My initial academic interest in the relation between religion and gender
led me to examine social and ritual roles of women, their image in Tuareg
cosmology, and the causation invoked to explain their illnesses (Rasmussen
1987, 1989, 1991a). I also examined how women adapted to contradictions
and stresses in their socio-economic roles (Rasmussen 1985, 1991b). I first
became interested in female spirit possession among the Tuareg while
intermittently in this region during my initial five years of residence in
Niger: near Mount Bagzan in north-east Aïr during the rainy seasons of
1977 and 1978, and in the town of Agadez for a year in 1976, when I
observed a number of spirit possession rituals in Agadez and in the
surrounding countryside.

From 1974 to 1979 I taught secondary school in Niger's capital, Niamey,
and in Agadez I was first a Peace Corps volunteer and later under local
contract for the Nigerien Ministry of Education. During that time, I was
involved in preliminary field research, curriculum planning, and the study
of local languages, Hausa and Tamacheq. I studied Tamacheq intensively
for one-and-a-half years with Monsieur Alitinin Ag Arias at the Centre de
la Tradition Orale in Niamey, and continued my studies informally during
independent travels and residence in the north of the country. Later, I
returned to conduct doctoral research near Mount Bagzan in 1983, through
the generous assistance of the Fulbright Hays Doctoral Research grant and
the Indiana University Grant-in-Aid, and again for three months during
the summer of 1991, with assistance from the Wenner-Gren Foundation for
Anthropological Research and a University of Houston Limited Grant-in-
Aid. I also had the benefit of suggestions and support from: Monsieur le
Directeur of the Centre de Recherches en Sciences Humaines; the Préfet,
Sous-préfet, Sultan, and Anestafidet (traditional leaders); as well as friends
in Agadez, through whom I was able to make contact with local leaders and
other residents and to settle in caravanning villages and semi-nomadic
camps, and eventually within the household of a Kel Ewey family. I resided
primarily in one village, and frequently visited other caravanning and
gardening centers nearby, as well as several other more distant oases and
nomadic camps.

The Bagzan region of Aïr was in many respects a delightful place to
conduct research. Its shady trees (numerous by local standards), dry air,

and nearby mountains protect it from seasonal temperature extremes, and although the days can be quite hot, the nights are usually cool. I made trips to Agadez for mail and supplies about once every six weeks by agricultural cooperative truck. Other travel was carried out on foot or by camel. The nature of my research topic required close and long-term residence. My decision to live in a tent helped to facilitate friendships among a people who, while not hostile, were initially shy, due to a combination of historical events (Tubu raids and French massacres) and my own novel status as the first American (or European) to settle there (most non-Tuareg typically passed through in a jeep with a tour guide). Furthermore, since women own tents and men own the increasingly common adobe house, and houses are also the usual choice of outside tourists, teachers, and government officials, my housing arrangement received widespread approval from local residents, in particular the women, thus underlining my role as essentially a guest and friendly student of Kel Ewey Tuareg culture. In the material that follows, all names have been changed to protect privacy.

Introduction

It was past midnight, and the Saharan sky was devoid of moon or stars. The desert winds scattered sand and dust into eyes, nose, ears, and mouth. Shadowy figures arose from mats, clutching at voluminous robes, sleepily weaving their way across the village among rocks and goatsties to the compound where there was to be a possession performance. Asalama, the woman in trance, sat silently in a shimmering white blouse as kerosene lamps flickered in the background. Slowly she arose from beneath a blanket and began swaying from side to side to the sounds of singing and drumming. Her motions became more rapid, and the audience praised her dancing. She then danced wildly, throwing herself from one side to the other, remaining seated all the while, until she flung herself to the ground, exhausted.

I first visited Asalama's compound with mutual friends who told me that Asalama suffered from *tamazai*, "an inner illness and a dangerous senti-ment," and the basis of possession affliction. Although Asalama's audience praised some aesthetic aspects of her possession performance, they also ridiculed her for appearing too often at possession ceremonies, for "craning her neck, looking for a man." Asalama's male cross-cousin jokingly warned that their sixteen-year-old female cousin, soon to undergo a possession ritual herself, "would become crazy, like Asalama." He said that Asalama was a *tamazel*, "someone who is bothered by other people, [someone who] can't sit still and be with other people . . ." Later that day, however, other friends told me that many women undergo these rituals, not because they are ill or a *tamazel* but because they "are touched in the heart by beautiful music." Yet despite local cultural values encouraging music and poetry, many residents expressed subtle disapproval of the ritual, warning young girls not to follow this path and become "crazy."

During my study of Tuareg possession rituals over the course of many

1

visits and a lengthy residence in the Aïr Mountain region of Niger, West Africa between 1976 and 1991, I gradually realized that possession was not simply the outcome of intense conflict, but also a stimulus for it. Local debates over its interpretation, moreover, were not limited to the immediate trance situation. Reactions to possession addressed more overarching claims to knowledge, authority, and personhood. In particular, possession imagery and the meanings it evoked became the focus of heated debate, suggesting that much larger issues were at stake. This led me to examine not only the nature of the immediate trance situation and the cure of individual cases, but also the long-term conflicts stemming from the interplay between the public and the personal in possession in general. Thus my goal in this account is to explore how far possession imagery connotes docile endurance and how far it generates critical social commentary.

The Kel Ewey Tuareg of north-eastern Niger speak of possessing spirits called Kel Essuf, or "people of solitude" – solitude in this sense connoting desolation rather than tranquility. Possession, considered an illness, is characterized by muteness, a condition described as "being in the wild" or "in solitude." The ritual cure for possession, by contrast, reverberates with sounds and visual images: the dancing of the woman in trance, the drumming and songs of curing practitioners, and the joking, flirting, and horseplay of the audience. Vivid tropes of personhood recur throughout the ritual as well as in local exegeses of possession illness and individual case histories. Spirit possession thus provides a lens for examining concepts of personhood enacted during the event, for these concepts are not merely reproduced but also reconstituted as objects of reflection by local specialists. Yet possession also acts within a larger social context, forming an integral part of a pattern in the transfer of knowledge and power. Through an analysis of the visual, verbal, and kinesthetic images in possession rituals, and through an examination of the conflicting local exegeses regarding the meaning of possession, I explore local concepts of personhood in relation to wider processes of social agency.[1]

In their local rural Aïr Mountain setting, approximately 150 miles northeast of the town of Agadez, the spatial organization of the semi-nomadic hamlets of Tuareg herders, caravanners, and oasis gardeners reflects a traditional social order while at the same time suggesting conflicts and contradictions. Internal divisions quickly become apparent in the contrasting features of the ecological and architectural environment. Household composition dynamics through time, and social hierarchies are apparent in the form and arrangement of residences. The distinctive elliptical dome-shaped nomadic tent, for example, set at a distance from a fenced-in compound containing other tent residences (an older nomadic tent, a few conical grass buildings, a rectangular grass reception room, and the increasingly common one-room mud or stone house), is the residence of a recently married daughter. Residents typically identify compounds by the names of the women who own the tents. Yet among the well-to-do, there has been a recent trend of adding houses constructed by men, which then belong to the male head of the household. These external characteristics of form suggest internal conflicts between generations and between men and women regarding marriage and property.

Additional features of Kel Ewey communities suggest at least an outward adherence to client–patron relationships. There are patterns of marked residential segregation and differences in wealth, both visually and spatially. The homes of nobles, chiefly and religious clans claiming descent from the Prophet, tributary groups, blacksmiths, and formerly servile peoples are often located in different neighborhoods. Clustered about the mosque are compounds of chiefly and marabout (Islamic scholar) households, neat and encircled by tree-branch fences (or, among the more sedentized, by mud walls) to keep out goats. The homes of smiths are generally older and dilapidated, and located further out. People of servile origin, whom nobles insist no longer work as slaves ("except far away, on Mount Bagzan"), but whom they shun nonetheless, together with families of ambiguous, mixed, or outside social origins, usually build their homes near the outskirts of settlements.

Tuareg men and women told me that the illnesses and depressions that cause trance are the result of spirits passed from mother to daughter. Possession curing rites, usually held publicly and late in the evening, are called *tənde n goumaten*. *Tənde* has three meanings: it is a mortar for crushing grain; a drum constructed from this mortar by stretching a goat hide across the top; and the generic term used for all musical events, including the spirit possession ritual, that feature this instrument. *Goumaten* is the plural of *gouma* in Tamacheq (a Berber language spoken by the Tuareg), and refers to both the patients or possessed persons at these rituals and the spirit (also called Kel Essuf) that possesses them. *Tənde n goumaten* feature: a drummer, generally a lower-caste individual, such as a blacksmith; a player of the *asakalabo* (a calabash floating in a basin of water, beaten with a cloth-covered wooden stick); a chorus of young women; and the *gouma*, or patient.

The curing rite is also a staged performance.[2] There is a large audience of both females and males, ranging in age from about ten to twenty-five. Audience, chorus, and patient evaluate the ceremony's effectiveness through jokes, songs, and gossip, and criticize singers for laziness, drowning out the solo singer, overwhelming the performance with too much crying and shouting, forgetting the lyrics, or failing to use "proper" Tamacheq (that is, filling in verses with vocables rather than using all the words, thus "distorting" the verse content). Only women learn possession-song texts. Curing practitioners consider healing to be an art form, and performers, audience, and patients alike recognize the importance of the aesthetic – music and song, in this case – in the curing of spirit affliction. Possession itself tends to occur in musical and festival settings: at weddings, at possession rites (sometimes among audience members), and when listening to recordings of possession rite music. Many possessed women are or have been professional singers. Much of the effectiveness of the cure depends upon artistic criteria: how well the drumming and songs are performed according to the precise rules of the ritual.

At the beginning of the ceremony, the patient lies prone beneath a blanket. As the songs and drumming quicken in pace and become rhythmically more elaborate, the patient rises to a sitting position and begins shaking her head from side to side, slowly at first, then faster and more vigorously, in what is called *asul*, or the head dance. Soon the motion includes the shoulders and upper torso. Throughout the rite, the patient remains seated, facing the player of the *tande* mortar drum, with the chorus on one side and the audience on the other. In her hand she grips a man's sword, holding it perpendicular throughout her dance. A female friend or close kinswoman covers her entire head and face with a black cloth (typically, only Tuareg men wear a veil, which covers the nose and mouth). At first, the woman in trance sits rigidly while the drumming and singing continue. Then she begins the head dance motion, swaying more and more vigorously, dervish-like, as spirits enter her body. Sometimes women in the chorus and audience join her in these trance motions. For several hours, chorus, drummer, and *asakalobo* player perform a varied repertoire of songs from the *tande n goumaten* ritual. Often the woman in trance places her hand(s) on the surface of the *tande* drum to absorb its vibrations. Occasionally, she indicates through non-verbal gestures that the spirit "prefers" one particular song to another. As the songs quicken and include more elaborate drum rhythms, ideally the patient receives praise and encouragement from the audience, and finally becomes exhausted, collapsing to the ground. Kel Ewey interpret her dancing as the spirit dancing, and her exhaustion as the spirits leaving her body.

Yet the Tuareg disagree about the cause, meaning, purposes, and consequences of possession. For some participants, "going to a possession rite is like going to a disco," and the aesthetic quality of the rite is an end in itself as well as the means to a cure. This element pervades contexts outside the immediate curing ceremony, and is the focus of a debate about the meaning and function of possession rites. Because the phrases "spirits are in her" or "she has spirits" may be said of anyone who is transported by beautiful music, singing and drumming style seem to be as important as the content and function of the songs.

Possession ritual has elements that anthropologists conventionally term "carnival," and, correspondingly, the cure requires jokes and play.[3] Rather than approaching the rite with reverence or solemnity, or regarding the illness with awe or anxiety, the Tuareg joke about the rite and even ridicule frequent participants. They also flirt and horse around during the ritual, gossiping and laughing among themselves. This playful element extends beyond the immediate ritual context: my women friends would refer jokingly to the kinks in my neck from travel as "spirit affliction," and children, with the encouragement of adults, frequently reenact the "cure" in play, complete with standing chorus, drummer, patient prone beneath a blanket, and tiny replica of the mortar drum.

Possession, characterized by an altered state of trance, and public healing rituals featuring song, dance, flirting, and jokes, is partly an end in itself and partly a means to other ends. The possession rite is also a forum facilitating the enactment of wider struggles. Among Tuareg, Islamic scholars scorn possession by spirits, but they also diagnose women for them, in treating a personal depression called *tamazai*. The danger of possession affliction becomes an opportunity for articulating hidden agendas, which, rather than referring only to the immediate circumstances of the possessed person, radiate beyond it to encompass the broader concerns of different interest groups. Early anthropological interpretation of possession trance as an altered state of consciousness that predominantly strikes selected categories of "deprived" persons is now widely regarded as an oversimplification.[4] This epidemiological perspective assumes that possession is deviant behavior, and results in a portrayal of its idiom as one of "muted" or "nonstandard" expression. Wittingly or unwittingly, this view encourages a perception of possession similar to previous perceptions of metaphorical expression as defective and illogical speech, akin to aphasia, rather than as an intentional and rule-governed phenomenon. Such a perspective does not pursue the metacommunication surrounding possession among local participants, who may or may not become possessed themselves. Nonepidemiological studies, however, have all too often assumed that the meaning of these rituals is consensual, and have treated them as aberration, paying insufficient attention to the conflicting definitions and viewpoints of persons representing different interest groups.[5]

We need to explore the expressiveness and intentionality of spirit possession for the audience and non-participants as well as for the possessed, who comment on possession in terms of the diverse contexts of gender, social stratum, and age. From this perspective, possession emerges as enabling, but not necessarily compensatory or manipulative, behavior. By focusing on both the symbolic and the epistemological aspects of spirit possession, I hope to illuminate important ethnographic and theoretical issues. For example, why is possession imagery consistently associated with women among the Tuareg? Why are certain gender-specific images used to express possession? And why is there such heated local debate over the meaning of possession? Central theoretical questions are how possession, serious and playful at once, stimulates the cultural construction of person-hood, and how possession then encapsulates personhood in all its depen-dency and contradiction. In exploring these questions, the gradually changing relationships between social strata and between men and women come into view. Possession enacts ambiguities in the relationships between the sexes, charged by issues of marriage and descent.

Most studies of altered states have tended to overemphasize the explicit curing function of these ceremonies and to equate curing with meaning, purpose, and performance style; either ignoring social context altogether or expanding it to crowd out other processes.[6] An analysis of possession tropes and metacommunication about them in terms of their effects, message and "style," in Hebdige's (1979) sense, as an interplay of cultural and subcultural styles, reveals an ongoing debate over person definition, and provides the key to uncovering the multiple meanings held for different participants. These meanings are expressed implicitly in form, style, and context of aesthetic expression and its unintended consequence, rather than overtly. Among Kel Ewey, the style of curing is as important as the cause, content, and result. Local exegesis reveals that these rituals effect transfor-mations from healing into processes having new meanings, in different contexts, for different participants.[7]

With these issues in mind, I focus not only on the multivocality of meaning but also on the contested meaning of possession tropes, and how they are used by non-possessed as well as possessed individuals to define personhood. Tuareg possession enacts a series of negotiations and promo-tions of social experience. The conceptualization, acquisition, and manifes-tation of spirits among Kel Ewey express different situations and vantage points, but in highly symbolic form. In locating these vantage points, I focus on the dialogue between possessed and non-possessed individuals, rather than solely upon the causal "arrows" of possession. My data show that trance among Tuareg represents neither rebellion nor social control, but rather a reconsideration of previous social relationships and a quest for new social relationships. Possession viewed from this perspective emerges not solely as a response to conditions, but also as a factor in creating or rearticulating them.

Michel Leiris (1934, 1958) and later Alfred Metraux (1959) have written famous accounts of the aesthetic aspects of possession cults. They described possession songs, dances, and music, as subjects of interest in their own right, but they did not frame this artistry in terms of wider social conflict or process, or in terms of how possession art relates to local knowledge areas and theories concerning personhood. My own work analyses the art of possession in relation to control and power in Kel Ewey Tuareg society. So rather than dwelling upon epidemiological or causal factors and relying on Western concepts of the person, I focus upon expression, style, and unintended consequences of possession in practice. The possession idiom, I argue, metaphorically encapsulates the ironies and contradictions of being a Tuareg. Art and affliction, performance and healing intersect with a number of key cultural values that contradict role expectations of social status in a community characterized by marked stratification of nobles, smiths, and formerly servile peoples. But the interplay of aesthetic form and social intent cannot be reduced to a consciously manipulative or directly causal connection. The art of possession emerges from relationships in the wider social order.

Possession rituals also provide a forum for discourse on healing and competition over claims to medical and other forms of knowledge in Tuareg society. These, in turn, act as a foil, revealing healing paradigms that are not uniformly equated with secularism, colonialism, or other "modern" influences, such as literacy or centralized state authority. This multiplicity of perspectives yields material that challenges the tendency in the anthropology of religion and systems of thought, on the one hand to generalize and establish polarities between "Western" and "traditional" or "non-Western" systems of thought, and on the other hand to demarcate boundaries or sequences between such domains as "magic," "science," and "religion."

It is above all in its curing method that *tamazai*, which often triggers possession, appeals to a power other than that of the Islamic God and marabout representatives. This appeal undermines the established hierarchies of dominance of marabout and noble men over women, but solely in the particular context of the curing drama. The subversion of hierarchy is an unintended consequence of other overarching conflicts, which have their bases in social class interests. Herein resides the principal threat of curing to Islam: in its aesthetic form, tropes, images of personhood, and dramatic effect, possession comments upon social hierarchies. This explains why curing rituals stimulate such controversy. Official male-dominated Islam is the medium of expression of wider conflicts, rather than the object of the rebellion in possession dialogue. Possession subverts style in the sense that it addresses broader issues including, but not limited to, official religion, by taking apart elements of local culture and reconstituting them. Its ritual process produces a kind of inverted social analysis or reflexive commentary about being a Tuareg, which includes diverse dimensions of personhood: Muslim/non-Muslim; male/female; noble/smith/former slave.

Tuareg spirit possession thus dramatizes contradictions between what Kenny terms "cultural myth and social reality" (1986: 8). Its ritual imagery not only encapsulates contradictions but also reveals compromises between ideals and actual conditions of existence. Possession imagery expresses a contradiction between the local ideology of the elevated and independent status of nobles – particularly women – and their actual position of economic transformation and uncertainty. On one level, Tuareg possession constitutes "engendered behavior." Since it is predominantly women who undergo curing rituals, the role of gender in possession has to be taken into account. But class and age also feature. With these issues in mind, I include in my analysis genealogical material, life histories, possession case studies, texts from songs and other oral traditions, household censuses, and epidemiological surveys of women, all of which relate possession to crucial life events, such as marriage and childbirth. A comparative analysis of images of possession and images of other life events reveals that both kinds of ritual dramatize the contradictory roles of women, refracted or mediated through kinship and social class. An analysis of the metacommunication between knowledge specialists about possession and alternative healing systems shows that possession expresses conflicting definitions of person-hood, and is the forum for articulating and exploring the identity of Tuareg women and also Tuareg identity in general. In fact, nowhere is Kel Ewey Tuareg personhood so clearly condensed into one discursive symbol than in possession.

Although the "language" of spirit symbolism reflects essentially a counterreality, possession imagery is constrained nonetheless by the knowledge-power system of the society at large.[8] The broader concern here is the role of symbolic mediation in the relationship of structure and practice of knowledge about the person. This study does not purport to show how possession is a tool that serves the immediate interests of specific participants. Nor do I analyze possession art and play as ends in themselves. Rather, I examine possession in a different way, on two levels: the first level approaches possession as a microcosm of the life course, blurring the boundaries between self and other; the second level uses possession imagery as a means to explore the relationship between aesthetics, healing, and ritual, identifying possession symbols with certain aspects of the social structure.

Possession by the "people of solitude" is the ultimate symbolic performance. The case study in chapter 1 which opens the discussion examines *tamazai*. Part I of this study considers possession tropes and symbolism in the *tande n goumaten*, and includes life histories of men and women who have been possessed. I look at the Tuareg belief system, their ritual and cosmology, and their interpretations of misfortune, and patterns of social organization, including gender. I analyze stories about spirits and illness, notions of power and causation, the relation of the individual to society, images of affliction and misfortune, notions of cognition and sentiments, and character acquisition. I look at how illness and personality classifications are established, the roles of specialists in curing (Islamic scholars, blacksmiths, herbalists), and their explanations of and responses to possession, tales about knowledge and destiny – particularly misfortune – and the relation of these latter to the cultural construction of knowledge about the person and healing.

Part II is devoted to aesthetic details of the spirit possession rituals, in particular how the social organization and cultural symbolic principles analyzed in Part I transfuse and pervade the intersection of art and power in the visual and verbal performance of trance. My methods here have more in common with analyses of possession through the lens of art and literary criticism rather than with epidemiological or positivistic methods. I take the position that possession is a culturally specific metaphor, not a universally distributed mental disorder (although I explore nonetheless Tuareg notions of mental states, including altered states conceived of as "normal" as well as those conceived of as "abnormal"). This idea of possession as metaphor leads me to return continually to a major theme in this book: exploring the relationship between the ideology of personhood and the enactment of possession, as the problem is addressed both through conflicting explanations of female curing and as it is manifested in possession tropes. Through an analysis of case studies interspersed with interpretations of transitional life events and ways of coping with conflicts and contradictions, I investigate the Tuareg sense of person, and how it alternately receives expression and shapes perception.

1

Illnesses of the heart and soul: the case of Asalama

Spirits of solitude bring illnesses of the heart and soul. In song verses used in spirit possession rituals, one who is possessed is referred to obliquely through the metaphor of an orphan (*golama*), a term also used to refer to a childless camel, and a female camel who has lost her young. Asalama, the blacksmith woman whose ritual served as a prelude to my quest for understanding possession, told me that this condition or illness afflicts the liver, the area just beneath the ribcage. According to Asalama, the liver is the seat of all sentiments – especially love and anger – and is the place where possessing spirits settle after entering through the stomach, which is the symbol of the matriline, associated in local cosmology with secrets as well as spirits.

Spirits are said to return often, circulating among regular hosts. During a visit to the house of a prominent marabout, I learned that there exist two types of spirit: black or blue ones (cured by the drum of the *tande n goumaten* ritual), and red ones (cured by marabouts). The former are like the "black monkeys on top of Mount Bagzan," who never approach villages, but remain on the fringes of the wild. The marabout indicated that, although spirits are equally dangerous to men and women, "women's spirits and men's spirits are not the same: the former prefer noisy *tande n goumaten* rites as medicine; the latter prefer the Koran." Most local explanations of possession included references to the stomach, the matriline, and women's spirits, suggesting that possession by *goumaten* or Kel Essuf spirits is distinctly feminine. The distinctive songs, head dance, and joking and flirting of the *tande n goumaten* ritual are also considered feminine. Tuareg men and women of all ages and social strata stated emphatically that only women should perform the head dance. Although men may be possessed, men's spirit illnesses are described as illnesses of

God, which require Koranic verses (rather than the drumming ritual) to cure them. In rare cases where men performed the head dance at the drumming ritual, they were described pejoratively as "effeminate." Women's spirit illnesses, in contrast, require the *tənde n goumaten* ritual.

Hence the paradox: concepts of disorder and disability are invoked to explain specific forms of behavior that are regarded as inappropriate, but possession is considered appropriate behavior for certain persons in specific situations. Men's spirits cause them to become antisocial or to go out and beat people, while women's spirits generally cause them to become depressed. Furthermore, the widespread disapproval (though not quite prohibition) of the drumming cure for men's spirits on the part of Koranic scholars indicates an undercurrent of power present in this "disability." The heart (*ewel*) in Tuareg culture is associated with courage and honor, and is believed to orientate the otherwise debilitated individual (for example, one who is asleep, or blind). The *ewel*, then, lends a kind of dignity to *goumaten* affliction. Local explanations of this condition at times imply cultural deviance and at other times cultural conformity, and local explanations of the cure incorporate both therapy and amusement. These alternating explanations suggest that the curing process – possession itself – is a vehicle for the transformation of experience.

Consider the case of Asalama. She is said to suffer from the severe depression called *tamazai*, which local residents believe triggers her possession attacks. At such times she is reclusive, rarely attending communal work parties (a central social and economic activity of the region), namedays, or weddings. (Indeed, during my 1983 visit, she did not fast during the Muslim fasting month of Ramadan, claiming that she was too ill.) Though Asalama is a blacksmith woman, in recent years she has done little leatherwork, except for the occasional camel harness, and she neither cooks nor serves food to nobles at their life crisis rites and celebrations, as is customary for smiths in their client–patron relationships with nobles.

Asalama is about forty-five. Her only surviving child is a daughter of about twenty-four by one of her former husbands (from whom she is divorced). This child, Amina, is also divorced; her ex-husband was Asalama's brother. Asalama had another child, now deceased, by her other husband, now also deceased. Asalama claims that for many years, the spirits of solitude prevented her from having children, and also caused her to have an abnormal child. Her first child, a girl, was born with a birth defect and died shortly thereafter. Asalama's first spirit attack occurred following the death of this child. Other spirit attacks occurred during my 1983 residence in her village (in February, during the cold season), and on several occasions between my departure and subsequent return to the region in 1991. On my most recent visit (1991), Asalama indicated that her attacks continued on a sporadic basis, but that she was now "bothered less often" by spirits.

Asalama belongs to the Kel Igurmaden descent group of Kel Ewey, and is of modest means (she has only a couple of goats). She has been widowed once and divorced once. Asalama is now the second co-wife of a smith who is also a practicing Islamic scholar in a nearby village, about a half-mile down the unpaved road. He has his first wife there, with whom he spends most of his time. This situation is a source of annoyance to Asalama, who, throughout my stay, seemed more cheerful during her husband's visits than during his absence. She considers marriage necessary for material support and for "help with general problems in life." Although her current husband, Romer, is a distant cousin, her divorced husband had been related to her more closely: his mother and her mother were sisters (a preferred mode of marriage, especially among blacksmiths), and their mothers had arranged the marriage. Despite her divorce, Asalama insists that, ideally, parents should choose the husband because it usually brings greater security. Marabouts explained to me the reasoning behind this custom: if parents choose the husband (in what is termed a "household or family marriage," as opposed to a "man's marriage"), the husband's family is obliged to help their daughter-in-law economically while he is away traveling. This support is not obligatory in the "man's marriage," which involves an independent and non-kin choice.

The immediate physical symptoms indicating Asalama's affliction were aches of the liver and stomach. She has a history of physical health problems, family deaths, and marital disruption, and her usual disposition is one of depression and even withdrawal around others. Although Asalama circulates occasionally among her noble patron households to announce news of births and marriages, her daily activities appear to be few. Her daughter, who lives adjacent to her compound, does most of the housework. Asalama's longstanding physical complaints include liver ailments, coughs, headaches, and eye problems, as well as problems during pregnancy. Yet her spirit possession cannot be attributed solely to these ailments; in June 1991, she was bitten by a scorpion, but did not stage a *tande n goumaten* ritual for it. Instead, she used a combination of traditional medicine, my Western-manufactured painkillers, and coffee to dull the pain and combat the venom.

Some of Asalama's relatives have also been possessed, including a female cousin, Halima, and a stepdaughter (the daughter of Asalama's husband

and his first co-wife). A few days after her 1983 possession rites, which were held on two consecutive nights, Asalama claimed that the songs of the rite had rid her of stomach and liver troubles. Two rites had sufficed for the time being, but she is afflicted frequently with *tamazai* depression, and often requests these curing rites; she is known as one of the most "habitual" patients. When I visited her, several days after her possession rites, Asalama still seemed to be listless and depressed. She hid her face in her headscarf and would not meet my eyes. Asalama claims spirits prefer some people to others, but she is not sure why. She says that her parents neglected her in her childhood and did not protect her regularly with Islamic amulets, for which reason she believes she has so many spirits now. Her definition of good health is "peacefulness, not being bothered, in equilibrium, being in family, nothing lacking in the heart." It is possible, however, to be born sick.

Asalama sat still during my postritual visit, declining to shake hands with anyone. Her dress was tattered and she wore no jewelry, partly because of her social status as a blacksmith and partly because of her self-image. Asalama often remarked to me that she was an old woman (*tamghart*), and did not "feel pretty" anymore. Pointing to her hair, she said, "It is grey." When I complimented her hairstyle, she said that it was "an old woman's hairstyle," and cheered up only slightly when I responded that it was, rather, "a married woman's hairstyle."

Asalama's family history is typical of other Kel Ewey (Kel Igurmaden) smiths. They originated on Mount Bagzan, and went south to Hausaland. Upon their return, they settled in a small oasis about six miles from the caravanning village where Asalama now resides, and then moved on to a neighboring village, eventually settling in Asalama's current village to work at the mosque. Despite her family's hereditary and social identification as smiths, Asalama's ancestors include a number of prominent Islamic scholars. Over the course of my visit, Asalama related impressions of her youth to me, providing some context for her spirit possessions.

Asalama's memories and impressions

I didn't know anything but how to play with other small children when I was young. When we were girls we either herded or wove palm fibers, or [made] leather necklaces [and] tassels, and the prettiest ones were taken and made into camel harnesses. We also made rope to pull camels [and made] leather sacks, and the young people made leather jewelry boxes, where women kept their stone necklaces. We used to gather palm fibers in Tazaguis [a nearby *oeud* or dried riverbed], and separated them. We blackened half the palms; these were woven into mats [and] tied together. We went to celebrations together with our girl friends, we went to songs.

I haven't traveled anywhere. Even little children don't know me. Our work as smiths is [large] leather necklaces, little leather necklaces, and harnesses. That's all the work I know. I have never made a large travel bag [considered more difficult to make], nor a woman's valise. When I used to go to the nobles' namedays in our village – when I arrived there – I did the work. At my noble family's [house], I worked. I prepared rice, wheat cakes, [and] macaroni at my noble's [house]. At the homes of those in Abardak, I sit down, I don't work [there], for that's not my [home] village. There, they [affines] bring me dishes; I eat, for I am a guest there. I don't prepare anything in Abardak [where Asalama's in-laws live].

I dress the hair of my noblewomen. Nobles don't know how to dress hair. It is smith women who know how – they dress nobles' hair, and they [the nobles] give their smiths one measure of millet. They [the nobles] also give them [the smiths] gowns. Even I used to do this [participate in the exchange].

My family [*tarik*, or female-headed domestic unit] and I fetch wood. I have only one daughter. She crushes grain, goes to the well, and pounds grain.

I have never been anywhere. Only to Tabelot [a village about twenty miles away]. When I went there, my daughter was very young. We went to Tabelot by camel. I left with my child who was ill [there is a dispensary at Tabelot]. I stayed there for several days. I don't like Tabelot. I only like my village, here. It's Ganni [Mouloud, the Prophet's birthday] that I really enjoy. The women mount donkeys, the men, camels. Of all the festivals I've seen, I prefer Ganni. Ganni is beautiful.

When I had spirits, I vomited a lot. I don't remember the first time well. I don't remember the persons who came to see me. I only remember from the time they had already begun the *tande* [music]. I vomited a lot. Then I saw people who surrounded me, doing the *goumaten* [curing rite] for me. I was a young girl then [between fourteen and eighteen years old]. I was at my mother's. At that time, I didn't have any children. I was very young. I wore the young married woman's headscarf when the spirits entered me. At the time, I was weaving palm fibers. I didn't do housework; I only wove palm fibers. For a long time, I have had spirits. They give me liver ailments.

The context of the curing ritual

During Asalama's 1983 curing rites, her cousin, Moussa, a smith and gardener from Abardak much admired for his skill on the drum, played on the first night. On the second night, his brother, Abdullah, took over because Moussa was tired. On the first day at sundown, Asalama was brought from her place of residence to the neighboring village a half-mile down the unpaved road to spend the hours before the ritual (which would begin at midnight) at the home of Abdullah and Moussa. A woman friend played the calabash floating in water (*asakalabo*), accompanying the chorus and *tande* drum. (Tuareg describe these two curing instruments as "in harmony together, as sugar is with tea.") The chorus, composed of young women friends and relatives from diverse social strata, sang songs to dull pain, induce sleep, and generally bring on relief. Asalama wore a white festival blouse, in order to "glow" in the dark. There is a ritual significance to "glowing white": spirits are said to like, and respond positively to, this contrast to the otherwise darkened setting. Throughout the rite, the audience and curers addressed frequent comments and questions to the patient during lulls in the music about the progress of the cure: "Is it better?" Generally, there was an informal atmosphere of chatting, laughing, and joking, even during the songs and drumming. Small schoolboys ran around the sidelines, some performing the *tande n tagbast*, a popular men's dance. At that time, residents were not yet used to my presence, and my tape recorder and I attracted a great deal of attention.

During the ritual, the musicians, audience, and trancers huddled together. At first the musicians and chorus "warmed up," and then proceeded formally with their performance after practicing briefly. The audience consisted mostly of young men, who wore strong perfume and dressed in their finest festival clothing. Many of these men circled around the ritual space during the ceremony, as they might do also at dances and festivals held on other occasions.

During Asalama's rite, another smith woman, Adaoula, went into a spontaneous trance; her recent complaint had been a painful molar tooth. Adaoula was in her late thirties, the mother of five children (the oldest of whom were teenagers), and pregnant with one more. Whereas Asalama's female relatives had arranged this ceremony for her after consulting with marabouts and herbalists, Adaoula did not seem to have received similar consideration from her relatives. Throughout the ritual, the chorus of young women sang possession songs from a repertoire recognized by most audience members. Song preference was indicated, through hand gestures, by the patients.

The aesthetic form and poetic content of the songs, in combination with drumming and audience responses, are said to have a therapeutic effect. Yet most Kel Ewey claim that, more than the words *per se*, it is the singing, clapping, and drumming of the possession songs that are linked directly to the cure. It is said that spirits are pleased by the drum calabash, ululation, applause, and the tonal quality of the music. Nonetheless, the verses themselves appear to be significant also, because they refer to such sentiments as love and nostalgia, as well as the need for approval and support. Throughout these verses, soloists call for applause, encouragement, and approval – crucial parts of the music, of course, but also an essential element of the curing process. The applause and singing are both linked to the overall well-being of the patient; both are mutually reinforcing and interdependent. The songs sung for Asalama also contained themes of youth. Possession songs generally contain references to young people and to relationships among women and between women and men. Allusion to youth and celebration is part of the treatment in that it invokes a pleasurable time in life, a time characterized by music, courtship, and festivals. Although Asalama is past the youthful phase of her life, she often speaks nostalgically of the festivals of her early years.

During the performance of these songs, with the accompaniment of the *tande* and *asakalabo*, the women in trance performed the head dance (*asul*), seated all the while, slowly at first, with the movement largely confined to the head, and then more vigorously, with motions extending to the shoulder area and downward until the dance involved the entire torso from the waist up. Asalama began her head dance after rising from a still, prone position under a blanket at the beginning of the rite. Adaoula joined her in the head dance several songs later. Both patients remained silent throughout the rite, participating neither in the conversation of the general audience nor in the singing of the chorus. After the conclusion of the first rite (at about 3.00 a.m.), there were complaints that it had not been "lively" enough, and the patients still were not cured of their spirits. The objective of the ritual is to make the patient so exhausted that she falls to the ground; only at this point is she considered cured. As neither patient had yet fallen to the ground, plans were made to hold a second rite on the following night. Moussa, however, said that someone else would have to replace him, for he was too tired. The next morning I heard Abdullah, the brother of Moussa, jokingly talking about how many men had gone looking for women after the ritual. It is customary for men to look for women after festivals of all kinds, including the possession rite, at night, after everyone has retired. (However, a man may be thrown out of a woman's tent if she does not like his attentions.) When young men discuss the spirit possession rite, it is this postritual courtship – rather than the curing rite itself – that they mention most frequently.

A second rite was held for both Asalama and Adaoula the following evening, and Abdullah played the *tande*. The pace of the songs was generally faster, and the head dance was more vigorous. The rite concluded first with the collapse of Asalama, and then with the collapse of Adaoula, indicating to the audience and chorus that the women were cured, at least for a time. Comments about this ritual were generally favorable; most people agreed that it had been livelier than its predecessor, and attributed this largely to Abdullah's drumming.

Analysis

Asalama's case of *tamazai* and possession is profound. Although her chronic state of *tamazai* is often linked conceptually to spirit affliction, not all intermittently possessed persons exhibit such extreme depression between possession attacks. Members of the community unrelated to Asalama and certain acquaintances tolerate Asalama's condition, but they also laugh at her behind her back and describe her as "crazy" (*attebek*; distinct from *anebzeg*, which implies permanent insanity). Residents generally agree that it is love and other worries that make her "crazy."

Asalama has a personal history of health problems and disruptions in her marital life: death, divorce, and currently polygyny (a form of marriage considered undesirable by most Tuareg women). Although women own property, Asalama, like many smith women, has few livestock. Her daughter's divorce not only removed important sources of economic security that her son-in-law's bridewealth and groom-service would have provided, but also stripped her of an enhanced social status as mother-in-law. As a result, Asalama lived in comparative social isolation – neither mother-in-law nor wife – for many years. She married her current spouse after nearly a decade of being single, and her current marital arrangement – being the second co-wife of a polygynist – is not favored by Kel Ewey women. Contrary to what has been reported about some other African societies, Tuareg women vigorously oppose polygyny, and the second co-wife usually represents a man's second choice: a contract with a close cousin to please his mother, a marriage of charity to help out a widow, or the result of any number of other motives that women find insulting.

Asalama has had no children with her current husband, but Rhaicha, the first co-wife, has had several. Although barrenness does not carry great shame or stigma for Tuareg women, Asalama's isolation and neglect are exacerbated by her husband's decision to spend a larger proportion of his time in residence with Rhaicha and their children. In accordance with her lone female status, Asalama refers to her home as *tarik* (an attenuated, female-headed household), rather than *eghiwan* (a complete and extended family among Kel Ewey; a camp among some other Tuareg groups). Although female-headed households are not rare in Aïr – particularly during caravanning seasons, when they constitute the basic subsistence unit – such households are neither typical nor ideal throughout the year. Ideally, the polygynous husband spends equal time in the residence of each co-wife. In reality, such equality does not exist. Ironically, the Tuareg strategy of dispersing polygynous households in separate villages, camps, or compounds in order to avoid the potential jealousies of co-wives defeats its original purpose. In practice, the husband resides in one village or camp longer than the other, thus dividing his time less equally than he might if his wives were to reside in the same or adjacent compounds.

Like many Kel Ewey women past their "youth" (which is culturally defined for women as being less than thirty years old and having no married children), Asalama fondly reminisces about her adolescent years, particularly the festivals and holidays of her youth, and the attendant music and dancing. She now avoids most nameday and wedding celebrations, citing her illnesses as an excuse. She avoids especially those celebrations requiring her services as a smith woman to her noble patron family. And though she speaks of going to Abardak as a guest, in fact she did not attend a nameday celebration held in Abardak in the household of Rhaicha and her husband for their baby. This event occurred during the cold season, closely coinciding with her depression symptoms and possession attacks in February 1983. Although Asalama claims to be cured as a result of the songs sung during the second consecutive rite, people say that she is always troubled in her heart, and she herself admits that she has "a lot of spirits." She talks with enthusiasm about the perfume, clothing, and jewelry worn at festivals, and says she likes the pleasant scents (preferred by spirits, and worn by young men at festivals as well as spirit possession rituals) in the air during the rite. These attitudes appear to conflict with her cultural role as an "older" woman, who would be discouraged from attending festivals and musical events due to behavioral restrictions (such as more frequent prayer and greater reserve, as well as the avoidance of evening festivals), and status changes associated with Islamic devotion and affinal kinship roles. Her behavior, however, allows her covertly to circumvent these norms.

Although Asalama says that her parents did not protect her with religious amulets during her childhood, she comes from a family of practicing marabouts of some prominence. (Blacksmiths, a hereditary, endogamous, occupational social stratum, may also become Islamic scholars.) Her husband is considered a "great marabout," and he tolerates his second wife's curing rites, a reaction not uncommon among marabouts whose female relatives request these rites. On the surface, however, marabouts voice opposition to the *tande n goumaten* possession rituals and attempt to limit them to smiths' neighborhoods, which, in many villages in the Bagzan area, are located far from the mosque. In the case of a possessed woman from a maraboutique family, the double-bind is apparent: these rituals are held by preference near the home of matrilineal female relatives, and such relatives, in the case of noble marabouts, often reside near mosques. Conflict arises also in the case of a smith family that includes practicing marabouts. In this instance, although the rite is held in the smiths' neighborhood, it is still opposed conceptually to Islam and marabouts, regardless of social stratum. Yet many of those people who are afflicted with *tamazai* use both marabout and *tande* drumming "medicines" to counteract spirits.

More importantly, their drumming cures also become the focus of social gatherings. Festivals are settings for license and temporary freedom from the constraints surrounding kinship and class roles. Many men told me that they purposely travel to rites of passage, curing rituals, and festivals at a distance to meet strangers "because women at a distance are more interesting than those [closely related] in their own region." At these gatherings, including the spirit possession rites, there is great importance attached to courtship conversation (Kel Ewey friends often nudged me to make conversation, saying that one is "lost" if silent at a gathering). Yet there is a contradiction between this cultural value and others, which emphasize hiding true sentiments or expressing them indirectly, through poetry, song, at festivals, and through go-betweens, such as smiths and ex-slaves. For example, a woman friend in casual conversation with me was ashamed to say that she preferred a particular village to her current residence (among Kel Ewey of the Bagzan region, most initial postmarital residence is uxorilocal), because the former was her husband's home, and a declaration of her preference for it would be tantamount to admitting that she loved her husband too much. One young woman was criticized in an evening gossip session for announcing plans to visit her fiancé at his home. Women are encouraged to grow more reserved and dignified as their avoidance relationships increase over a wider social sphere, when their children reach marriageable age. At this time, triangle relationships and tensions emerge between mother, daughter, and daughter's husband, and between sibling, husband, and wife in initial uxorilocal residence and groom-service.

The secret, repressed sentiments underlying the affliction and the feminine aspect of the cure were what residents most emphasized. Spirit possession is a metaphor for illicit, prohibited sentiments, feelings that are considered shameful. These may concern love for a forbidden person or activity, or they may consist of anger toward a person for whom one should feel affection and solidarity. The possessed person comments on aspects of Tuareg society in her key role in public curing rites. On the one hand, she inverts the features of women's social status to achieve a greater social whole; for example, for dramatic effect she often clutches a man's sword during her possession trance. On the other hand, she exaggerates women's social status in the hyperbolic motions of the head dance. She obliquely exaggerates men's roles in her headdress and sword at the same time that she inverts women's roles. Thus she stands outside the particular divisions of Tuareg society. She transforms the major social categories of gender, age, and kinship, transcending them and facilitating their redefinition for others as well as for herself.

Asalama's case was explained as a personal vulnerability that is regarded with indulgent tolerance rather than outrage by other Kel Ewey. Yet throughout there are also hints of power assertion by the possessed. Possession enables the afflicted to relive a satisfying social role (in a festival setting, dressed up, with music and perfume, joking and flirting) without its attendant obligations and with minimal loss of face. This occurs both within the possession event and within the larger social setting, through possession images and through their reverberations in personhood, knowledge transfer, and systems of thought. Being secretive about sentiments is part of Kel Ewey cultural values; possession reverses, but also ultimately reinforces, norms of personhood in a debating discourse, conveying them in tropes that alternately invert and exaggerate identity.

PART I

IMAGES OF POSSESSION

2

Inversion and other tropes in spirit possession rituals

There are numerous elements of reversal, or symbolic inversions, during the possession ritual that are apparent in the singing, dance motions, and ritual paraphernalia of the event. Possession songs begin only after sunset, when restrictions on behavior are relaxed, and when patients usually emerge from their tents (or, more rarely, are brought to the curing site away from their compound). After sundown, the usual roles and relationships in Tuareg society are overturned: affines may interact with less reserve; men and women, regardless of marital status, may flirt; and old women may dance. It is a time of courtship and sociability among different social strata, a time when spirits and the devil are believed to be walking about. Many Kel Ewey place a positive aesthetic value on dark colors and simple styles, but at the evening *tande* there is, in contrast, an emphasis on colors and textures that glow in the dark, showing up from afar.

Spatial arrangement

The layout of the event and the spatial arrangement of the audience also display a marked contrast to the daily social and ritual patterns among Kel Ewey. Rather than the usual distance and reserve, performers, audience, and trancers all huddle together. Instead of the typical highly stylized and formal greetings, there is an emphasis on spontaneity, camaraderie, and mutual support. People frequently speak openly to and about individuals in the chorus and audience, and inquire about the progress of the *gouma*. At various times, the singers insert jokes into the songs about the patient, other singers, various members of the audience, or individuals not present at the ceremony, but known throughout the area. For example, a song entitled "The sentiments of my soul" includes the following community references in its verses: "Friends of my village, you must applaud and give me a good

25

voice ... The song is an orphan, its lacks fans ... Those who dance from evening until sunrise, who shout from evening until dawn ... I count on the day that they visit me at noon ... Khamadodo's camels, the color of ostriches that resemble each other ... I accompany them up to Azaoua ... Little camels, crying in the shadow of small trees." Other verses comment critically on social divisions as well as individuals: "Young boys stop Iwillemeden women, slaves stop Balkoranan women. Silimana, the woman who looks for men, is the one who extends her neck, supported so as not to break her back."

These last verses refer satirically to the possessed woman during her head dance. Silimana was mocked for craning her neck, presumably in search of a man. Several informants, a prominent marabout in particular, asserted that women organize the rite "in order to attract men." Furthermore, *goumaten* spirits are said to be attracted to women, which suggests a connection between spirit possession and romantic love. In daily life, young women are not supposed to reveal a romantic preference, and older women should be preoccupied with prayer, not with love.

Body imagery, states of being, and social identity
References to the body and states of being reinforce this point. Songs at possession rituals refer repeatedly to the liver, the location of love and anger. Love is tied to Tuareg concepts of gender, class, and age roles. In the second cited song, for example, young boys (immature men) are said to like Iwillemeden women, and slaves are said to like Balkoranan women. The Iwillemeden and the Balkoranan are two divisions of Tuareg, rivals of the Kel Ewey confederation. The Iwillemeden inhabit the region around Tahoua, south-west of Agadez, and the Balkoranan live to the west of Agadez, near the oasis of In Gall. A certain Khamadodo is praised through a reference to his camels, which are said to be a two-tone color, like that of ostriches. The patient's need for guidance is also conveyed here with the phrase "supported so as not to break her back." The body and its states of being thus enter musical performance in poetic imagery, as an arena for conflicts revolving around gender, age, and class identity.

Many terms in song verses address either females or youth; for example, "young people of my village," "youth," and "young people singing songs." There are also images of social stratum and descent. These are prominent in many song verses, especially in one that mocks groups associated with specific social strata: "The Kel Eghaser, that with which they belt themselves while on camelback, [is] the *alechou* and *percale* gown. The Kel Nagarou, that with which they belt themselves while on camelback, [is made] from palm fibers." In these brief verses, two Tuareg groups are contrasted. The Kel Eghaser, who originate from the Iferouan region, are considered to be of predominantly noble status; the Kel Nagarou, from the Auderas and Tewar regions, just west of Abardak, include both servile groups and nobles. This song praises the Kel Eghaser, asserting that they are not only more "noble" than the Kel Nagarou, but also wealthier: the Kel Eghaser belt themselves with fine cloth, while the Kel Nagarou belt themselves with palm fibers, which dry up quickly and deteriorate. The song also expresses a woman's preference for men of the Kel Eghaser because of the qualities associated with noble status, and disdains men of the Kel Nagarou because they possess qualities opposite to those of the nobles.

Another recurring image is the neck: "Since I was born, oh, young girls, for the sake of God, for the sake of God, for only tonight I bear it on my neck! My neck, oh, my soul is old. I am upset without having a [bodily] illness, [rather, I have] an illness of the mouth." The neck is where spirits are believed to perch, before settling in the head, after travelling upward from the liver. The neck is the central focus of the patient's dance. The mouth is also alluded to here, in the context of a type of sorcery, specifically, antisocial behavior called *tawarna n mawan*, or "illness of the mouth." This behavior is said to evoke a state of jealousy between two parties. Kel Ewey say that one cause of spirit illness is conflict between people, which results in mental depression (*tamazai*), and is aggravated by *tawarna n mawan*. Illness of the mouth consists of gossip and rivalry in interpersonal relationships, such as the competition between two women in the chorus, namely Rhaicha and Hana, who are rival song artists. When spirits intrude upon the social world, they may take the form of jealousy, which disturbs the usual patterning of identity and self-expression.

Gender and sexual imagery
There is not always a sharp distinction between the physical and the psychological symptoms of illness. Rather, the significant distinctions are between causation (by social, natural, or unknown agents) and intentionality (the presence or absence of ulterior motives of the patient). Marabouts are credited with the ability to produce medicine against certain spirits and jealousy, but these marabouts may also possess negative powers. Kel Ewey speak of "bad" marabouts, who intentionally infect certain places (usually in the dry riverbeds or desert areas between villages and camps) with a "bad fate" by burying charms there. However, while these conditions and powers are perceived negatively by many Tuareg, they are often alluded to

satirically during *tɔnde n goumaten* rituals, as part of a broader social commentary on relationships critical to Kel Ewey social structure. Some jokes in the songs needle singers for not participating enough, or for being distracted from female solidarity by the male audience. Consider, for example, the following selection:

> My friends, who are with me,
> Applaud the young men well.
> God, calm me,
> As you have calmed the *anage* tree,
> Which is on a sand dune.
> Young people, applaud the camels.
> The shields are suspended
> In order to protect us,
> The soul of he who walks.
> This interests blacksmiths as well as nobles.
> I implore God, who brought me into the world,
> He who made the sun,
> God who brought me into the world,
> And who is going to take me to my country Takriza, Agalal, Anou-neqrin
> Young girls of the Kel Tates, protect me,
> Guard me throughout life.
> Alas, have pity for someone in love.
> When they are attacked, even maraboutage does not get rid of it,
> Nor the sorcerers of Kano,
> Nor the Tubus of Kewar, nor those of Bilma Sougou.
> Oh, my soul! The switches of love are nineteen in number.
> The *aza* and the *abaka* trees pierce the liver
> Like straw which burns quickly from hot iron.
> Young women with me, some have been distracted by the men.
> Others have been sold for billfolds.
> Others have been sold for tobacco.
> Others have said I am not beautiful, I am not pretty.
> But I do not care about the looks of night and day.
> Adawoula who is light-complexioned
> And who made gold anklets.

These verses include subtle "digs" at other women for being vain and vulnerable to male pretenses of wealth, for being tempted by material goods, and, in the immediate performance context, for being distracted from singing (which is but a symptom of the larger weaknesses summarized above). The solo singer warns against succumbing to passion and abandoning song, the implication being that the young girls must be strong, like the *anage* tree, which grows in the Tewar *oeud* on sand dunes. Animals eat this plant year round, for it is durable and grows even during periods of drought. Additional images of strength and protection abound in the song's references to God, shields, and remedies of marabouts and sorcerers from diverse ethnic groups and regions. The *tənde*, in principle at least, is supposed to be a curing event, in which the energized performance of music for the purpose of exorcizing devils is the explicit goal. But people attend this ceremony for a variety of reasons, as the playful reproach of the verses suggests.

Other song verses are less subtle in their criticism, and take on a ribald tone. One song describes a sexual encounter between a man and a donkey:

Young women
For the sake of God, applaud.
Tomorrow is the departure
For the marriage between the donkey
And the houseguard.
Spoiled *koura*,
Which covered the donkey.
Small amulets swinging behind the donkey.
Whom is this song for?
It is for the houseguard.
His radio is left suspended.
Spoiled *koura*.

Koura is a very expensive cloth, worn traditionally by the nobility. The cloth (and, by extension, noble descent) is spoiled or degraded by association with the houseguard's act. Many Kel Ewey men who go south to Nigeria on caravans each year remain there for a time working as houseguards, but this career is considered less prestigious than herding or caravanning, and is beneath the dignity of the nobility. Nonetheless, many prefer this to gardening, an occupation more closely identified with servile groups. The image of sexual obscenity may express the tension between the ideals of social stratum and the reality of economics: the contradiction between a desire to maintain traditional ideals of pure descent and conduct associated with noble status, leisure, and luxury consumer goods, and the economic necessity to perform low-status occupations.

Audience interaction and inversion
Additional behavior that normally would be considered improper or even licentious is expressed in the core image of the possession songs. As in many other African possession idioms (Hausa *bori* rites, for example), the possessed are described as "mounts of the gods." Kel Ewey say that spirits mount the possessed, using the Tamacheq term *ewaren*, which denotes

mounting a camel or horse. Throughout the ritual, there is increasingly licentious behavior in the audience, including poking and pinching, much of which concerns the efforts of young men to attract the attention of young women, often members of the chorus. Men in the audience perform the *t-hum-a-hum* sound, an accepted Tamacheq phrase, onomatopoeia referring to a guttural, rasping sound said to "address" or "be about" spirits, and occasionally beam flashlights on women's faces, while the women pretend to be irritated or not to notice the intrusive beams of light. They also make blatant physical and verbal passes at women, which, in other situations, would be considered highly insulting. (On one occasion, in fact, the village "crazy man" mimicked possession and lay down beside the real patient.) Young children beat on improvised drums and often imitate the head dancing of the possessed. Boys place lizards on each other. In general, the people present at a possession ritual address each other as *anebleg* (friend), rather than the more formal terms of direct address.

Throughout the joking and laughter, the patient remains subdued, with the exception of her head dance and the evocation of the spirits. Although it is the audience and the musicians who speak, joke, and sing, however, even the possessed person displays behavior normally uncommon, if not prohibited, for women. Contrary to the usual value in Tuareg culture placed on concealing one's true desires, the patient indicates non-verbally her song preference. She also holds a man's sword perpendicular to the ground, upon which she leans as she dances, in order to "cut and separate spirits" – it is the metal, in particular iron, that scares off spirits. (Both young and old patients do this, in spite of the belief that a sword held by a menstruating woman will have a detrimental effect on its male owner's virility and prowess in warfare, and despite the view that elderly women need less protection against spirits than younger women.) The dancing of elderly women presents a further inversion of normal behavioral roles. Older women usually do not dance in public, particularly not in mixed company, and especially not at events featuring ribald behavior and suggestive entertainment. Also in contrast to usual practice, female patients wear the black veil which is similar (though not identical) to the face-veil typically worn by men in everyday life. In other contexts outside the possession ritual, there is not much interaction between different age groups, but at the ritual seemingly irreverent conduct and interaction between age groups abound. Young boys horse around freely on the sidelines, sometimes dancing like grown men, sometimes causing considerable mischief. They wear men's veils (usually not worn until a man is eighteen years of age or older), and carry long sticks to simulate the men dancing with lances. They speak without reserve to adults, often teasing them, but this behavior provokes little reprimand during a possession ceremony.

Rituals of reversal in wedding symbolism

The songs and other behavior during the *tande n goumaten* display the inversion typical of "rituals in reversal," which have been the subject of much anthropological attention (Gluckman 1965; Handelman 1990; Beidelman 1971, 1974, 1980).[1] Yet the possession ritual has many parallels in symbolic content with rites of passage. These two seemingly contradictory strands are integrated into a unified whole through the spirit possession idiom. The tensions between the inversion and the correspondence of symbols in the spirit possession rite and other domains of Tuareg culture (rites of passage in particular) reflect certain contradictions in social relationships. A number of authors (Douglas 1975; Turner 1982; Kapferer 1983; Schechner 1985; Stoller 1989; and Handelman 1979, 1990) explore the role of the ludic in ritual and drama as an oblique attack on form. In a similar manner, Gadamer's observations on the transformations of art, ritual, play, and games (1975, 1986) provide a useful framework for analyzing the transposition from the presentational media of the rite to the drama. In Tuareg possession rituals, this transpositional process is evident in dominant symbolic parallels with the life-crisis rite of marriage.

The most striking parallel is the association of the initial body posture of the possessed person with the behavior of a bride prior to the marriage ceremony. At the beginning of a possession ceremony, the patient always appears in a prone position on the ground, with her entire body covered by a blanket or cloth. This is also the dominant symbol at weddings, seen in the central image of the wedding tent. For the first days of the wedding ceremony, the bride lies prone beneath a blanket in her mother's tent. During this phase of the wedding, for several successive nights the mother of the bride and other close older female relatives construct, take down, and reconstruct the marriage tent (*edew*). This tent image is associated with both the curing rite and life-crisis rites, nearly always in the context of festivals featuring mixed-sex sociability. In fact, courtship takes place within the tent; hence its underlying association with romantic love, outside of as well as within marriage. During the nightly conversation and tea-drinking among friends in the newly married couple's tent, incense is passed around, and each individual holds his or her robe over the head, tent-like, in order to saturate it with the burning fragrance. Incense is used in courtship, but it is also said to protect against spirits, and thus is used in possession ceremonies. Several patients told me that one symptom of their illness was a strong desire to smell beautiful fragrances, like perfume and incense.

For at least part of the possession ritual, then, the patient enacts the role of the metaphorical bride beneath the blanket. The blanket covers her, tent-like, as it does the bride in her nuptial tent. The possession songs also contain marriage tent imagery: one song text refers to the central wooden post of the tent frame: ("well-attached branches of the tent"). The image of well-attached branches refers to the mother–daughter relationship and its enduring qualities, before and after marriage. Initial residence among the Kel Ewey is near the bride's parents, and in the Bagzan region where I conducted my research, this often continues in practice even after the couple may choose to move after two or three years of stable union. Furthermore, during this initial period, the groom must perform services and give gifts (typically foodstuffs and household items) to his mother-in-law on demand. This triangle between mother, daughter, and daughter's new husband frequently becomes the focus of intrafamily conflict.

Women say that the main reason that the bride lies covered in her mother's tent is that "she is ashamed [reserved]" (*tela takarakit*). They are less explicit about why the possessed person lies covered during the curing rite. Some explanations point to her state of possession, saying merely that "spirits are inside her" (*goumaten a teha*), or that "she feels solitude" (literally, "she is in the wilderness" – *essuf a teha*). Others mention a kind of shame felt by the possessed woman, but do not elaborate on its cause. Yet it is evident that shame is associated with the initial phase beneath the blanket, before the patient rises to a sitting position and begins the head dance. It thus appears that the patient undergoes a kind of transition from reserve (*takarakit*) at the rite's beginning to lack of it as the rite progresses, which corresponds to the idea of the transformation of initial suppression of self-expression to the almost unrestricted unleashing of expression in joking relationships. Throughout this transformation, the audience continues joking and laughing, more like the familiar behavior of a courting relationship than that of marriage. Trance behavior is thus identified with ambiguous or liminal states. The image of the beginning of the rite, when the patient lies prone beneath a blanket and later is fitted with the black veil and white tassle as she rises, is parallel to the bride's seclusion in her mother's tent, when she also wears a tassle, signifying her reserve and also serving to protect her from spirits that are believed to menace the new household (initially headed by the mother-in-law).

The possessed patient beneath the blanket is also in a liminal state, and may experience some shame from the association of this performance with transition in social position (from adolescent to married woman, or from mother to mother-in-law), and with change in behavior (from the joking of cousins to the reserve of affines and elders). The possessed and the bride both undergo a transformation of social identity – but simultaneously, in the conflation of opposites, rather than sequentially. Possession, like marriage, constitutes a rite of passage, but not in a linear sense; rather, spirits are representations of the person that are incompatible with accepted definitions of self. These "unacceptable" representations are accommodated during possession.

The institution of courtship has strong parallels with the curing rite. Courtship is highly formalized and the subject of much preoccupation and speculation. Like courtship, *tənde n goumaten* usually takes place at night, and its central events, also like courtship, are music, poetry, and conversation. The same term (*eljimat*) is used to refer to conversation both at the curing ceremony and during courtship. *Eljimat* consists of jokes and games, with an emphasis on verbal wit, and takes place during courtship in the girl's tent. Though the *eljimat* of the possession ceremony takes place out in the open, it features nonetheless elements very similar to those of courtship: a sociable atmosphere, an audience of mixed company, and strong perfume and fine clothing. Indeed, as noted earlier, courtship often takes place immediately after the curing rite, in the privacy of a woman's tent. The suitor is expected to enter by surprise and awaken the woman, much as the songs "awaken" the patient from beneath her blanket during the curing rite.[2]

The alternating frames of non-serious joking and serious healing seem to parallel the frames associated with relationships over the life course that are transformed: for example, the transition from the courtship phase (involving a degree of sexual license and frequently illicit liaisons) to marriage (featuring behavioral restrictions and economic obligations). The transition to marriage also affects kinship behavior: the joking and horseplay associated with cousins become the reserve and formality associated with in-laws. The initial posture of the possessed, with its visual symbol of the covered bride and the marriage tent, highlights not only the transition from joking cousin to reserved affine, but also the transformation from active motherhood, with children, to successful motherhood, with married children and affinal relationships connected to their marriages. Just as successful wifehood implies a reserved relationship with one's husband in public, successful motherhood implies a reserved relationship, as a mother-in-law, with one's son-in-law.

There is also a parallel between the curing rite and courtship in the personal choice exercised in both contexts. The *gouma*, by refusing to dance, indicates her rejection of certain songs or their style of performance. Likewise, during courtship a girl may reject a suitor by reacting negatively to his attempts to enter her tent. In both contexts here, women are transformed from normally reserved members of the community who, despite their high status and ownership of property, must restrict expression of personal sentiments, into articulate agents who make direct statements of personal choice. In other contexts, such acts are strongly discouraged. Adolescent girls, since they are of marriageable age when bridewealth negotiations are delicate, are not supposed to reveal their personal preferences; rather, they can reveal only their veto of a suitor. Ideally, Kel Ewey express a preference for marriage within the same social stratum and between persons classified as cousins. In practice, however, most marriages are between either distantly related or completely unrelated persons. (I was told by certain smiths, who negotiate nobles' marriages, that marriages between close cousins seldom last long, for such persons usually have been raised together, and find the transition from cousins to husband and wife difficult.)

The curing rite thus provides an occasion for persons from diverse social strata not only to mix socially, but also to reassess their social predicament, which often results in directing "digs" at each other. The early years of Kel Ewey marriage typically are extremely brittle, and feature much conflict in domestic relationships. A married couple is not viewed as an independent household unit until bridewealth obligations are met by the husband and he is accepted by his parents-in-law. A mother-in-law is capable of breaking up her daughter's marriage if she dislikes the son-in-law. As a result of this tentative situation, newlyweds are seen frequently at evening festivals, and may continue to participate covertly in the flirtation that takes place at these gatherings. Indeed, if one's spouse is away for a long time, the remaining spouse is considered to be temporarily available, almost as if he or she were single. In this sense, marriage in its early stages is contingent upon the groom's behavior, almost a continuation of courtship: the groom must continue to provide gifts and services for the bride and her family, the couple is allowed to use the nuptial tent only at night, and the groom disappears from his in-laws' camp or household during the day. This attitude, combined with the emphasis at possession rituals and other festivals on personal display and appearance (sartorial finery, strong perfumes, flashy make-up), seems to encode the temporary suspension of marriage and affinal ties during possession.

As the curing ceremony progresses in its alternating sequences of non-serious, ludic, and serious healing frames, it becomes a counterpoint code, expressing the double-binds of cross-cutting and contradictory relationships between members of different kin categories and social strata. Often it is held near the patient's mother's home, underlining the belief that *goumaten* spirits are inherited from mother to daughter. This location and illness etiology, and the kinship relationships it represents, symbolizes tensions surrounding marriage in Kel Ewey society. The *tənde n goumaten* counterbalances these tensions in several ways. It requires or encourages situations and behavior opposite to those valued and expected in other everyday and ritual contexts. For example, poetry and song are considered excellent vehicles in which to express those sentiments that cannot be addressed directly. In this way, the reserve required in certain social relationships (between affines, between husband and wife, between older women and their sons-in-law) can be temporarily relieved by the poetic admission of typically prohibited feelings (such as one's romantic preference, or one's hostility toward an affine). These feelings can thereby be expressed during the *tənde n goumaten*.

The divergence between occupation, socio-economic status, and traditional social stratum creates yet another kind of tension when Kel Ewey decide to marry. Given this divergence, it is often difficult to find an appropriate spouse in a society that favors class endogamy, and it may be difficult also for a Kel Ewey groom to meet his bridewealth and brideservice obligations. Once again, the *tənde n goumaten* ceremony relieves the tension by representing and parodying expected behavior. Jokes and inversion of role-playing are interspersed with dominant symbols of reserve (covering, veiling) paralleling those of life-crisis rites, representing an accelerated, condensed image of life situations in which significant structural ties are alternately highlighted and shadowed, asserted and suspended. Throughout the ceremony, there is a symbolic opposition between courtship, illicit love, and joking (during which property and affective ties are contained within the maternal tent) on the one hand, and marriage, childbearing, and in-lawness (during which the groom is alienated from the maternal tent and social behavior is reserved) on the other. It is no accident, then, that women take a greater interest in singing in the curing rite when the patient is a close relative, and that men are more likely to attend when the patient is from a distant location or kin category.

On a performative level, inversion in possession balances kin and class restrictions and hierarchies through wise-cracks and insults. It allows for the temporary release of kin and class restrictions and of gender- and age-based roles and relationships, but solely within the performance context of the songs. Some men state openly that they attend celebrations such as weddings and namedays – and *tənde n goumaten* rituals – far from home precisely because of the enhanced opportunities that these events provide for extramarital affairs. Indeed, they say that attending these events is "like going to a disco" elsewhere. However, the spirit possession rituals differ from other Tuareg celebrations in that no money or gifts circulate, attendance does not depend on monetary or other kinds of contributions based on one's social relationship to the other participants, and communal work or other kin- and class-based obligations are not required. The *tənde n goumaten* rituals serve as an occasion for meeting people, particularly those of the opposite sex, "with no strings attached." The singing during the curing rite provides a degree of choice, an opportunity to establish ties that would be off-limits in other situations. This view was illustrated clearly in the case of one young man who attended regularly the frequently held curing rites for an elderly woman named Silimana. Silimana had several daughters of marriageable age, one of whom the young man wanted to court. In everyday life, this man was afraid or ashamed to enter Silimana's compound, precisely because of the daughters' status as potential marriage partners and their mother's status as his potential affine, and his extreme reserve toward her. In addition, it is the parents of the couple, along with marabouts and blacksmiths, who arrange marriages among Kel Ewey. This factor added further to his embarrassment, because of his fear that the mother would reject him as a potential spouse for her daughter. At the evening curing rites of the mother, however, he felt free to approach the girl of his choice and flirt openly with her.

The curing ceremony, then, can be interpreted as a kind of carnival in which individuals transcend the normal social boundaries encircling marriage and affinal relationships. From the male point of view, the wife and mother-in-law are central figures in this scheme, toward both of whom reserved public behavior must be maintained. From the female point of view, as well, there is a suspension of belief in social norms of reserve: for engaged adolescents, of restricting expression of personal sentiment, and for older women with marriageable daughters, of attending evening musical festivals. But there is no clear-cut opposition between men and women in this respect; suspension of belief or assertion of belief does not fall consistently into one or the other gender category. Rather, it seems dependent on context. The alternate suspension and assertion of belief for women is shown clearly in the analysis of this ritual in terms of the two polar relationships that dominate women's lives: the joking relationships with cousins, on the one hand, and the reserved relationships with affines, on the other. *Tənde* patients often describe themselves as "not participating fully in women's lives." Many of these women, in fact, do avoid weddings, nameday celebrations, and other events, such as communal work projects. Is their lack of participation in these events the cause, purpose, or consequence of this sporadic illness? Evidence suggests that *goumaten* illness is sometimes used as a means of seeking refuge from the duties and obligations of age and kin, and from class relationships which feature joking as well as those that feature reserve. Duties of joking relationships include gift-giving at namedays, preparing food or providing other services at rites of passage, and cooperative work in tent-construction between close female cousins, or between nobles, smiths, and former servile groups. While joking relationships offer relaxed familiarity on the one hand, they can also become stressful: for their obligations of reciprocity often conflict with one's socio-economic situation and inclination. It is interesting to note that several spirit possession ceremonies coincided with, or closely followed, weddings and nameday festivals, and that some possessions actually took place at these events.

The non-serious elements and the symbolic parallels with serious rites of passage and structural processes express and counterbalance extreme tensions in the avoidance and joking relationships of both men and women, associated with affines and cousins, respectively. On the one hand, it enables individuals to express sentiments, relax, and to mix with whom they please on the basis of achieved rather than ascribed criteria, figuratively to "drop the veil." It allows them to include themselves and to approach when it suits their purpose; to narrow the distance in reserve and avoidance relationships. On the other hand, it enables individuals to opt out, to exclude themselves, when this suits their purpose, from obligations of joking relationships. It permits the creating of distance in these latter relationships when they become claustrophobic. Thus kinship and social stratum are focal points of reference throughout these processes. However, ritual tropes also address gender and age issues. These latter are seen clearly in women's inversion of headdress, the associated symbolism of head and hair during possession, and the head dance with its more general aesthetic code of "swaying tree branch."

Head symbolism: headdress inversion and hyperbole
The head comprises several key tropes that recur throughout Tuareg spirit possession. Head symbolism and other tropes elaborated into possession aesthetics entail a culturally produced and reproduced discourse about

forces constituting the person. Thus they provide a useful point of departure for examining how social configurations of gender, age, and class are continually realigned, in two domains of experience: agency and power, and aesthetics. Tuareg possession tropes and the aesthetic forms embodying them illustrate how ritual transforms contradictory gender, class, and kinship experiences. During possession, the woman in trance wears a white cloth band on her head and a face-veil, made of dark but usually iridescent indigo-dyed cloth. Despite some parallels with the men's customary face-veil, the headdress of the possessed woman is different in two respects. First, unlike the men's face-veil, this headdress is not limited to covering the face, but drapes "tent-like" over the entire head. And second, it is not called by the same name as the men's face-veil: the women's veil is termed *ijewaren*, and the men's is called *tagelmust*. It is interesting to note here that the women's ritual face-veil is never referred to as *afar* (the term Kel Ewey use to designate the headscarf women wear daily). Significantly, the women's face-veil appears not solely as an inversion of women's daily attire, but also as an exaggeration of men's – particularly noblemen's – daily attire, thus serving as a doubly allusive symbol. During the ritual, a white band is attached over the veil by a girlfriend or female relative soon after the possessed woman has risen to a sitting position from her initial prone position beneath the blanket, as she begins to perform the head dance to the music. Usually, with the exception of the dark indigo fabric of the headdress, the possessed person will wear colors that shine in the dark: for example, her blouse consists of white or shimmering fabrics. Women do not wear face-veils in everyday life; these are men's accessories. In fact, the patient's headband resembles closely that worn by a young bride during seclusion in her mother's tent. In form, it is also similar to a popular leather tassle hair ornament, which is often decorated with cowrie shells (considered by Kel Ewey to symbolize fertility) and worn by women in everyday life.

Men never wear women's headscarves, and, in the rare case of a man undergoing the *tande n goumaten*, he would never don the woman's *ijewaren*. Rather, a man's standard attire within and outside rituals is the *tagelmust*. Although the *tagelmust* can be arranged in a variety of styles in accordance with personal preference, it is never draped, *ijewaren*-style, to cover the entire head and neck.

The meaning of veiling, its inversion during trance by women, and its everyday function for men, can be understood best by comparing both types of headdress. Many symbolic anthropological treatments of covering, masking, and adorning the head, face, and hair attempt to find universal, psychological explanations for this behavior. Studies that focus specifically on hair often assume that covering the hair displaces the focus of sexuality from the genitals to the head.[3] With few exceptions (Derrett 1973: 100–103; Obeyesekere 1981), most approaches do not explore why or how this occurs in a particular society. Interpreting ritual inversion and hyperbole in possession requires examining the extent to which a headdress may signify sexuality transferred to the head, dominance or subordination, and a closer look at the nature of local attitudes toward male and female sexuality and gender roles. The meaning of gender and class inversion, hyperbole, and head imagery during possession emerges from local interpretations of relevant core meanings, such as examining the relationships among men, women, and other parties, or among humans, spirits, and God. In local exegesis, there are Koranic bases for core meanings as well as individual explanations of core meanings. These have referents in men's and women's roles at official levels of social, political, and kinship organization and in formal authority positions, as well as in other influences, such as informal networks.

Situational meanings demonstrate how particular meanings emerge from the framework of core meanings. Individuals select meanings to fit the situation and even change them by playing with the system. For example, the different contexts of festival, courtship, life-crisis rites, and encounters with authority figures all entail variations in the situational meanings of Tuareg headdress. Relevant here are the local uses and the symbolic connotations of hair. Depending on the context, hair can be a beneficial or a dangerous power. For example, Kel Ewey believe that a woman may expose the back of her head and allow her hair to trail down her back if she is single, in courtship, and at a festival where neither her father nor her brother is present. But if she is married, pregnant, or nursing a baby, such behavior is considered dangerous, for it is said to cause birth defects and to dry up a mother's milk. In general, the wide variety of Kel Ewey headdress expresses life stage, class, and gender. Tuareg men, especially marabouts, shave their heads upon passing from youthful manhood to status as older males with children of marriageable age. Young adult noble men in some divisions traditionally wear distinctive long braids. A woman's life stages are marked by separate coiffures and the presence or absence of head coverings. There are also temporary hairstyles and headdresses for certain ritual states, such as a baby's nameday or a mother's forty-day seclusion after she gives birth.

Both headdress and possession are important features of transition and rites of passage among Tuareg. In this respect, there are important parallels between Tuareg headdress and masks in some other African societies: both are prominent symbols in life crises and transitions. Like masks, Tuareg headdresses are simultaneously agents of social control and avenues of escape from control,[4] and both masks and headdress are central to rites of transition and social conflict. They symbolize rejoicing in ambiguity, because the goal for Kel Ewey is not necessarily clarifying ambiguity, but rather preserving it to advantage in social relations. In headdress, ambiguity is maintained purposely, rather than overcome, in order to protect person and property in times of transition.

Thus there are important links between head covering and gender organization over time: the perceived capacities of men and women over the life course are put into practice and condensed into one central symbol of head covering. While possession clearly addresses diverse experiences and viewpoints in Kel Ewey culture (particularly those of social stratum, which cross-cut the experiences of men and women), and while possession includes in its dialogue non-participants as well as participants, the performance itself is predominantly female, and, as such, speaks clearly to gendered relations. As Moore (1990: 13) points out, gender may be seen either as a symbolic construction or as a social relationship, and the challenge is to translate local categories without distorting them, while simultaneously examining what men and women do in material, daily life. With these considerations in mind, local tropes and aesthetic forms of possession are woven into the present study, with the hope of avoiding the ethnocentric Western assumptions and epidemiological analyses that have plagued some studies of female possession (Lewis 1966, 1971; Shack 1966; Curley 1973). At the same time, the differences between men's and women's versions and elaborations of Kel Ewey Tuareg culture must be addressed, considering carefully both the observed gender asymmetries and the sometimes contradictory local constructions of personhood (Boddy 1989: 4–5). In my view, possession discourse is largely an elaboration of these notions and their outcomes; thus it is precisely this heterogeneity of local theories that can illuminate, rather than constrain, interpretation. The local discourse, then, can speak for itself.

Kel Ewey Tuareg of either sex and of diverse social origins consider men and women to have basically different natures. Women are considered to be more prone to depression and spirit possession than men. Men, especially marabouts, say that women are more "upset by little things," and that "women remember, men forget." There are different avenues to prestige for women and men: women derive much prestige and security from mother-in-law status, and men derive much prestige from Islamic scholarship.

Headdresses in standard and inverted forms express these dual avenues of men and women, as well as the multiple branches off these avenues that allow flexibility and other options according to more specific distinctions of age and social stratum. Yet headdresses frequently represent only a part of the total message communicated by the adorned body. They emphasize, reinforce, or restate messages that are also contained in the total set of body decorations or conveyed by other means. As Biebuyck and Van den Abeele observe (1984: 21–23), headdresses are independent of dress. They are combined easily into complex composite sets, which enables their elaboration in possession as well as in other rituals and daily interactions. In effect, "the wearing of different hats" surrounds the transformation of person over time, embodied by inversion and hyperbole. In this process, headdresses are part of the vestimentary outfit, yet they have a somewhat independent existence and meaning. They draw special attention to the head, to different parts of the skull, and to the hair, providing more specific indicators for both sexes: age, marital status, class, kinship, moods, crisis situations (jealousy, revenge, property transfer), socio-ritual transitions, as well as conceptions about health, fertility, potency, restraint, and dignity.

Tuareg headdresses appeal to the senses in a variety of ways, often through valued materials and colors. One way Tuareg differentiate social status, for example, is in the manner in which certain jewels are attached to the coiffure. The wife of a chief or marabout wears them fixed on her forehead; women of other social segments wear them on the right temple; and a Daga Tuareg woman would display them on her left temple. Tuareg headdress seems to be a metaphorical statement about notions of personhood. According to Turner (1967: 28), dominant symbols can be conceptualized in polar terms: "At one pole is found a cluster of significata that refer to components of the moral and social orders . . . At the other pole, the significata are usually natural and physiological phenomena and processes."

Considered collectively, the Tuareg veiling of head and hair is a dominant symbol, and certainly exhibits polar properties. Multivocality allows covering the head to suggest different meanings to various participants, at different levels of experience, on different occasions. But establishing that head covering is a dominant ritual symbol exposes only one dimension of meaning. What is more interesting are the multiple uses of the headdresses beyond these specified ritual contexts. For example, they are used ironically in ludic and carnival social settings, inviting joking, flirting, and courtship. There seems to be a transformation among different performative "registers" or "frames" of drama, ritual, and play – a concept that has been discussed by Gadamer (1975, 1986), Turner (1982), and Schechner (1985), but which has not been explored fully or linked to processes of spirit possession. Tuareg social relations are articulated through symbolism and aesthetics (both within ritual and outside it), and social action in terms of discourse style. They constitute, to borrow Ong's term, "a key refrain" (1987: 10) of the possession idiom. What new entity here is associated with the symbol in this emergent refrain? How does it relate to its use and meaning in possession and other contexts of person definition? The performance of metaphor in ritual joins separate domains of social life to greater effect and with greater affect than when these domains are considered separately in their ordinary aspects.

There are tropes of both social and ritual contexts in which headdresses are central features. These are underlined in men's face-veil wrapping rituals, everyday social interaction, courtship, festivals, marriage, and women's possession rituals. The tropes, and their potential analogies, suggest a series of questions regarding the separation of the sexes, the boundary-marking function of headdress, the reliability of form in communicating meaning, and the types of distinctions that Tuareg consider most important.

In an attempt to explore some of these questions, let us examine the function and significance of the veil more closely. The adolescent boy's first wearing of the veil is a family ritual occasion that marks his initiation from adolescent to adult status. Throughout adulthood a man is rarely unveiled, whether he is travelling alone, asleep, or with other people. Women, in contrast, do not wear a veil, but a headcloth (called *afar, ekerhei*, and numerous other terms), which is also taken up around puberty. Most authors (Keenan 1977; Casajus 1987) consider the headscarf to be quite different from the veil; the headscarf is black, much shorter than the veil, and is not wrapped around the head, but partly draped over it without concealing the face. My own data indicate that this contrast between the headscarf and the face-veil applies only to young women of childbearing age. I noticed that older women often manually raise the side of the headscarf to cover the mouth, and, in the presence of affines, elderly women fasten the headscarf over the nose to resemble the men's face-veil (Rasmussen 1987, 1991a). Today, the most formal style and fabric of the men's veil, the indigo *alechou*, is worn almost exclusively for ceremonial and festive occasions, particularly rites of passage, and then predominantly by the noble social stratum. Significantly, the veil donned by the possessed woman is also indigo, suggesting some parallels with the symbolism of men's veiling, such as the metaphorical adoption of a new status or the guarding of a property transfer. The formal material stands in contrast to the simpler *khent*, worn by men for some ritual occasions as well as for everyday use, and in contrast to the most common type of veil now worn by all Tuareg men for general use – the *echchach* – which is white, black, or dark blue (not indigo) in color. *Echchach* is made of manufactured muslin, which is much cheaper and readily accessible in the shops of the Mozabite merchants in Tamanrasset and Agadez.

Men's and women's head coverings suggest distinct yet interrelated meanings when considered semiotically as well as functionally.[5] This is manifested in the covering of the mouth, nose, and brow when in the presence of foreigners, especially women and parents-in-law, particularly mothers-in-law. The men's face-veil and the women's headcloth are similar in form and shape, they serve the same social function, and they have complementary or analogous meanings. Yet the position and style of an individual's veil is more than a reflection or communication of expected role behavior in a particular social situation. The self is to some extent concealed; as Murphy (1964, 1967) recognized, the wearing of the veil by Tuareg symbolically introduces a form of distance between their selves and their social others.

These observations open up new perspectives on the use of headdress in Tuareg possession. The position of a man's veil signifies the degree of respect or deference that is expected of a particular social position. Between two actors, the one to whom respect is owed will usually wear his veil lower, so that the lower the veil, generally the greater the role status. The man's veil is worn higher in the company of parents-in-law, senior kinsmen, and elders and leaders. However, there is an inversion of this pattern in other social contexts: highest status can be symbolized by a veil in the highest position when worn by a chief or a marabout, and lowest status can be symbolized by a veil at its lowest position when worn by smiths and former slaves. Generally, for example, chiefs and marabouts wear veils at the highest position. Smiths and former slaves tend to be careless with the veil when not in the presence of parents-in-law or senior kinsmen, allowing it to drop below the chin.

A summary of differences and similarities between the two headdresses is necessary in order to illuminate its alternately inverted and hyperbolic qualities in the possession ritual. A woman who has self-respect does not exhibit the nape of her neck and also hides a small part of her hair, at least when she goes out to visit. In the presence of older persons and strangers, sometimes a young woman will bring a corner of her headscarf over her mouth. However, the female headscarf differs strikingly from the men's face-veil in several respects. Men must devote much time and effort each morning to winding the material of their face-veil (more than ten meters long). All day long, men never cease to readjust it. The woman's headscarf, in contrast, is a much more modest piece of cloth that is placed on top of the head in a detached fashion and kept in the same style most of the day. There are, however, marked exceptions to this rule in ritual conduct and before affines, elders, marabouts, and male strangers. Thus the practice of veiling is not exclusively reserved for men. Normally, the cloth that covers the woman's head does not hide her face; it is perched on the hair. But in front of strangers, especially men, as well as before affines (in particular the parents-in-law), the woman intermittently hides her mouth with one corner of the material that she wears on the head.

There is a plethora of local slang to designate the woman's headscarf, depending on region and texture. For example, *alechou*, in its first sense, is the name of the fancy indigo-dyed cloth imported from Hausa regions to the south, and the complexity of its manufacture makes it very expensive. Men also wear face-veils of indigo, called *tagelmust n alesshu*. In addition, although there is a term to designate wearing the men's veil (*anagad*), there is no such term for wearing the women's headscarf. It should also be noted here that the wearing of the woman's headscarf is not as strict as the wearing of the man's face-veil. While a woman should not expose her hair in public, it is unthinkable for a man even to display his face. Upon my suggestion that men might show their faces, a male friend who is a resident of Agadez, where traditional attire still predominates, exclaimed with astonishment and horror, "What! Expose my teeth and tongue . . . especially while eating, to women?"

A woman never covers both head and face permanently. She must cover her hair to be proper in public, except during her hairstyling, which is done by smith women who are attached to noble families. She must also wear her hair in neat, tightly woven braids. This was clearly demonstrated to me once on a visit to a close friend, Tita, a young noble woman who was a renowned singer and also frequently possessed. I was surprised to find Tita braiding her own hair, because nobles depend on smiths to perform this service, as they are considered more skillful at hairdressing. I was still more mystified to see this self-hairdressing while Rhaicha, a smith woman, was sitting nearby watching. After I inquired as to why Tita was dressing her own hair, Rhaicha told me that smiths were not supposed to dress hair on this particular day, as a sign of respect for a deceased mythical ancestor who had died and left an inheritance on that day. When I complimented Tita on her beautiful hair, however, and remarked that she need not take the trouble to dress it since it looked fine freely flowing, Tita remarked that a Kel Ewey woman, especially a noble, would never go out with undressed hair, even if she had to dress it herself. For the Tuareg, hair flowing freely about the shoulders and neck is very sensual, for either sex, and would be considered an inappropriate style for a noble woman in public.

To attribute Tuareg veiling and hairdressing solely to sexual modesty is problematic and contradictory, however. Men wear the veil outside social interaction, such as when they are alone and when they are sleeping. A woman's popular hairstyle leaves the neck exposed, and a modern man's face-veil seen in towns (but never in the countryside) consists of transparent gauze setting. Although women's and men's everyday headdresses are distinct, they are analogous and complementary in meaning. Their link lies in the transformation of kinship and marriage over time, as expressed in aesthetic and ludic uses of the headdress. The wearing of the veil during the possession trance condenses these meanings into one central visual symbol.

Men begin to wear the veil at about twenty years of age. A Tuareg proverb states that "the veil and the trousers are brothers." Before being veiled, the young man is called *amawad*; after the veiling, he is called *amangad*. The veiling ritual marks the passage to the status of an adult male eligible to marry. Formerly, the first face-veiling was always followed by a week of seclusion, similar to the seclusion of a newly married couple. Today each family determines whether they wish their son to be secluded after veiling, and the father of the family decides when the time is appropriate. Sometimes a *tande n emmnas*, or camel race, is held in honor of the occasion, and when the young man goes visiting, people give him small gifts. During this time, the man is veiled very strictly, like a groom. As *amangad*, men can go to war, attend meetings, visit young women at night in their tents, and carry the sword. From the age of about forty onward, men shave their heads as a step in attaining a more respected status.

The link between female veiling and marriage exists, but is less explicit. A young girl takes up the headscarf when she begins to be available to suitors. She considers it attractive, but its first wearing usually features no precise ritual or seclusion. An exception to this, according to older Kel Ewey women, is that the girl's grandmother may place it on her head for the first time as she nears marriage. One woman in the village where I lived who had never married did not don the headscarf until she was past adolescence, when an old woman dressed her in it. She told me that if a woman is still single by the time she is about thirty years of age, an old woman should give her the headscarf. Otherwise, a husband will often give a headscarf to his new bride.

Women's headdress, then, while sometimes donned upon reaching adolescence or approaching marriage, does not always coincide with these life stages; nor does it coincide with a woman's first menstruation, although I noticed that some Kel Ewey women did begin to wear the headscarf at this time. Women may marry without having covered their hair, but the new bride will receive headclothes from her husband upon their marriage. This custom suggests that an engaged or married woman should cover her head, yet Kel Ewey never affirm this, and married women sometimes go uncovered.

Ludic and aesthetic aspects of headdress
Both forms of headdress express not static kinship but transition and changing access to property over the life course. In their external aspect, they are cosmetic. Men consider the veil to be "pretty," and feel more attractive when veiled. In Agadez, one new fashion of men's face-veil, transparent netting, runs counter to the traditional modesty norms underlying the wearing of the veil. The transparent veil promotes display rather than concealment, and is related to flirtation and sexuality. Possession song verses praise a traditional veil style, which flows back over the shoulders. The aesthetic and affective qualities of the man's face-veil are evident during courtship, during which time a man will take great care in his dress (particularly his veil), the display of his sword, and his camel. In such situations the veil preserves his self-respect and also creates aesthetic appeal.

In addition to the serious, functional aspect of headdress, it can also be used ludically to subvert expectations. Non-serious, ludic aspects of Tuareg headdress reveal its dynamic character, and provide further insights into women's veiling during the possession ritual. Headdress communicates the possibility of role conflict and the intent and disposition of actors, reducing ranges of social stimuli but not entirely concealing identity. The intent is not always serious. It allows the individual to "play" with the system and still protect the self-image, and in this respect acts as a personal fortress. A young married man may mockingly exaggerate his veil when an older woman enters, thus expressing sarcasm about her authority. Women may exaggerate covering their mouths with their headscarves upon the approach of their in-laws, as a joke. Men may allow nieces and nephews to play with their face-veils. During courtship, at musical festivals and mixed-sex gatherings, a suitor may race his camel near a woman, snatch her headscarf, and run away with it. Then all the men scramble for it, and one returns it to the owner. During weddings, there is a game in which any woman may try to tear off the veil of any man, once he is inside her tent. Whoever wins the struggle receives a prize of perfume from the loser.

Uses and styles of Tuareg headdresses in different contexts reveal additional linkages among possession, rites of passage, and the everyday social construction of gender and personhood over time. In particular, the inversion of headdress in trance reveals its relation to the men's face-veil wrapping ceremony, weddings, and namedays, and to the jural changes these encode through the life course of either sex.

Headdresses of both men and women act as alternately ornamental and concealing; they express the identity of the wearer in both hyperbole and understatement. They suggest alternating concerns with freedom of association among diverse social segments and kinspeople outside official marriage (such as flirting and courtship), and official marriage and property interests. They convey reserve and proper decorum, important noble cultural values. These qualities are not possessed in equal measure by everyone, and Tuareg believe that contact with the unreserved rubs off: children, smiths, and former slaves of either sex have the least reserve, and men and nobles possess the most. In fact, nobles of either sex are seen as the embodiment of reserve. Age is the most important factor in determining reserve and decorum, then comes social stratum, and the least important factor seems to be gender. The transitional points in life, when individuals take on roles guarding the transfer of property, necessitate reserve and respect. During these times, in particular, the face-veil and headscarf are emblems or props in a kind of masquerade to protect self, status, and property interests.

Kinship, descent, inheritance, and property encoded in headdress
In Tuareg social life, there is a proliferation of rules for social behavior based on two seemingly extreme modes of conduct: one is based on *takarakit* (reserve) and the other is based on *adelen* (joking). These two forms of behavior dominate most roles and relationships between different kinspeople and age groups to a greater extent than gender. For example, a woman friend of mine, whom I shall call Talbissout, hesitated to enter a tent where men had congregated. Before entering, she covered her face partially with the headscarf, greeted the owner of the tent, and inquired as to who was inside. These steps were taken not because she was timid before them as a woman before men, but because some of the men were possibly her affines, and such a possibility would require her to behave with *takarakit*. Likewise, another woman, Zeinabou, shyly raised the corner of her scarf and declined to drink tea with a group of guests in my tent, not because they

included men but because they included "guests from the other village" (that is, likely affines). Discretion must be observed toward elder persons of both sexes, but more particularly toward the father or relatives on the paternal side, and toward spouses in public. This discretion occurs during daytime sociability as well as during rituals, and includes name teknonymy (not using each other's names), refraining from eating together, modest dress, full or partial face-covering for either sex, slow gait, and low voice pitch. All festivals, courtship, and possession rites take place at night because "only then may in-laws be encountered without shame."

The basic residential and kinship unit is the household (*eghiwan*), which consists of the nuclear family (in earlier times it also consisted of slaves), and which is the basic unit of production, distribution, and consumption. Its animals are managed by female and male adult heads, as both women and men own and manage herds. The caravan trade merchandise of each household is kept separate. Though the *eghiwan* is the basic residential unit throughout most of the year, it is in fact highly flexible, and goes through processes of fission and fusion according to season and subsistence strategies. The nomadic tent (*ehan*) of the married woman remains hers in case of divorce; thus, although a man may end up without a tent, there is never any danger of this for a woman. Yet there are competing pressures among the semi-sedentized Kel Ewey, in that men own the mud house (*taghajemt*). Oxby (1978) and Casajus (1987) report a kind of endowment (*elkhabus*) among the Kel Ferwan Tuareg, which appears related to the *akhuderan* of the Kel Ewey, in that it is also intended to compensate for Koranic rules favoring men. According to the *akhuderan*, heirs to a wealthy donor's herd must be female descendants of women. The owners are named by the donor, and the property cannot be sold. But such cases are often ambiguous, and I was told that they are now being challenged by brothers who attempt to have their sisters' *akhuderan* herds converted to Koranic inheritance through the intervention of marabouts.

Gender, relations between the sexes, and headdress
Three characteristics of Kel Ewey Tuareg kinship impinge upon the definition of person and gender in headdress. First, the cross-referential nature of kinship creates loopholes and ambiguities for actors in social interaction. Second, kinship engenders conflict for Tuareg because of the emphasis on politeness to certain persons based on kinship ties on the one hand, and the need for close cooperation based on relative socio-economic position on the other. And third, the way in which men and women relate to their immediate kin is quite different: men relate to a wide, extended family

(*eghiwan*) and descent group (*tawsit*), while women relate more on the level of household (*gara*, defined as "those who eat together" by women, and as "fence enclosure" by men) and the female-headed, matrifocal domestic household (*tarik*).

Tuareg cultural values about gender in everyday life emphasize ambiguity rather than clear definition in the social system. A kind of masquerade ensures the appearance of nobility in aesthetic style: proper decorum, reserve, and refinement, both visually and verbally. The daily headdress of both sexes embodies these values. Tuareg consider dress and ornaments (which include both human jewelry and camel trappings) central to self-definition. As nobles personify the values of reserve and refinement, and, not surprisingly, as nobles disdain manual labor, Tuareg dress and ornaments imply freedom from manual labor. For example, rings are thought to emphasize long, fine hands that work neither tooling leather nor tending herds; elaborate hairstyles that require a smith stylist imply leisure time and status; and voluminous robes communicate wealth and a disregard for "working uniforms." Dress and ornaments are not the only indicators of prestige, leisure, and prosperity in Tuareg society; other markers are fatness (which has become more difficult to attain as pastures diminish and domestic slave labor dwindles), voluminous but constricting clothing, and heavy jewelry. Increasingly, there is a contradiction between the cultural ideology that values freedom from manual labor and a correspondingly high social status, and the greater prosperity and independence possible for individuals of lower social strata who choose to do the tasks disdained by nobles precisely because these tasks bring in more money.

Despite heavy manual work, such as going to the well, adolescent and newly married young women are encouraged to give the appearance of prosperity and ease by devoting a large part of their time to sociability, which includes drinking tea, socializing with friends of both sexes, making palm-fiber mats for tents, beaded bracelets, and polishing silver jewelry. They spend many hours on beauty routines, such as applying henna to their hands and feet, and styling their hair. During the first two or three years of marriage, while the new husband is completing his bridewealth payments and providing his parents-in-law with household gifts, there is an emphasis on personal adornment for the women of the household, and gifts brought back from caravans or other remunerative work are proudly displayed. Much of the couple's prestige derives from the husband's generosity to his wife and her household, as manifested through gifts. Items received by one young bride during the first year of her marriage included five indigo headscarf cloths, silk material, several short bolero-style blouses, incense, perfume, and two pairs of leather sandals. In general, these presents are of aesthetic value. Indigo cloths for the headscarf are an important gift; they are displayed before friends and relatives in the home of the bride's mother. During this time, the guests not only praise the cloths but also ask many questions about their cost, exclaiming how beautiful they are, and how jealous others become upon seeing them.

Tuareg men, in contrast, never receive face-veils as presents from their wives. Men's face-veil wrapping occurs before marriage, and is ritually performed by a marabout who recites Koranic verses as he winds the cloth around the young man's head. Men are supposed to cover their faces, cross their arms, and can neither eat nor drink when women are present after they have received the face-veil. A Hausa schoolteacher from the south related some of his difficulties in adjusting to a man's life among the Tuareg: when he ate in front of Tuareg women, they were astonished and loudly reproached him; when he bared his chest in public, they became upset; when he washed in front of them, he was chastised; and when he wore short pants (rather than long pants), he was admonished. Tuareg men are generally "ashamed" before women and speak in low, hushed voices in front of them, while women, on the contrary, often tease men. Frequently, when I talked with women and children among the Kel Ewey as a guest in their compounds, the men of the family would sit with their backs toward us and their veils on. Older men, in particular, usually remained inside the tent, and quickly fastened their face-veils upon my approach. They also avoided eye contact during greetings. Even after a long association in friendship and many visits, these barriers were only partially lifted.

For both men and women, covering the head connotes transition in jural status, although the men's veil style (which occurs in subtle form among elderly women as well as men) is accompanied by more restrictions. Yet despite the rigid and clear-cut role expectations for persons of different kin relationships and social strata, there is ambiguity in men's and women's jural status as they age. This is expressed in verbal art motifs reversing modesty and reserve norms. In one tale I collected from a young boy of servile origin, women discover they are married to monkeys instead of men after their mothers pull down their husbands' pants (Rasmussen 1990: 91–92). Numerous legends depict women as formerly wearing the face-veil, while men wear the women's wrapper-skirt (but never the headscarf). These legends link the wearing of clothing with name avoidance and reserve (Rasmussen 1990: 89; 1991a: 112), thus representing the conflict between joking and reserve, and the difficulty both sexes experience in the transition from cousin (joking) to spouse (reserve) to in-law (reserve and avoidance). In social life, the adjusting of the headdress and name avoidance manifest this difficulty. Although the regulatory norm is close cousin marriage, most Kel Ewey admit that this occurs rarely, and when it does, it usually ends in divorce. Cousins are frequently brought up together, and thus feel more like brother and sister than husband and wife, making the transition extremely difficult from the joking and friendly premarriage relationship to the reserved and respectful relationship of husband and wife.

Dress, ornaments, and jural responsibilities
In early childhood, small girls imitate adult chores through play with dolls and miniature tents. At about eight or ten years of age, they start to help their mothers seriously with domestic tasks, such as herding, cooking, fetching water, gathering palm fibers for mats and firewood, and mat-weaving. Between the ages of about ten and twelve, young girls occupy a liminal phase, during which they are said to be "neither *tabarart* (girl) nor *tekabkab* (teenager)." At this time, they still wear the long gown (*tekatkat*) and a girl's hairstyle. Although their ears will be pierced at this age (by a grandmother or maternal aunt), they wear neither the woman's large decorated hoop earrings nor the woman's bolero-style blouse (*aftag*) until adolescence, which is marked by the start of menses. The headscarf, as noted, is not donned by women until just before or immediately after marriage. Upon adolescence, young girls experience a sudden increase in domestic workload and responsibilities, diminished only temporarily during the early days of marriage.

In general, adolescence marks a change in dress for girls. They begin to wear the adult wrap skirt known as *teri*, large earrings called *chizobaten*, and various Islamic amulets. Very small children who are being weaned, adolescents, and brides all wear these amulets in abundance, but older children before adolescence and very old persons wear fewer amulets. A smith friend told me that Tuareg believe that adolescent girls are especially vulnerable to spirits and misfortune "because they are so highly valued and loved by their parents at this time, and spirits, jealous, want them, too." Extremely elderly women are believed to be safe from spirits, and thus do not need to wear as many amulets. In fact, traditionally, an elderly woman temporarily replaces the bride during one phase of the wedding ritual "in order to attract all the spirits [who would otherwise attack the bride] onto herself" (Rasmussen 1987). The five life stages when individuals are particularly vulnerable to spirits and misfortune are at birth, around weaning, during adolescence, as a bride, and as a new mother.

In the social system, adolescent girls and older women classified as past the childbearing age occupy statuses that are complementary to each other. This complementarity emerges clearly in ritual. Adolescent girls only attend night-time festivals, never the namedays and weddings held during the day. Elderly women, in contrast, fulfill their ritual obligations toward affines during the day (such as food preparation and formalized greetings); they return home at sundown and do not appear at the evening festivals. One elderly woman – the mother of several frequently possessed daughters, a former singer, and frequently possessed herself – told me that the reason older women stay away from the evening festivals is because they are old and because their in-laws attend these festivals. It is interesting to note here that preadolescent girls are seen as equivalent to elderly women in ritual events. On Islamic holy days, only little girls and post-childbearing women follow men and boys to the prayer ground on the outskirts of the village; adolescent girls and young childbearing women must pray at home. While small girls do not wear the headscarf, however, older women usually do, even exaggerating its style when they become mothers-in-law.

Thus, like the tent, draping and headcovering appear to protect and envelop women. Since very young girls and very elderly women usually do not have their own tent, headdress conveys the protection of their jural status and access to property at times when these are uncertain, or vulnerable to competition, jealousy, and ambiguity. Such situations arise just before and just following marriage: precisely the time when engaged or newlywed girls take up the headscarf, and older women exaggerate it. Significantly, men wear the face-veil throughout adulthood and they are always concerned with the tent, as they may be ejected from it at any time by the female proprietor.

Part of the tension between the sexes and marital instability undoubtedly derives from men's prolonged travel, but it also has sources in structural contradictions in Tuareg society. There is a great uncertainty between the sexes precisely because of the wide range of permissible social interaction: men are permitted to visit women in their tents – even recently married women – ostensibly for conversation. Courtship allows for the manipulation of marriage and descent norms, and also produces ambiguity. Romantic love, descent, and motherhood are mutually exclusive. This is most strikingly illustrated in the tacit permission for illicit affairs, and in the effective counterbalancing of this permissiveness in the taboo against illegitimate children. These contrasting expectations seem tied to Tuareg polarities of woman as cousin and woman as affine. Indeed, contradictions abound between descent and inheritance patterns, between the position of women in cultural ideology and their actual place in economic domains, and between the ideal of a monogamous nuclear household and the pull toward an extended polygynous household in a semi-sedentized setting.

It is not surprising then that in local ideology, Tuareg conceive of gender and class differences in terms of vulnerability to one's emotions and the display of sentiment (that is, the lack of reserve). Men, especially nobles, are not supposed to argue openly with women, and are not supposed to become as easily upset by "little things." Noble masculine pride emphasizes the ability to control the self (specifically, to hide one's true sentiments). Men are encouraged to be "cool" rather than "hot" or less controlled (like women), and to talk things over before resorting to violence. However, women are actually under more pressure than men to be coy and to conceal their emotions because of the constant gossip and ridicule to which they are subject. This restraint is particularly crucial regarding a woman's love preference in her adolescence and during her engagement and marriage negotiations. It is at this time, not surprisingly, that women take up the headscarf.

Headdress, then, seems to be a metaphor for protection, for concealing and controlling one's inner self. Feelings must be contained with reserve, or channelled in playful joking, such as sham fights between cross-cousins when they tear off each other's veils or headscarves. Women, especially noble women, are believed to be physically as well as emotionally weaker than men, and thus more susceptible to illnesses caught from exposure. One such illness, *afo*, is characterized by severe headaches, which are believed to result from sitting in the sun's or moon's rays, especially without a headscarf. Another illness, *ezziz*, causes bloating, and is said to come from sitting on warm sand (even after sundown) or standing on it in bare feet.

A link emerges between male and female headdress, the importance of reserve and concealing one's feelings, tent ownership, a more general access to property, and jural adulthood through time. These aspects of Tuareg life are reflected in changes in headdress style. Older men and women emphasize the veiling of the head the most at the time they negotiate the marriages of children and women, and when they construct the nuptial tent for their daughters' dowries. According to Tuareg, the marriage of children depends on the conduct of the parents; thus, mothers should keep their hair covered with the headscarf, and mothers-in-law should cover their mouths "like men who wear the *tagelmust* veil" (Rasmussen 1987).

The nomadic tent and headscarf are both associated most prominently with marriage, motherhood, and mother-in-law status. The nomadic tent is most prominent during the childbearing years of married life, and, as noted earlier, the young married woman's mother constructs the tent for her; she owns the tent at this point and keeps it even in case of divorce. Although elderly women are considered experts at tent construction, much later in life they often lack a nomadic tent, and end up living in grass huts adjacent to their daughters' compound. Significantly, they drop the headscarf in private, except when encountering affines in rituals. At times when the tent is the most prominent concern, headdress is also most prominent: at the time of marriage, during jural adulthood and childbearing, and, in exaggerated form, during the possession trance. Both bride and groom wear the indigo veil high on the face during the wedding ritual, as do mothers-in-law during weddings and other rites of passage. In informal everyday social interaction, there is more flexibility about the position of the headdress, depending on one's company, the message one wishes to convey, and one's jural status. The term for a married woman of childbearing age who is the female head of the household is *tamtot n ammas*, which literally means "woman inside" (as in "inside the tent").

Thus the human head is elaborated to convey one's personal position with respect to descent, inheritance, and property, and property determines shame and openness. Intelligence (part of a child's inheritance from the same-sex parent), property, and descent need varying protection during different life stages. Children do not cover their heads; they do "not yet have a head." Intelligence, in turn, is tied to principles of descent and social stratum. To say that someone has either no head or a black head (*eghef wa kawala*) is to call the person stupid or childish. Kel Ewey also say that "children have no shame." Thus their acts are explained by their place, and the attributes of this place, rather than by their individual responsibility or motivation. Children are not considered full social persons, either in morality or in intellectual capacity. They neither eat with adults nor initiate greetings to adults. They are seldom washed, and are often given left-over scraps of food. Children are not socially distant from anyone; indeed, they are encouraged to have close contact with many related and unrelated adults. Children and slaves, significantly, go unveiled and wear no headdress, and smiths are lax about both veils and headdresses. Changes in headdress signify altered personhood, and a new social status, with all its responsibilities. A headdress change may proclaim maturity and responsibility for actions, including those actions committed during trance. They underline the need to protect social differentiation, jural status as property owner, and the beginning of a new distinction. Headdress in its serious and non-serious modes therefore illuminates its ritual inversion, revealing a spectrum of varying states of vulnerability centered about the head, but also affecting the hair and other parts of the body.

The body in concepts of person
Tuareg associate different parts of the body with aspects of personhood, character, and states of being. The stomach (*tedis*) represents the matriline, which is also where spirits enter. The liver (*tessa*) is where sentiments are located, and where spirits rest temporarily. The head (*eghef*), the seat of intelligence, is also believed to be the eventual destination of spirits, who affect memory. Hair is considered to be the outer manifestation of intelligence; *isagan*, the name of a particular hairstyle, also means "one who hears something interesting." Small boys of noble status sometimes wear a hairstyle called *alegin*, a tuft high on the back of the otherwise shaven head, which is said to enable the Prophet to lift the child up into heaven if he dies. This tuft is more generally a sign of firstborn and noble status. Generous and abundant, yet also controlled, hair is associated with "pure" noble origins, and nobles often mock ex-slaves for their close-cropped hair. A group of Tuareg known for noble heritage, the Imazghaden, who live about three miles from Iferouan to the north-west of Mount Bagzan, are praised in possession song verses for their abundant and beautiful hair. Luxuriant hair is thus a part of the aesthetic of jural adult status: specifically, a married, noble, tent-owner.

Marabouts wind a white cloth around the head when diagnosing for spirit possession, identifying the head as the object of ritual divination. Extremely unkempt hair and head are identified with insanity; insane persons in Tuareg society typically have long, matted, untrimmed hair and an ill-fitting or carelessly wrapped headdress. One image used to describe spirit possession is *eqqan eghef*, which means disorientation, or, literally, "taking off of the head." The term for the sideways head and shoulder motion during trance is *asul*, or head dancing. This dance motion is also associated with flirting, specifically with illicit love outside marriage, which constitutes a threat to official endogamy and descent-based social stratification. The motion is thus seen as lack of self-control because it evokes rebellion against social norms that threaten property.[6]

The mouth (*imi*) is the major source of vulnerability to evil (as in *awal*, which means powerful speech or gossip, often viewed negatively as "evil mouth"). The eye (*shet*) is also associated with evil (as in *tehot*, which means jealousy or "evil eye"). For example, sorcerers of the evil eye and mouth are warded off by good diction and by covering the orifices, as well as by avoiding certain places or by moving one's tent or livestock pastures. Victims of *tehot* or *awal* often display eye and ear maladies. Spirit possession, however, often begins with a headache or with "liver" problems, even though spirits are also believed to perch on the neck of the possessed, which association is expressed in possession songs (*irin*) through the slang for bearing a burden. Thus threats to the tent and property manifest themselves through vulnerability of the mouth, and the higher one's jural status, the more intense the threats, which require correspondingly strict protective measures, namely, concealing the sentiments.

Headdresses are thus used in different contexts to reinforce notions of male and female personhood over time. Women's daily wearing of the headscarf and their gender inversion of it during possession are emblems of alternate containment and exposure of the self, to protect against threats to property and jural status during transitions throughout the life course. Feminine veiling is prominent in flirting, courtship, and festivals, in marriage and motherhood, in jural adulthood as mistress of the tent or "woman inside the tent," in mother-in-lawhood, and in close partnership with men in official Islamic observance until old age prevents their active participation. The *tamtot n ammas* or "woman inside the tent" is also the woman inside the headscarf. The headscarf expresses variations of women's status and prestige according to context: social stratum, kin role, and, most of all, age. It may become similar in style to the men's face-veil when brides and mothers-in-law exaggerate the headscarf at life crisis rites. (As noted, however, very elderly women may drop it in recognition of successful "retirement" from these concerns.) Thus there is no simple dichotomy between headscarf and veil in terms of subordination and dominance in female/male roles. In some contexts, the headscarf signifies subordination and respect; in others, it signifies high status and prestige; in others, it represents modesty and shyness toward strangers; in still others, it may represent perceived threats to property. It is also used aesthetically and ludically, to tease and flirt, as a manifestation of cleverness or "having a head."

Head covering is linked directly to transformed jural status, when one attempts to consolidate one's independent household and property as a spouse (actual or virtual), which requires proof of the prudent observance of ideal adult qualities. The closer adherence to veiling practices, such as that of women in female possession trance and for both sexes during the wedding ritual, represents protection in times of proximity to spirits. Therefore, spirits are a metaphor for threats to status and property.

Gender inversion of headdress by women in trance thus suggests the nuanced and dynamic, rather than clear-cut and static, meaning of possession tropes, and partly explains their relation to social reality. Women's ritual veiling is a graphic example of how possession imagery provides social "cosmetics" or buffers in situations not only of ambiguity, but also too-sharply demarcated roles where one wishes to create ambiguity. Inversion conveys submission to social convention, but at the same time empowers. It symbolizes protection of property, a manifestation of jural status of person: as the Tuareg term it, veiling is "proof of reserve."

3

"Like a tree branch swaying in the wind": the head dance

In possession, tropes, aesthetic form, and the social expression of power are interrelated. This is illustrated most clearly in the multivocality of the central simile or motif appearing in possession imagery that is also pervasive throughout Tuareg visual and verbal arts: a balanced swaying to and fro, compared metaphorically to "a tree branch swaying in the wind." This image in art, associated with femininity and nobility, is idealized as the "most beautiful" aesthetic style. It recurs in song and poetry, in the drum pattern called *talawankan*, in dress style, in the fringe and tassels of leatherwork, and in the sideways "head dancing" performed by the woman in trance. Outside possession, it appears in the popular men's dances *dilélé lé* and *achelub-chelub*, as they approach a chorus of women at festivals. In addition, this image is used to describe altered emotional states.

This association between verbal, visual, and kinesthetic modes of understanding is demonstrated in the head dance, viewed against the backdrop of Tuareg visual arts and spatial/temporal orientations. Both within and outside the possession setting, these mixed codes interlock. The singing of women is considered incomplete without the shouts of men; storytelling is accompanied by the hand gestures of the teller; and some instruments must be played together, such as the *asakalabo* and the *tonde*. (Kel Ewey smiths, prominent musicians at the possession ritual, told me that "the *asakalabo* is to the *tonde* what sugar is to tea.") Yet the interpretation of poems and tales does not always have a one-to-one correspondence to dance or gestures, which makes the interpretation of the swaying visual image particularly interesting.

The swaying tree branch motif in possession and throughout Tuareg aesthetics seems to be an antidote or counterbalance to the noble cultural value of reserve or *takarakit*. This is suggested by evidence from contexts of use: the motif occurs in situations where it fills the need to circumvent structure. In this respect, the image of "wind" is significant: for some spirits are said to reside in the wind. Thus this core image, in visual, kinesthetic, verbal, and aural forms, refers metaphorically to deviating actively from norms, especially in its flirting imagery. It accomplishes this in a number of ways, as a kind of subcultural style. The aesthetic code that integrates all this in one key image conveys a message about concerns of descent, prestige, and status in relationships between men and women, and among the different social strata in Kel Ewey Tuareg society.

As discussed previously, an attempt at an interpretive analysis of altered mental states is problematic. A symbolic analysis of possession tropes only mystifies these problems further unless it focuses upon social conflict and power assertion. Possession tropes suggest ways in which art defining the person is used to assert social power: how mixed codes are used to express dominance and subordination, purity and pollution. Yet the relation of decorated personal facade to underlying social process is neither self-evident nor direct.

Many authors (Langer 1953; Gadamer 1975, cited in Weinsheimer 1985; Hebdigé 1979) have opened up new perspectives on transformations occurring among the different frames of modalities of symbolic and aesthetic expression. In my view, these perspectives illuminate, but do not fully resolve, two aspects of this problem: (1) the stratification and hegemony of power; and (2) the style and arbitration of form. Art asserts power via the selection of style. Tropes and aesthetic styles in Tuareg possession reflect and express, but also rework in alternating discourses and socio-political differences. The terms art, aesthetics, and symbols are not used interchangeably here; rather, these images of possession embody "art," as in Langer's concept of "the making of a symbol, as transparent and taking on literal significance and evoking feelings. . .as virtual space, entirely independent ... a self-contained, total system ... and infinitely plastic" (Langer 1953: 75). Implicit in this approach is a view of art as a metaphor for social relationships and processes of transformation, rather than static forms and structures.

Possession tropes provide a key to understanding how possession art is associated with the acceptance of, and the participation in, the dominant ideology by those subordinate to it, and how it is used to manipulate social order. It is the semiotic that governs selection of a style in a given medium that is the goal of this analysis. Who is the arbitrator of style and form in artistic expression? Nobles, nominally the most prestigious group and the commissioners of many consumer art objects characterized by the "sway-

ing tree branch" motif? Blacksmiths, who manufacture most art objects
and play prominent roles in spirit curing? Marabouts, who diagnose for
spirits, and who insert protective Koranic verses into the decorative metal
and leather objects made by smiths, but whose Koranic amulets are
temporarily removed during the spirit possession drumming cure? The
understanding of possession tropes thus requires an examination of the
multiple codes or modalities throughout Tuareg culture, identifying their
correspondences in kinesthetic, verbal, and visual orientation, in relation to
socio-political codes. This central pervasive metaphor of the swaying tree
branch is associated with purity of form and radiates out into the wider
symbolic system.

The connection between art styles and politics has been recognized by
several scholars (Weber 1958; Benjamin 1968; Baxandall 1972; Hebdigé
1979). Less understood is the role of this connection in the transformation,
or alternatively, the reproduction, or ontology. In Tuareg aesthetic values
and behavior surrounding the core image of balanced swaying, there is in
several respects what Weber terms an "elective affinity of a style of life"
(Weber 1958). Art is used as decorative display of beauty, and style is an end
in itself, in accordance with what Benjamin calls "exhibition value"
(Benjamin 1968), in which the ritual or cult value of art is emphasized in
religion, healing, and in rites of passage throughout the life course.
Exhibition is more highly valued among Tuareg nobles, but this appears
imposed upon all social segments during rituals bringing them all together.

The recurrence of Tuareg possession tropes in mixed aesthetic codes
suggests a relationship between the "elective affinity of a style of life" and
other worldly orientations, in political, religious, and economic contexts of
Tuareg social life. One interesting aspect of Kel Ewey Tuareg society is the
existence of an aesthetics to the style of life of the different segments of
society. Tuareg conduct politics through art forms. There is, for example, a
kind of "aesthetic" of social class: namely, concepts of beauty and preferred
styles of expression, self-presentation, and performance associated with
each social stratum (Rasmussen 1985, 1986). Physical body types, dress,
cooking and eating patterns, housing decor, ritual, festival and musical
styles, and jewelry designs are identified with different social strata. For
example, whereas nobles take pride in the neat and clean orderliness of their
tents, surround them with fences, and keep them in regular repair, smiths
generally inhabit old, crooked tents, seldom enclose them, and leave their
materials to rot. Nobles arrive at life crisis rites and festivals dressed in their
best; whereas traditionally smiths, at least in rural areas, are supposed to go
clad in ragged, shabby clothing. An Agadez smith told me that until

recently, although smiths manufactured jewelry, they "disdained" it, and refrained from wearing as many pieces of jewelry as nobles typically wear, especially at festivals. The music of nobles, smiths, and ex-slaves also displays marked differences; while nobles may surreptitiously enjoy drumming, ideally they express a preference for the "classical" music of the *anzad*, a bowed, one-stringed lute, and dance with reserve; smiths and slaves, by contrast, play music with a strong percussive accompaniment and also perform distinctive dances.

Among noble men, the ideal is slenderness and grace, and among women, the ideal is fatness; noble men ridicule ex-slave men for being fat and clumsy. They also ridicule ex-slaves for their preparation of a dish called *eghajira* (a dish made of dates, millet, and goat cheese that is the centerpiece at life crisis rites): when nobles serve the dish, all the date pits are removed and the ingredients are finely ground; smiths and other servile classes occasionally leave in some date pits and grind the ingredients coarsely. Nobles prefer to eat with spoons and ladles, and they mock other social segments for eating with their fingers, especially when they have the socioeconomic means to eat with dining utensils. Nobles also criticize certain pieces of jewelry as not being fit for their use. For example, when I wore a marbled agate stone I considered attractive, a male noble friend in Agadez told me that a noble would never wear marbled agate, even though it is pretty, for nobles prefer the dark opaque agate because its quality is considered superior. My Malian Tuareg women friends in Niamey explicitly praised "thick, fat, and dense" jewelry pieces, denigrating the lighter versions made at the museum for the tourist trade. When I wore a woman's blouse with the sleeves sewn closed for convenience and attractiveness, noble men and women in rural Aïr expressed shock, emphasizing that blouse sleeves should always be loose, billowing in the wind. Likewise, deep indigo dye is highly valued, not only on cloth, but on human skin. When I washed mine out early in my residence, nobles again were horrified, as they considered the cloth's beauty now ruined.

Therefore, to be "like a tree branch in the wind" is part of a generalized mixed aesthetic code. Viewed against the backdrop of broader, overarching themes in Tuareg aesthetics, possession tropes have bases in an elective affinity of lifestyle. Mixed codes synesthetically extend from visual and verbal forms into domains of sound and motion.[1] Dick Hebdigé (1979) discusses how a culture's symbolic system pivoted on the sound of reggae music. The sound was intimately bound up with the notion of culture, and if the system was attacked, then the community itself was symbolically threatened. The music thus became hallowed ground, to be defended against possible contamination by other outside groups. Hebdigé calls this the "symbolic defense of communal space" (Hebdigé 1979: 39). In Tuareg possession tropes and art forms, ideology is signified in form and acted out by cultural agents. In aesthetic forms, it is thus possible to map out patterns of rejection and assimilation between the different interest groups in Kel Ewey society: nobles and non-nobles, marabouts and smiths, men and women, and elder and youth. The styles valued and disdained represent a succession of what Hebdigé terms "subcultural forms" in local aesthetics (Hebdigé 1979: 44). These can be read as a series of deep structural adaptations that symbolically accommodate or expunge a foreign presence. It is on the plane of aesthetics – in dress, dance, music, rhetoric of style – that one finds dialogue between interest groups most subtly and comprehensively recorded, albeit in code. By describing, interpreting, and deciphering these forms, one can construct an account of the person in terms of the exchanges that have taken place between Kel Ewey Tuareg social divisions, which appear in condensed form in the possession idiom.

In material culture and music, oppositional values serve to symbolize and symptomize in new contexts the contradictions and tensions played out in Aïr Tuareg culture. For example, the dress and ornaments of the possessed woman are ambiguous in origin. On the one hand, her sword is normally a masculine accessory, for Kel Ewey women never carry swords. Her face-veil is also part of the male – noble male, in particular – prerogative. Yet, as seen, elderly women also veil the lower part of their faces in certain situations. The poetry of the songs is very ancient, described by residents as "old Tamacheq," while the accompanying drumming was introduced more recently, and is from south of the Sahara and of servile origins. Thus there is a dialectical interplay in possession tropes between male/female, noble/servile (dress, music, style), and older/more recent codes, embodying aesthetic themes common to both manifestations. Of central concern to both masculine and feminine gender identity are themes of dominance and servitude, but their direction extends to class roles in addition to opposite sex and kinship roles. It is the process of constructing meaning, rather than unidirectional cause or consequence, that is important here.[2] Through possession tropes, players enacting the possession process create a counterdiscourse in which experienced contradictions and objections to the ruling ideology are obliquely represented in style.

Dance and communication in Tuareg festivals and possession rites
It is instructive to proceed here from the starting point of dance, and then analyze its relation to other codes and the aesthetic of the swaying tree

branch. These images relate to person definition and political power because dance motions are visual representations (which respond to the auditory representations of the drum patterns) of other images and themes in Kel Ewey Tuareg culture, such as decorative arts, ritual, and poetry. The images emerge from local concepts of space and time, critical aesthetic judgments, body motions and gestures, particular dance styles in Kel Ewey Tuareg society and their contextualized meaning, visual and verbal skills, notions of beauty, and visual and aural art (leather fringes, tassels on the veil of the woman in trance, current fashions in dress, images in poetry and in songs of possession). Throughout these manifestations, the concept of swaying is pervasive, described as "supple, yet strong, like a branch swaying in the wind," and "balanced and harmonious."

The possessed dancer, perhaps the strongest manifestation of the swaying branch image, becomes the song as she dances; she literally "catches the song." Her head dancing is, in fact, the rhythmic pattern of the poem, song, and drum, and can take the place of the constant reiteration of this pattern. The motion also pervades Tuareg life outside the context of a curing rite: individuals do the head dance spontaneously while listening to music on the radio or on a tape recorder, babies and small children are encouraged by their mothers to perform the motion as a musical game in time to crushing grain, and adults imitate the motion jokingly to describe emotional or physical states involving the enjoyment of music. Tuareg say that both the rhythm and the words are important in possession curing, which suggests a closer examination of the meaning of "swaying" in this context, or, more specifically, how power is constructed through this motif. The combination of words, drum patterns, dance and other motions, and music are related to each other and to empowerment in an overarching aesthetic.

Central here is not only the role of dance in general, but local notions of movement among Kel Ewey. Although young people of both sexes dance among Kel Ewey, there are distinctive patterns and styles for young men and young women. For example, young men more often dance facing an audience at evening festivals where courtship takes place, marking either life-crisis rites or national holidays. In one popular men's dance performed at evening festivals, pairs of men brandishing lances or swords approach a standing chorus of women of all social segments and a seated drummer. As they approach in pairs, the dancers perform a vigorous sideways kicking step, stamping and digging into the earth with their feet and swinging their legs to the side. Throughout, there is an emphasis upon the aesthetically pleasing swaying motion of sleeves, veil, sword, and amulets. Men's dancing is explicitly competitive, and is a showcase for masculine pride;

male dancing is connected with courtship, for its aim is to please women and to display strength, and, by extension, male prowess.

Kel Ewey women's dancing differs from men's dancing in that they rarely perform in pairs in front of an audience of the opposite sex. For example, noble women occasionally dance in public, but usually in a tight, closed circle facing each other. Smith women perform a buffoon-like dance during their application of henna to the bridegroom just before his wedding, when they receive gifts from noble guests. In this dance step, the smith women assume the posture of begging, which nobles say conveys the smiths' "self-debasement" and smiths say is a "blacksmith theatre."

Women do not usually brandish swords or lances outside the head dancing of possession trance when the dancer, clutching the sword, is the center of attention and is being judged for her competence. The sole exception (aside from during trance) is in a dance that elderly women perform in the company of other women at the unofficial nameday ceremony for the week-old baby, in which they hold pestles in the same way that men brandish lances. This dance performance is held at the mother's tent the evening before the official men's naming ceremony at the mosque (Rasmussen 1987).

When I asked why most women don't dance in the same fashion as men, vigorously stamping and leaping, local residents of either sex and all social segments replied that "men are strong, supple, and graceful." In courtship, men take on the burden of performance, and women's singing and clapping are said to inspire and reward them (similar, perhaps, to the way that men's shouts are said to inspire women's singing). Thus, dancing is an expression of cultural gender typifications among Tuareg, concerning body positions and motions related to praise and self-esteem. Men's and women's dancing, analyzed in diverse contexts, and taken together with the concurrent drum patterns, decorative fringe, and tassels, all display a similarity in their overarching aesthetic, which is based on class as well as gender. The power is embodied in the dancer, in the same way that divine power is located in amulets. The central space and time of the dance, like those of possession, serve as a stage on which Kel Ewey present themselves to each other. Held in the evening, far from mosques, and often on the edges of the camp or village, dance, like trance, is outwardly a public version of the person. The dances of men and women and different social segments seem complementary; they contain messages about flirting and courtship, as well as about client-patron relationships. Yet in its expression of an overarching aesthetic code, as well as in its connotations of morality and etiquette, dance projects inner concepts of self and of the conflicts surrounding the person: to dance is to seek something. The evening festivals that mark life-crisis rites draw in groups from outside the village or camp, so that all the members of the inside group are encouraged to present the group and themselves positively, through dance. The guests are often an assortment of affines, members of different social strata, and travellers from more remote areas. The encouragement, judgment, and praise or rejection of an individual dance performance circumvent the more typically ascribed traits based on descent and class.

Beidelman (1986: 59), in his description of the Kaguru, observes that dancing and drinking are modified extensions of sexuality and alimentation, which two, in turn, are often equated. In Tuareg society, although these equations are made less explicitly, eating is a euphemism for sexual relations (as it is in many African societies), and feasting takes place during daytime rites of passage. During evening festivals and courtship, however, eating is shameful, for the emphasis during those times is on skillful conversation, poetry, song, and dance. Among Tuareg at evening festivals, the individual projects the self to the stranger as a potential and actual suitor through singing, dancing, and chatting. Assembling strangers and members of diverse social segments permits behavior normally not condoned within the household and class boundaries. Residents, outsiders, cognates, neighbors, affines, and diverse social segments mingle like one large household. Dancing is the public enactment of private attachment, thus making one's private goals public.

Head dancing during possession trance objectifies political power in a manner similar to cabbalistic words: both have unknown power, yet both refer to political power. From the moment the possessed begins to perform the head dance in the trance state, the spirits mount her. One reason given for the few men in spirit possession rites is that the swaying motion of the head dance is considered feminine. Yet the possessed woman's head dancing in some respects inverts the usual pattern of male exhibitionism and female modesty in dance. As long as a woman does the head dance during the trance, it is the spirits that are dancing, rather than the possessed person, which allows for face-saving. Thus head dancing is intentionally ambiguous, open to multiple interpretations, in that it contains elements of both reinforcement and reversal of the norms of gender typification. The dance begins sedately and slowly, and at first is limited to the head; as the drum patterns become more complex and rapid, the head dance becomes more vigorous, including the lower neck, shoulders, and eventually the entire torso, from the waist up. In the Bagzan region, where I observed most rituals, patients almost never rose to a standing position to dance with their feet; the rare occasions when they did were attributed by audience members to a "particularly strong case of spirits."

The head dance may last from half an hour to four hours, and will come to a close typically in the early hours before dawn. Throughout the ceremony, the motion is regarded explicitly as a performance, and possessed persons and audience alike invariably refer to it as a dance rather than as a reflex response or hysterical fit. The audience frequently encourages the dancer and also judges her curing progress according to how "well" she dances. Only if the patient reaches her goal – that is, becoming so exhausted from the dance that she falls to the ground – will she be even temporarily cured of spirits. This state of exhaustion can be reached only if the music, drumming, singing, and audience response are harmonious and balanced. Women who are possessed frequently, however, say that this cure is often merely temporary, because spirits tend to recur in certain individuals regardless of the frequency with which they perform the curing ritual.

Some families are ambivalent about kinswomen who dance the *goumaten* ritual frequently; they admit to being a bit ashamed because there is something undignified about the head dance. Men chuckle slightly when acknowledging female relatives' frequent participation, and male friends told me stories of how husbands had attempted to discourage their wives from doing this dance by ridiculing them or (rarely) beating them, but to no avail. Men say somewhat ruefully that "you can cure women or spirits, but not of wanting the *tande* or wanting to dance." Significantly, men who perform the head dance are ridiculed by people of both sexes and all social strata.

Although some Kel Ewey families, especially the marabout clans, regard dancing and possession with disdain, women are not required to obtain permission to dance in public, and still enjoy a large degree of social freedom. However, at specific times in life, such as during engagement and in later affinal roles, such conduct is viewed with ambivalence. The head dance – in contrast to the headdress, which can be seen as a personal fortress – reveals one's inner sentiments too openly, and the image of the swaying tree branch is associated with flirting, love, and courtship. This behavior runs counter to definitions of females as behaving in a dignified and reserved manner (rather than meek or subjugated) during engagement and marriage. Despite the surreptitious practice of accepting suitors, and in contrast to the free social interaction between the sexes, secrecy and dignity normally surround these practices when the participants are engaged, or when their children are engaged. In addition, marriage and bridewealth require delicate negotiations; too overt a preference shown for a particular suitor is feared to complicate bridewealth negotiations. For example, if a suitor is considered only barely acceptable, in some groups there is a penalty fee, which translates into higher bridewealth payments. In the initial stages of courtship, at least, a woman's preference must be shown indirectly, through subtle greetings, hand signs, poetry, and song images, or by using friends, smiths, or ex-slaves as go-betweens.

One young woman I knew who was frequently possessed, whom I shall call Hadia, was engaged to a young man, Abdou, who was a distantly related cousin from a neighboring village. Long before the wedding took place, during unusually protracted bridewealth negotiations, Hadia sent word through a girlfriend that she planned to stop by her fiancé's home to visit the following day. That night, during a tea-drinking gathering of relatives, friends, and neighbors, a smith (who acted as an important go-between in marriage bridewealth negotiations) gossiped about this incident, ridiculing Hadia for her open display of sentiments. He described her with the slang phrase "she is on the outside," a euphemism also used to warn someone when a portion of the undergarments show. He explained that "she never should have announced her intention to visit so boldly like that, in advance; to do so is shameful [*takarakit*]." Although her conduct in itself did not represent grounds for cancelling the marriage, it still caused general disapproval and scorn.

During the public context of the dance, friends and relatives demonstrate their concern for the patient and commit themselves to assisting her in her attempt to be cured. Thus the aesthetics of trance motions provide a forum for the "safe" expression of the patient's needs and personal sentiments on the one hand, and her friends' and relatives' responsiveness on the other. At the same time, they underline the possessed person's value to the opposite sex, according to Tuareg criteria, as a person who is beautiful, graceful, and competent in her role as dancer, singer, and musician at festivals. Throughout, there is room for the elaborate manipulation of norms in indirect communication; for example, through hand gestures and body posture. Dancing, hand gestures, and body postures are all part of culturally acceptable conduct during courtship and festivals, when more direct means of expression are not always advisable.

Hadia underwent a series of *tənde n goumaten* rituals, all of which took place during her lengthy engagement to Abdou. During this frequent dancing of the *goumaten*, it was rumored that she was impatient to marry Abdou, but was in conflict with her mother over the negotiations (her family hoped for substantial bridewealth). Viewed in this context, the aesthetics of possession as embodied in dancing and gestures enable the display and demonstration of sentiment that would be valued negatively in other contexts, where the traditional noble values of reserve and dignity are expected. Although the noble aesthetic code predominates in the specific dance style of all possessed women, regardless of their social origins, the accompanying ritual paraphernalia such as sword, face-veil, and public exhibitionism, invert and reconstitute this dominant aesthetic code.

The core image of the swaying tree branch, which appeared in one of the drum patterns and in numerous songs at possession rituals, connotes resilience, and is defined primarily by a slow drum rhythm. The term *azel* denotes both branch and song in the Tamacheq spoken around Mount Bagzan, and may also refer specifically to a song of the *talawankan* (swaying tree branch) drum pattern genre. Many possession songs refer to the *tadeine* tree, which has supple branches that bend but do not break, and which are used to make camel saddles. Through this image, the dancer is encouraged to be like a branch of this tree. As *azel* refers to both song and branch, the image is extended to represent the rhythm of the song moving through the dancer like the wind blowing through the branches. Kel Ewey women singers and transcriber-assistants of either sex told me that song is like a branch in the wind, swaying, smooth, and balanced, like the dancer in trance.

Additional references to the swaying image appear in other possession songs. In *idoukal*, which is a song genre characterized by the personification of a geographic feature, there is a song that mentions the plains of In Gall as a metaphorical reference to the palm of a hand. Transcriber–assistants explained this to me as meaning, by extension, the caress of a lover's hand. Here, the swaying motif is linked to personal, romantic love. This song also mentions *elangé*, an old way of wearing the face-veil in which the veil trails behind the shoulders. Although this is a much-admired style of face-veil and is considered flirtatious, it is seldom seen today because it requires a lot of cloth and is thus expensive. Here, the swaying motif is linked to socio-economic status and prestige. In the same song verses, there is also a reference to the patient's neck: "I promise to sing ... on my neck ... until tomorrow." The neck represents here the stem of the swaying branch, and plays a central role in the dance. This image also refers to the neck's burden: the spirits, which are believed to perch on the patient's neck throughout the ritual.

The cultural aesthetic of swaying also appears in leather fringe, and is mentioned is poems and possession songs. The possessed woman often wears a tassel over her veil, which may consist of leather or simply white cloth, but in possession trance is always suspended freely. Outside of possession, young women generally wear a leather hair ornament that sways flirtatiously across the back. Thus the swaying motif recurs throughout different visual, aural, and kinesthetic contexts. Recall here, also, that the head dance is often seen as flirting, as "craning one's neck to look at a man"; associations of vanity and flirting reverberate throughout this code when it is seen synesthetically. In effect, the possessed woman becomes the embodiment of *talawankan*, a kind of human fringe swaying like the tassel on her veil.

Leather fringe and tassels have a multivocal range of associations. On the one hand, they appear frequently in the dress and containers of the older hunting and nomadic culture, contrasting with the sedentism and external Sudanic associations of indigo cloth imported from Kano, as well as the North African and European origins of cotton cloth. On the other hand, leather, like the *tande* drum also, has become identified with domestic servitude, multifunctionalism, and manual labor. While men conduct living animal sacrifice, women, smiths, and slaves handle leather hides. Yet another dimension of leather is its closeness to *al baraka*, or blessing power, because of its association with elements of living things, specifically milk and blood. In other writings I have described how many noble Kel Ewey women continue to observe menstrual taboos restricting physical contact with leather hides (Rasmussen 1987, 1991b), which emphasizes the complexity of the role of leather in the symbolism of the swaying tree branch. Like other variations on this theme (the *asul* head dance, the *talawankan* drum pattern, the hair ornament and tassel, and the men's dance step), the leather fringe appears to be an integral part of being noble and pastoral. Most important, however, is the fact that leather is identified with sexuality, and is associated closely with women in their economic, reproductive, and ritual roles. It indicates women's covering, containment, protection, and support specifically of children, and more generally of "purity" of heritage.

Several incidents vividly illustrated these notions to me. A Kel Ewey marabout remarked that a young nursing mother who wears the decorative leather hair tassel called *azumi* will cause her milk to dry up; and masculine theories of conception and birth describe the woman as being "like a leather sack" or container for the baby (Rasmussen 1987). There are warnings in local cosmology about spirits confusing skin waterbags with babies and stealing babies instead. Yet Tuareg women's roles are not limited to their reproductive fertility or childbearing. Why, then, is the idiom of fertility and sexuality used in reference to female personhood throughout the swaying tree branch motif, particularly as it appears in possession imagery and leather ornaments?

Form and style are most meaningful in terms of the socio-cultural contexts in which they are observed. The swaying tree branch motif communicates a hierarchy of power throughout visual, verbal, and dance imagery, within and outside possession. Among the social statuses and symbols in Kel Ewey Tuareg personhood, there are tensions between flirting/courting and official marriage, between vain displays of emotion and property and the more typical and expected reserve about them, between nomadism and sedentism, and between art as assertion of power and art as servitude. In this scheme, women of all social segments play central roles. In Tuareg visual ornamentation, gender roles, and sexuality, the swaying motif associated primarily with noble men and women in general encapsulates the relationship between social organization and body symbolism, between public and private symbols of personhood. It mediates external information and individual emotional states. Aesthetic images and tropes in possession show the capacity to command "imports" from the worlds of external social segments and the opposite sex, and exaggerate or invert them, thereby directing them toward reproducing the personal and social order of the possession state.

The swaying motif, as evidenced in leather ornamentation, not only signifies flirting and provides a counterbalance to the noble constraints of reserve and shame, but also represents a source of security and esteem for Kel Ewey women. Among Tuareg, the manufacture of leather ornaments is left entirely to women, usually – though not exclusively – blacksmith women. In the Bagzan region women of all social strata, who are usually elderly and past their childbearing years, tan, pound, and soften hides; and smith women dye, cut, embroider, and otherwise decorate the hides. A newborn child's goatskin cradle is constructed by the grandmother for the firstborn, and subsequently by a smith woman attached to the noble family. Goatskin is tanned locally with the *tamat* or acacia tree seed pod, and dyed with red maize leaf or indigo. The decoration of the goatskin is enlivened by fringe, tassels, a bright red color, and often the combination of bright red and turquoise. In some regions, leather sandals held in the hand during delivery are believed to promote easy childbirth. Five or six cowries attached to a triangle of leather are said to bestow fertility on the wearer. Children occasionally wear the protective amulet of a date sewn into their leather hair ornaments. This practice parallels the use of dates at the baby's unofficial nameday ritual, when an old smith woman carries dates, millet, and goat cheese in a potsherd during the procession of female relatives of the baby on the evening before the official naming by men at the mosque. In both cases, the *al baraka* of dates, leather, and milk are believed to transfer on to the person who is the focus of these rituals. (Interestingly, at the unofficial female nameday ritual, the women give the child a name that is different from the one given by the father and marabout at the mosque the subsequent day.)

Leather, although associated with fertility and sexuality, clearly is also part of different aspects of women's roles, and underlines their socio-economic and ritual powers beyond motherhood as well as their procreativity. To pastoralists, leather is indispensable to everyday life; it constitutes the basic material for habitat. Hides are linked to the creation of the domestic unit, to marriage, to the life of the nuclear family. Leather utensils are also a unit of measure for grain sale. In their culturally refined form, leather containers, ornaments, and utensils protect life. Women's leather-work is more richly colored and decorated than men's, and has a greater abundance of fringe. Leather fringe is associated with the economic utility and security of the domestic unit and includes, but is not limited to, the seeming constraints of servitude and procreativity. The use of leather accompanies changes in life stages, and helps symbolize and transfer power.

Turner has pointed out that the power of symbols in human communication "inheres not only in shared languages, but also in individual crafting of speech through tropes: metaphors, metonyms, oxymora ... (and in) manual gesticulations, facial expressions, bodily postures..." (Turner 1982: Introduction). These diverse sensory codes have been identified with ritual and drama (Gadamer 1975, 1986; Turner 1982; Schechner 1985; Handel-man 1990) and with politics (Benjamin 1968; Baxandall 1972; Hebdige 1979) in their multimedia and multivocal dimensions. What needs to be done is to situate the mode of presentation more clearly in socio-political contexts of the transformation of meaning. If comparative symbology is to do more than merely investigate cultural genres in abstraction from human social activity, ritual symbols must be analyzed in a time series in relation to other events, not merely demonstrated as multivocal. My search for a more dynamic framework that goes beyond multivocality includes linking tropes of color symbolism and aesthetic style, and then takes this approach further by examining how the full range of modalities in multivocality and mixed codes are used in different contexts and how they are transformed and used in social agency: essentially paving the way for linking aesthetic and socio-political domains.

Among Kel Ewey, the color red (*wa zeggere*) is not associated explicitly with blood; in fact, blood is often referred to as black (*wa kawale*). Red is used to describe the light complexions of certain groups claiming noble descent, Arabs, and other outsiders. There is no single meaning for red but, by and large, the notions of transition and ambiguity as well as power and danger seem widespread in African associations of red. But Tuareg also regard red as visually beautiful. So red leather fringe is both beautiful and dangerous, and thus emerges as an iconic differentiation of states, mediating between life and death. Used in combination with the iron of the sword clutched in trance, leather repels spirits. This association of repulsion stands in contrast to the idea, attached to the aesthetic code of swaying, of leather fringe attracting the attention of the opposite sex. Hence the coexistence, in possession aesthetics, of two contradictory images: attracting humans and repelling spirits.

These images come into sharper focus when they are related to time and social agency. They convey the tensions surrounding marriage and inheritance. A woman inherits jewelry, leather, and ornaments from her mother throughout her life, and also receives presents of jewelry and other ornaments from her mother and her husband when she marries. Kel Ewey say that these gifts express how highly parents and suitors love and value the adolescent engaged girl. Yet there is also the belief that this love also endangers the girl, for the state of marrying may cause spirits to be jealous of her and occupy her, attempting to carry her away. This is one explanation of an engaged adolescent girl's spirit possession. There is an important social facet to this explanation, for only the prosperous own decorative belongings, and this makes them vulnerable to the jealousy of human neighbors, who are believed occasionally to cause the destruction of person and property.

Thus there is a linkage between the symbolism of the aesthetic code, sexual symbolism in ornamentation, and socio-economic status, when the analysis of their multivocal qualities is extended into wider domains of hegemonic action concerning gender and class. Among Tuareg, both sexes and all social segments are much given to vanity and vestimentary display, whenever means exist to achieve this, and this trend becomes apparent in the idiom and imagery of possession. Humans, as well as spirits, like shimmering indigo-dyed cloth, bright red tassels, and graceful dancing. What attracts and repels spirits is the mirror image of what attracts and repels humans, and brings about admiration, respect, and prestige, but can also cause feelings of envy, hostility, and spite. This complex relationship with status symbols is played out in possession aesthetics and its oxymoronic transformations. Among the Tuareg, there is the cultural ideal of "beautiful things in association with beautiful persons" as markers of good taste, high social status, and prestige. What nobles value in aesthetic form is the rarity of the material worked, such as the quality of wood or metal, and the particular effort of the artisan or smith as demonstrated in technical expertise. All of these elements point to the prestige of the patron or the consumer.

Hence the display value of the ornaments, ritual paraphernalia, dance movements, and musical sounds of the possession rite becomes clear. Even for non-noble patients (perhaps particularly for these persons), these objects and motions constitute a construction of person based on noble ideals of restraint, good judgment, and choices in abundance. Self-concepts derive from exclusivity: the display value of ornaments projects an individual who knows the quality of materials and appreciates painstaking workmanship, and who takes pride in wearing the ornaments, or in listening to and judging the music. Vestimentary display is central to possession as one more variation on the presentation of self at rituals and festivals. These mixed codes provide a forum for revealing rank, as aesthetic tastes and form are directly tied to descent and socio-economics. The direct marking of these is problematic, however, because sources of prestige and sources of wealth do not always coincide in the same person or activity. Furthermore, the accumulation of wealth in the form of beautiful art (whether visual ornaments or aural praise songs) also brings obligations of support in client–patron relationships.

Many nobles can no longer meet these obligations easily. During my residence, I was always careful to refrain from wearing more than one blouse during two or three successive days, except at a festival, for the display of extra belongings invites pressure to take on clients in patronage relationships. Additional problems derive from the contradictions inherent in placing women high on a pedestal in accordance with noble cultural values and ideology, and their partial dependence on men for material goods in an increasingly sedentized and monetarized economy: the discrepancy between the cultural emphasis on social freedom for women before marriage, and the increasing pressure to behave with dignity and reserve as the universe of affines increases upon a woman's marriage. Possession aesthetics enable individuals to display themselves in terms of a concept of person that is compatible with traditional norms of respect that might be difficult to uphold in daily life. Possession trance, with its centerpiece of the swaying tree branch motif, enacts a fantasy in which private symbols of personhood are given public expression in a "safe" environment.

Being like a tree branch swaying in the wind conveys messages about the person caught in a maze of contradictions. This motif throughout Tuareg aesthetics constitutes an antidote or counterbalance to the noble cultural value of reserve or shame. There is evidence for this in the motif's recurrence in social contexts where it fills a need to circumvent structure. Images of wind and earth (spirits) and wilderness or solitude surround the possessed person as she dances. Therefore, a positive valuing of performative competence through motions described metaphorically by an image of resilience and balance are of central importance to the possession cure. This suggests that there is a link between positive self-concept and aesthetics (music, dance, and visual arts) in Kel Ewey Tuareg culture, provided there is positive reinforcement during possession. This process has the effect of providing a new, if temporary, social status and change in social identity and self-concept. During trance, in its mixed visual, aural, and kinesthetic codes, individuals are able to enact behavior that ranges from the reserved to the flamboyant, with audience support and encouragement providing social sanction. However, there is much more involved in trance than a cathartic discharge of tension. Tuareg concepts of performative competence in the head dance and its associated poetry, music, drum patterns, dress styles, and accessories serve to structure or reconstitute what would ordinarily be regarded as an undignified outburst by most Kel Ewey, particularly nobles. This process takes place in the controlled context of local criteria for performance of possession as art, specifically dancing, in the relationship between the woman in trance, the audience, and the musicians. Tuareg aesthetic codes constitute a set of symbols through which the woman in trance is able to express conflict and to structure its overt symptoms into artistry. These tropes bring coherence to the experience of solitude.

The Tuareg dance therefore differs in important respects from some other cases of possession, where dance is interpreted as an expression of anxiety and tension.[3] As shown, in Tuareg possession dance is part of a more generalized system of artistic achievement and courtship activity; it is therefore a positive expression of this aesthetic, as well as an indicator of the negative tensions associated with the conflict between concepts of person, immediate situation, and performance competence. The head dance is both a symptom of illness and a part of the cure. When the woman in trance is cured, observers note with satisfaction that "she has danced well." Yet there is a decidedly normative dimension to her performance as well, in that persons in trance also internalize moral and religious ideals associated with the aesthetic image of the swaying tree branch: resilience, harmony, strength and grace under pressure, and suppleness. Swaying in the wind also suggests deviating from norms, however, or at least the possibility of yielding to temptation and potential disorder. Several women friends told me that spirits are "similar to men, in that they like women's singing, dancing, perfume, and pretty clothes." Spirits in the wind are transformed from malevolent figures, who torment the possessed who sways in the wind, into benevolent ones, who "like" the dancing, music, perfume, and dress of the woman in trance. This process occurs through the concept of gradually improving her dancing, which is supposed to become more proficient and "prettier" with time.

The images that the Kel Ewey frequently use to describe a state of trance are the same as those used positively to evaluate visual art, poetry, song, and other dancing at festivals: suppleness is greatly valued. Therefore, through dance comes a release from the confinement of noble cultural values of shame and dignity as well as a reaffirmation of status and prestige. Tuareg women say the head dance image in particular "transports them beyond themselves." This remark suggests that the head dance enables individuals to overcome obstacles, to extend themselves beyond constraints, and, temporarily, to redefine themselves. The image is oxymoronic, bringing together opposites: it is appropriate in some contexts, inappropriate in others, a strength as well as a weakness. It is by defining the head dance in terms of its aesthetic beauty and performative competence that the possessed acquires dignity and meaning.

Display, power, status, and prestige

Kel Ewey view music, dancing, and visual art in terms of local expectations of the client–patron relationships between nobles and smiths. In rural communities, the performance of music and the manufacture of jewelry, leatherwork, and amulets is always embedded within a very personal social relationship between the individual (usually a noble) who commissions the art and the specialist (usually a smith attached to the noble) who designs it. The more abundant and sumptuous the fringe on the leather, by implication, the higher the status of the wearer or commissioner. At rites of passage, the drumming and praise songs performed by the smiths become more elaborate as nobles contribute more gifts. Kel Ewey value both the quality of the material and the skill of the craftsmanship, but the most consistently recurring motif in everybody's discussion of art is subtlety and "knowing good quality." The image of delicate swaying is pervasive and emotionally charged for Tuareg, and it is no accident that the local preference is for fringe on leather ornaments and for billowing sleeves and tassels on clothing. The leather fringe, tassels, dance motions, and songs are foils, or, to use Baxandall's term, "répétiteurs" for each other (Baxandall 1972: 49).[4]

In Tuareg aesthetics, the way things move is more important than their physiognomy. In moral conduct and etiquette values, the emphasis is upon sedate, slow, almost stationary movement and behavior (particularly among nobles). Certain pieces of jewelry and amulets are considered more beautiful and effective if they swing back and forth, suspended pendant-style. Yet such motions must at the same time be controlled. Dancing should be strong but graceful; oral tales must be accompanied by hand gestures, which must be restrained (except for the excessive gesticulation expected of smiths); and songs must be lively and flowing, yet the voices must be delicate. Hair that is worn freely is considered beautiful, but also, as shown earlier, too sensual for public display. In general, art must be set into motion to be complete, but if the movement is unrestrained, it is no longer considered dignified, and is associated with a lower social status.

The ideal of restrained movement is seen clearly in Tuareg hand gestures. Some hand gestures are used for the purposes of secret communication (usually for flirting and courtship) during festivals and rituals. These hand signals indicate the acceptance or rejection of a suitor. Extending this technique, men in rural areas flirt by training the beam of their flashlights on women's faces at nightly festivals, including the possession rite. But rather than showing emotion, women caught in the beam are supposed to pretend to ignore it. The performance of head dancing by the possessed distracts the audience sufficiently so that men and women can engage in this communication surreptitiously. The Tuareg handshake is restrained in a similar fashion. Its duration and repetition increase according to relative social status and length of time since last meeting. The hand is extended and retracted several times, during which time questions are asked and answered regarding personal health, family, work, and mental and physical state (standard inquiries in most African verbal greetings). In gestures of pouring tea, the restraint and control of motion is also evident: tea should be poured from high above the glass and make a wide billowing descent toward the glass, but should also display precision and grace by hitting the glass neatly. The aesthetic motion of swaying emerges as a billowing expansive gesture that expresses feelings and emotional states in a deeply significant way. The cognitive styles relevant to these practices are firmly rooted in social process and practice, responses to the contradictions and conflicts inherent in Tuareg life. Although these interrelationships remain largely unexplored in the ethnographic literature,[5] this aesthetic code is essential to understanding Kel Ewey social dynamics and how these are addressed in possession rituals, for it corresponds to a socio-cultural code in its hierarchical associations.

Cognitive skills, and time and space orientations
Dance, drum patterns, song, dress, and leather and metal ornaments encode social processes as well as emotional states. The head dance in

particular represents a stylized physical expression of feeling that also enters into visual and aural art. These practices revolve around specific temporal, spatial, and stylistic efforts to maintain the separation between different strands of identity: sacred and secular, noble and slave, male and female, nomadic and sedentized, reserve and freedom of expression. The dichotomy between secular and pious gesture can be seen in the contrast between motions of festival, spirit possession, sociability, taletelling, and decorative arts, and motions of prayer, Islamic ritual, and ritual paraphernalia. While the head dance and fringed tassel emphasize abandon, standard Islamic prayer is characterized by rigid body positions and gestures.

Fringe, the *talawankan* drum pattern, and head dancing are linked to physical environment and to spatial organization. But the swaying motif is more than merely a microcosm of more general nomadic movement in space. The aesthetic of swaying pervades dance, drumming, body postures, hand gestures, and ornament, referring to orientation and direction in social space as well. Thus the head dance is identified with feminine gender role typifications. Kel Ewey women are the designers, builders, owners, and users of space and residence, as well as the people who exercise jural rights over the tent and its furnishings. Women weave baskets and mats, and make containers out of hide. The weaving of doum palm leaves for tent mats and containers is one of their most important tasks, and one that they consider to be boring and monotonous. Women make bed mats and wind screens, and tan and tool leather. In addition to all of this work, women create music, song, and poetry.

The images of possession reveal, in a compressed form, the manipulation and enactment of the categories that Kel Ewey use to deal with the physical, cosmological, and social worlds. In curing rites, there is an oxymoronic process of boundary-crossing in the swaying tree branch metaphor's reconstruction of social reality. Its motions and responses dramatize the progression from disorder to order. The possession head dance symbolizes loss of control and danger at the same time that it represents beauty and grace. In a similar fashion, dance embodies relations between domestic/public and wild/alien domains. The Kel Ewey household is a fenced, bounded social space, which fact is acknowledged by outsiders, who must never enter without a formal greeting. Yet the house is not private. The swaying tree branch motif in Tuareg art and ritual is a manifestation of the same cultural logic.

4

Illnesses of God: personhood, knowledge, and healing

Spirit possession rites and verbal art imagery do not occur as discrete entities, but as a continuous code. Ritual and mythology are mirror images of each other in their articulation of issues surrounding concepts of self. Both address healing in their interconnected themes of suffering and social conflict, and both draw upon the same symbolic repertoire and imagery. Both encapsulate the contradictions of the individual/society relationship.

The local etiology of spirit possession as being inherited from mother to daughter reveals ways in which structural sources of conflict affect domestic cycles, marriage, and descent. An examination of possession tropes has shown that internal well-being is inseparable from external well-being, social stratum, and kinship roles. Among Kel Ewey, despite the cultural preoccupation with the relationship between fertility, maternity, and nurturance, social status and descent cause tensions between spouses on the one hand, and among mothers, sisters, and daughters on the other. The domestic unit enacts in a microcosmic form the larger conflicts pertaining to economics and descent. These issues have emerged as central concerns in images of possession and in concepts of person. Illness, misfortune, general suffering, and the responses of others to these phenomena are linked to one's position in the social structure.

These themes of suffering and their concomitant tensions are played out further in verbal art, such as storytelling and singing. Plots often portray women in situations of domestic conflict who inflict illness on others, the consequence of which is usually represented in the tale by the slaughter of livestock. The tales contain symbols that are also present in possession song verses and possession etiology, such as references to the liver, heart, or intestines, emphasis on shame or respect, references to certain trees and plants for healing and sustenance, and recurring themes of orphanhood.

The structural oppositions implied by these references seem clear: health/ illness, love/hate, hunger/nourishment, and kinship/orphanhood. The diversity of the images of feminine nurturing and fertility in these tales implies that the relationship of descent, social status, and economics in a given household is potentially problematic. In many tales, there are indirect references to marriage ("bull weddings" where a bull is offered by the groom to the family of the bride), animal sacrifice, marriage preferences, forms of ownership and inheritance (specifically *akhuderan* or "living milk," which refers to the livestock herds that women inherit and thus own), and body symbolism. Throughout much verbal art, there is also covert reference to the devil: in Tuareg myths and cosmology frequently portrayed as grasping his victims with his fingernails.

The tales allude to marriage, property, and inheritance, and a common theme is the domestic or class conflict caused by the contradiction between a woman's rightful ownership of livestock and her frequent lack of immediate access to it. A tale entitled "White cow" highlights many of these themes. In this tale, there is a "Cinderella" theme of an orphaned girl who is mistreated by her stepmother and stepsister, and who receives nurturance from a white cow she meets. The cow provides the girl with food in secret until this is discovered by the stepsister, who spies on them and brings some food provided by the cow home to her mother underneath her fingernails. The mother places a date-pit in her cheek and claims to have a sore molar tooth, insisting that the meat of the white cow is necessary in order to cure it. The cow is subsequently taken away and slaughtered by the father. In this tale, there is allusion to the archetypal "wicked stepmother," who denies food to her stepdaughters while favoring her own daughter, as well as an evocation of the domestic rivalry between women: for example, when two sisters are married to men of unequal economic means, who contribute varying amounts to the women's parents' granary.[1] (The rivalry is important here because in Tuareg familial relationships, sisters are supposed to share close bonds.)

The tale's explicit message is to criticize individuals who neglect adopted children. Similar to the themes of some of the choral songs sung during the possession ceremony, the tale represents a cry for love from someone who is "orphaned." As children are usually adopted on the matrilineal side, the process of orphanhood, adoption, and neglect can be seen as expressing a wider situation, in which place of birth and descent differ from place of residence and subsistence, as do the ties dispersed over these domains. Kel Ewey say that fathers of children who are divorced or widowed, step-mothers, and co-wives often neglect children. On another level, being an orphan in Kel Ewey society may be experienced figuratively, through being cut off from social ties and economic resources. Throughout, there are hints of structural obstacles to the acquisition of personal property and to forces threatening affective ties. In this respect, the cow is significant. A cow or bull is given by the family of the groom to the bride's family at a special wedding called *aduban n ezger*, if the bride's family requires such an offering. If the bride's family decides not to slaughter it, the cow or bull is not placed in the bride's herd immediately, and remains with the groom for a time. The "White cow" story alludes to the need to protect *akhuderan* herds, which, in principle, may only pass to women (usually sisters and nieces) and cannot be sold, and to the increasingly common practice of men disputing this property and attempting to have marabouts convert it to Koranic (male) inheritance.

Another problematic aspect of livestock inheritance for newly married women is that the bride's livestock remains in her mother's herd until the marriage is considered stable enough for permission to be given by the bride's mother to disengage the daughter's herd. In "White cow," the daughter benefits from the cow indirectly and secretly. The white cow itself symbolizes the nurturing role of matrilineal ties as well as the noble ideal of purity. In the tale, at first the white cow nurtures surreptitiously, until it is taken away and slaughtered by members of the father's household. The mother, by allowing the white cow to be removed from her stepdaughter, has withdrawn food, and, by implication, affection. The father, by slaughtering the daughter's property and source of sustenance, has shown himself to be wholly without love. Thus the love and nurturing of the matriline are opposed here to the jural and economic power of the patriline; descent is not necessarily where the money is. The tales that focus on illness, domestic conflict, orphanhood, and adoption are mirror images of themes in possession and, as such, articulate major contradictions in the life experiences of Tuareg women.

Another tale, entitled "Chief of the date palm," further elaborates these themes.[2] In a more macabre plot, a stepmother of two orphaned children, a brother and sister, feigns illness and requests that her husband slaughter one of the two children. The children escape temporarily, under the protection of a chief of the date palms where they seek shelter. Eventually the woman discovers them, and attempts to drown the girl in a stream, but the boy, her brother, saves her with the aid of animals, upon whose tailhairs the sister climbs up out of the stream. This tale also contains images from possession songs: orphanhood and unripe dates. Once again, a new stepmother mistreats the children from her husband's previous marriage.

The deceased real mother is eventually replaced by the chief of the date palm, who adopts the children. Thus, a founding ancestress dies, and her children are taken into the care of, first, a wicked stepmother and, subsequently, a new official male authority figure. A brother and sister are in distress. This imagery, recurrent throughout Tuareg verbal art, evokes the situation of ancient Kel Ewey matriliny subsumed under the more recent patrilineal bias of Islam. Yet the important role of motherhood and nurturance are underlined here, albeit by the device of a negative example, as in the first tale. Maternal ties can be subverted by selfish motives, which are evident in the behavior of the stepmother in feigning illness in order to slaughter the stepchildren. The brother eventually saves his sister with the assistance of animals, another widespread theme in Tuareg folklore, evoking ancient matriliny and also evoking women's inheritance forms to counterbalance Islamic forms.

Thus there is the idea of social control, kinship obligations, and the channeling and constructive use of household property. Domestic tensions center on the conflict between mother figures and children. But the ties between mother and child and between sisters normally are considered to be close, which is why these tales portray antisocial acts: the tales reinforce norms through inversion. They also express underlying structural sources of tension between maternal and paternal ties, between property transfer and use. Therefore, to say "I am ill" expresses conflict over personal legitimacy and property concerns as well as physical well-being. Discussions of illness and the art of healing constitute power struggles, and direct attention to the debate over possession and conflicting local explanations for and treatments of illness.

"Folk" and specialist theories of possession
With few exceptions (Obeyesekere 1981; Comaroff 1981, 1985; Ong 1987; Boddy 1989), anthropological studies of possession have generally tended to neglect the relationship of possession to more overarching issues of the sociology of knowledge in terms of local ontology and paradigms. There is a need to focus more intently on this dimension of possession, since it reveals a local system of logical explanation in its own right, thereby escaping the tendency in some anthropological studies of religion to portray non-Western systems of thought as quaint or primitive versions of Western psychology and medicine. Ironically, the same approach that has perpetuated this tendency has also provided some important insights into the possession process: the emphasis on the case study method.[3]

While extended case studies are crucial for an adequate understanding of the stages of possession and its etiology in relation to social process, unfortunately they detract attention from other, equally illuminating sources of data: namely, local theories of possession formulated by those who, like the anthropologist, stand at some distance from possession. Such distance, while incomplete in itself without a complementary emphasis upon the inward experience of possession, facilitates nonetheless a serious understanding of possession as part of a logical system, rather than as an isolated, sensationalized phenomenon, exotic even within the society of its own occurrence. Two main currents of thought among Tuareg illustrate these points: informal gossip and anecdotes about possession by the unpossessed and by non-specialists; and the formal transfer of knowledge about healing among specialists, including – but not limited to – healing practitioners and diagnosticians of possession. Among Kel Ewey, possession etiology, symptoms, and responses to spirit affliction are the object of much debate and speculation in daily gossip and conversation. In relating anecdotes about possession residents interject their own theories about its meaning.

Local anecdotes contain competing interpretations and explanations of possession, which reflect deeper social divisions. For example, two male gardeners and marabouts visiting me for tea one evening related an incident about a woman singer in a nearby village. They said that just before marrying, she claimed to have been bitten by a scorpion on her big toe: "She insisted on staging a possession rite. As this could not be done quickly, her relatives played taped recordings of a previously held ritual. The woman was cured on the second playing of this taped ritual. Afterward, there was no sign of the original scorpion bite." My visitors noted that the reaction to someone else's request for a *tande n goumaten* ritual was less favorable: "The husband of the woman requesting it became angry and beat her. She was eventually cured of these spirits, but by the beating itself rather than by the *tande*." When I expressed my surprise at the seeming nonchalance with which this beating was related, since wife beating is rare in rural Aïr and is viewed with strong disapproval, the men replied that "because the beating was intended to cure the affliction, it was probably necessary." Tuareg believe that sudden fear can heal some afflictions, especially those involving paralysis and muteness, which are common symptoms of possession. This belief is illustrated in a tale I collected and analyzed elsewhere (Rasmussen 1989), in which a paralytic and a blind man are cured of their disabilities by fright after encountering a monster and subsequently escaping and fighting among themselves. My Tuareg assistant in Niamey, the capital, corroborated this by explaining that, in milder types of illness or physical disorders, residents may attempt to cure afflicted individuals by startling them.

Another anecdote concerns a case of asthma, which was locally interpreted as spirit possession. The widely-traveled, French-speaking residents who related this story to me had some secular education, and recognized the difference between the physical condition of asthma and its local interpretation in the possession idiom. Some years earlier, in the town of Tahoua, a center of Adarawa Hausa and Tuareg populations located midway between Agadez and Niamey, an American Peace Corps volunteer had been stricken with an asthma attack. When the victim's companion tried to help her breathe by holding the respirator up to her mouth, he was restrained by local bystanders because they interpreted her symptoms to be an attack of spirits. As noted previously, Tuareg believe that during the active phase of trance, anyone who touches the possessed person will be killed. As a result of this cultural response to the overt symptoms of asthma, the volunteer died.

A story suggesting a common cause of possession was related to me, on my visit to a nearby oasis, by two young women friends I shall call Hadiza and Tamo, both of servile origins. A young woman named Chimo "ran wildly" in the desert, with neither cause nor destination, on her first possession attack. Chimo was about twenty years old, of servile origins, and resided with her divorced and widowed mother, selling mats and herding goats for a living. Her spirit afflictions returned occasionally thereafter, and sometimes were treated with arranged rituals, and at other times gave rise to spontaneously occurring rites. Although her immediate complaint was a headache, it was discovered later that Chimo was pregnant out of wedlock. Kel Ewey defined this instance as spirit affliction, but initially no ritual was held, and Chimo was married by her relatives, against her will, to a man other than her lover. The women who told me this story emphasized that having a secret love was the usual cause of female possession: "Her illness was caused by her wish to hide the truth of her desires."

I later witnessed a possession ritual held for Chimo, in which the songs referred to the possessed individual in a much more explicit way than usual. Here are some sample verses of the possession songs directed at Chimo: "God, who is ours, watches over us/There is one who watches over us/The friend watches over you/Why have you abandoned her?/She [Chimo] is not resting in the shadow of God" and "Why love him who does not love you?/ Wherever he goes he causes gossip about you among enemies." In this last verse, Chimo is being warned against the open expression of unrequited love.

These vignettes suggest that possession arises from a complex interplay of physiological symptoms and social processes, in which marriage and illicit love are involved. Although one anecdote features an outsider stricken with possession-like symptoms, all include an overt physical manifestation that is interpreted as having an underlying psycho-social cause, or that is simply considered to be destructive to others. In many cases, the purported motives are viewed as antisocial.

All segments of Kel Ewey society have their own interpretation of the ritual. Although Koranic scholars profess opposition to the possession ritual, they sometimes participate indirectly by diagnosing for spirits prior to the rite, and often provide follow-up treatment with amulets upon the conclusion of the ceremony. Several women told me that the healing ritual is cheaper than seeing a marabout, but this economic explanation does not fit in with the frequent combination of the two healing practices: diagnosis by a marabout, the possession rite, and then seclusion with a marabout again, followed by the application of protective Koranic amulets (never worn during the possession trance and drumming ritual itself) to reinforce the cure.

Even Kel Ewey children are aware of the moral and psychological conflicts surrounding the affliction and the ritual: small schoolboys told me that a *tande n goumaten* is required "for those women who are irritable." An Agadez merchant told me that afflicted persons "have red eyes," do not eat, and often stop speaking, instead expressing their ideas with their hands, as if they were deaf or mute. Many men claim that women undergo the ritual in order to cure their "taking off of the head" or disorientation. A gardener told me that ripening barley brings on such attacks. A teacher cited discomfort from the hot season as the probable cause. Both male and female informants claim that such women "do not know where they are going." Women, however, also tend to emphasize other factors. For example, the mother of four sisters I knew well who were all frequently possessed stated that women undergo these rituals "because only women do the head dance, whereas men dance on their feet." Silimana, whose possession was subject to ridicule by youthful residents due to her advanced age, provided several interesting observations about the possession ritual:

Not only "sick" women do the *tande* cure, but also those transported by beautiful sounds. Many women are struck by spirits when they hear this [*tande*] drum, and are also cured by hearing it again, but during an organized ritual. Yet spirits are not in the music itself; rather, some persons already have spirits present in them and thus fall into trance more easily when they hear beautiful music. Such persons react strongly to songs and music, and to the events at which songs and music are featured: festivals following life-crisis rites and Islamic holidays.

Many other residents indicated that these rites increase in frequency during periods of plentiful food, such as when there are frequent wedding festivals, camel races, and visits among different groups. Their explanation for this was that people at such times eat well and feel like enjoying themselves through music and dance. Another elderly oasis woman patient of mixed origins told me that Kel Ewey believe that spirits walk about on Fridays and on important Muslim prayer days. They seize people who are most vulnerable at these times. She added that her own spirits tended to attack at such times, and that she "did not feel well mostly on Fridays or Muslim holidays."

The complexity of the relationship between female possession and Islam among the Tuareg is supported by the comments of other women I knew well who had been frequently possessed. Asalama, the smith woman whose case was documented earlier, ruefully said that women do this "because, unlike men, women since their childhood are not protected by maraboutism." She confided to me that her parents had not protected her adequately with amulets, but that they had done so with her brothers. The mother of the four frequently possessed singers whom I knew well elaborated on women's lack of protection by stating that women, unlike men, do not carry swords, which leaves them unprotected from spirits, who fear metal in general and iron in particular. A young, newly married woman patient who lived near me, whom I shall call Marhaba, felt that "women become possessed because they study [the Koran] less." Marhaba's own possession coincided with the break-up of her marriage when her husband suspected her of infidelity during his absence on caravans to Nigeria. He announced this suspicion and his demand for a divorce in a letter to Marhaba's parents. Marhaba, not surprisingly, came from a family of distinguished marabouts. But while this is a trait of most Kel Ewey in the Bagzan region, not all residents become possessed here, and there are Tuareg who become possessed who are not from famous maraboutique families.

Possession cannot be attributed solely to antipathy toward marabouts or toward Islam. Nor can it be explained only in terms of the correspondence between patterns of possession and local explanations, such as the assertions that spirit attacks are associated with problems of love and marriage, although this correspondence is supported by many case histories. In general, statistical data alone tell us very little. For example, while data from my wider sample of possessed women revealed that a high proportion of those women were married to men who were marabouts, gardeners, and caravanners, this reflects the male occupational trend throughout the Bagzan region of Aïr, and thus applies to the husbands of non-possessed women as well. Most local men are marabouts, gardeners, or caravanners, or combine these occupations pragmatically. Likewise, while possessed women come from diverse social segments with a slight majority of nobles, this also reflects the general class composition of the region: nobles, smiths, and former slaves are all represented among Kel Ewey, and, as observed, many families of mixed descent claim noble origins. Thus, neither statistical analysis nor rebellion against Islam add significantly to our understanding of Kel Ewey possession; indeed, both perpetuate the tug-of-war between theories of ethnographic particularism and universal explanations.

Throughout these explanations of spirit possession, both men and women assign psycho-social causes underlying the overt physical symptoms. However, male residents assume more readily that women are consciously manipulating or strategizing in the preliminary stages of *tamazai* depression. In this respect, Kel Ewey men resemble some anthropological theorists who contend that "female deprivation" is the main cause of possession. For example, some young men claimed that women "have a ritual because they want a husband." A few elderly male inform ants, members of the village council and generally respected and deferred to, gave me a disapproving look and sternly insisted that women do this "because they want to get out of work," but this explanation was vigorously denied not only by female patients and non-patients, but also by younger men, schoolboys, and many husbands of patients. The patients' husbands also asserted that women "want songs and pretty clothes featured at the rite." – However, contrary to what has been reported about *zar* spirits in Somalia and Sudan (Lewis 1966, 1971; Boddy 1989), the spirits possessing Tuareg women do not ask for presents. Residents of all ages and social segments and of either sex stated that women underwent possession rituals when they had a hidden love. This message is expressed metaphorically by such phrases as "being tempted by the *tande* drum" and being a "habitual patient." A primary school director compared possession to alcohol, calling it "an escape for those with low self-esteem." Women, in contrast to men, are more apt to cite these conditions as causes but not motives, and to refer to possession as a manifestation of these causes, without necessarily having a conscious, strategic purpose. Residents of either sex with more secular education tended to offer different explanations: they elaborated on psychological explanations by saying that some individuals had more vivid imaginations than others, and that such people would be more susceptible to spirit attacks. These people also said that "being filled with thoughts" could bring on attacks. Individuals with secular education or training in other traditional healing practices asserted that frequent patients are "less logical" and "more sentimental" than other people. (Interestingly, this characterization of the possessed person does not deviate very much from the Tuareg traditional belief that creativity is associated with solitude and mental illnesses: an insane individual was said to have composed beautiful poetry in the solitude of the *oeuds* outside villages.) Yet these conditions in and of themselves are not seen as lapses; to become defined as such, they would have to be followed by a *tande* cure.

Several trends can be detected from these observations. First, there is a common thread throughout the various local explanations: the secret, repressed sentiments underlying the affliction and the public cure. Residents insisted that although the spirits produced physical symptoms, the illness was essentially "of the heart and soul." When I inquired about arranging *tande* rites for such problems as migraine headaches and sore throats, friends told me firmly that these would not be cured by *tande* rites because they were not illnesses "of the heart." Furthermore, the reasons for women's use of the ritual cure are economic, religious, aesthetic, and psychological in nature. These explanations constitute much of its social basis: as the subject matter of metacommunication about possession, rather than as its cause. In my view, these explanations must be taken into account and accorded a value equal to that of actual cases of possession recorded statistically. The local explanations locate personhood in knowledge–power systems, and acquire meaning when integrated on the one hand with the symbolism in previous sections, and with the details of spirit possession on the other.

Throughout competing explanations of the meaning and purpose of undergoing *tande n goumaten* rites, residents implicitly classify forms of knowledge. There is a subtle opposition between logic and sentiments, science and myth, truth and falsehood. Tuareg culture dichotomizes sentiment and logic similar to the way in which Western culture splits art and science, and this dichotomy has ramifications in areas of knowledge and healing that shed light on power relations. There is a relationship between possession and claims to knowledge and competence, which in turn are linked conceptually to social status. Cultural typifications of social stratum, age, and gender encourage drawing upon different inventories to respond to calamity, and promote different ways of expressing the human condition: for example, consider the differences between men's and women's songs and dances. In this sense, possession is part of the art of expressing the human condition. Most men cannot and do not do the head dance. Marabouts assert that women's possession spirits attack "little people," while the spirits of the illnesses of God attack "great people." Spirits of either type are believed to return and circulate among those regular hosts who tend to attract them. Spirit illness is linked to character, which in turn is linked to descent. One can be born with the tendency to become possessed, a tendency that occurs in certain families more than in others. Spirits are considered contagious, and are believed to be able to transfer themselves through a mother's milk. In fact, some more secularly educated individuals (for example, male agricultural extension agents) told me that a study of possession was badly needed in Niger, not because they considered it to be an esoteric or "quaint" "folk" religious topic, but because it was viewed as a public health problem! In their opinion, possession was not taken seriously enough by the "modern" medical establishment, as represented by hospitals and clinics.

Specific situations may provoke this "natural" susceptibility to spirits, bringing out into the open an otherwise latent tendency. For example, spirits may strike when the individual walks in the wrong place. Such emotional forces as love, anger, gossip, and "bad words" are believed actively to produce bad fortune, and, as a result, *goumaten* possession among women. Men's spirit affliction, in contrast, is seen as arising from intense religious devotion. Marabouts emphasize that spirits are equally dangerous to both men and women, but that men's spirits and women's spirits require different types of curing. Marabouts compare different spirit illnesses to different ethnic groups: they describe "illnesses of the heart" and "illnesses of God" as "like the races of people." Thus physical and emotional states, their definition and the methods used to deal with them, are linked with one's position in the power structure by framing them in local variants of anthropological theories of religion, healing, and art. Within Tuareg society, it is in the interest of certain groups to define possession as deprived and calculated behavior; for others, it is better to define possession as an individualistic, psychosomatic illness; for others, it is considered highly symbolic communicative art; and for still others, it is seen as part of an evolutionary progression from "sentiment" to "science." All these explanations are connected, in local conceptualizations, with descent, prestige, and status. They depend, for their formulation and perpetuation, on knowledge–power relationships.

Illnesses of god: science and myth, diagnosis, and the control and transfer of knowledge
Power struggles pervade discourse on illness and on the art of healing, which can be seen in the lack of consensus about the meaning of spirit

possession within Tuareg society. Possession and conflicting interpretations of its imagery serve as a forum for hidden struggles and agendas.
Among Kel Ewey, healing specialists from diverse social segments control
access to power through alternative channels of knowledge. Underlying
their rival claims to competence, larger issues are at stake. Control over
healing serves as the major instrument of intellectual coercion in the
transfer of local sacred and secular knowledge. Distinctions among healing
knowledge specialisms evoke, in certain respects, the art/science and myth/
history split of European cultural traditions. Alternative forms of healing
are available to all Tuareg, but there are internal as well as external
pressures on these healing systems and on the choices among them, which
come from indigenous social organization and recent administrative
organization.

Medical knowledge affects the cultural construction of self/societal
relationships through musical performance, dance motions, and verbal art
texts that address illness and healing. Competing claims to professional
credibility are defended most fiercely in specialized healing domains, and
receive expression in conflicting theories of possession and images of
personhood. The content and practice of healing thus provide a forum for
evaluating forms of knowledge as myth or science, thereby indirectly
mapping the social status of the person. Specialists transmit their knowledge of healing and notions of personhood through verbal and musical
performance containing critical commentary on knowledge; namely,
through women's possession curing songs, and through the Islamic litur-
gical music known as *ezzeker* sung by men, during which they occasionally
become possessed. As commentaries on illness, these texts reveal wider
struggles surrounding social divisions of class, gender, and age. They serve
as boundary markers and standards for distinction, rather than as primary
causes of possession.

Tuareg healing methods, and the texts they employ, express local
knowledge and power hierarchies, infused with notions of truth and
falsehood. Different interest groups rank certain versions of knowledge
more highly in their perceived hierarchies of truth. For example, men say
that "women tell lies and children's tales [*imayen*]" while men tell history
(*idámen iru*), and that women's possession songs are "not science" while
men's *ezzeker* songs praising God are derived from Sufism, and are thus
identified with the "science of the Koran [*taneslema*]." Reserve and secrecy
characterize certain types of knowledge: for example, noble male creativity
is identified with solitude. Good male poetry and singing must take place
outside villages and away from groups of people toward whom reserve

behavior is practiced. Openness and lack of reserve characterize other types of knowledge; not surprisingly, Tuareg of all social segments say "smiths and slaves have no shame," so their drumming apprenticeships take place in public. These contrasts affect local perceptions of women's solitude during the possession trance. The cultural opposition between prayer and song is also relevant here, for although many possession song verses articulate a dichotomy between prayer ("science") and secular song ("art"), these two categories are not seen as mutually exclusive or isolated.

In the anthropological literature, these knowledge–power hierarchies are widely identified with the so-called sacred–secular split and literacy (Horton 1967, 1983; Goody 1977). However, the attempt to find universal trends is problematic because, all too often, it results in rigid ethnocentric classifications. To escape the pitfall of evolutionary ranking, it is useful to focus on the internal divisions within Kel Ewey society, and find the general implications therein. For example, in the transfer of medical knowledge, why does the established local intelligentsia find some sources of knowledge and transfer channels more threatening than others? The possession idiom provides a forum for disputes about wider power struggles in Kel Ewey society, for both men and women are players in this game, although they are not necessarily juxtaposed along gender lines. At issue are such questions as who owns specific forms of knowledge, to what extent does this ownership coincide with power, and whether other resources come into play. Tuareg healing specialists present competing versions of personal health as models for social relationships.

What is most interesting here is the manipulation of truth-falsehood oppositions within a diagnostic setting, as well as the source and limits of credibility, and its relation to the sacred–secular and myth–science distinctions suggested in possession imagery. In the struggle over definitions of personhood, the concept of the possessed woman's solitude inverts social status distinctions in Tuareg society. Perceived hierarchies of truth are connected to social hierarchies as some versions of knowledge become defined as truth and others as falsehood. Traditional apprenticeship situations, as well as themes of illness, curing, and learning in verbal art tales and in individual life histories, indicate that the creation of knowledge is separate from its transfer, and that different channels of knowledge transfer are associated with different social strata and varying levels of prestige and influence. While some apprenticeships, for example noble men's sung poetry, occur in solitude away from villages and camps, only in the presence of age-mates due to the cultural value of reserve, these verses are disseminated and modified in public performance over a long time.

Although noble descent groups traditionally composed and held copy-rights to certain forms of sung poetry, their attached blacksmiths could recite them. An analysis of the roles of different knowledge specialists – herbalists, marabouts, diviners, smiths – in transmitting medical knowledge reveals how notions of truth and falsehood are constructed by specific agents and are then associated with different persons.

Among Tuareg, different kinds of power are available in gender, age, and class divisions, and each has an impact on the practice and transfer of medical knowledge. The practice and content of ritual and oral arts in the transfer of healing knowledge reveal Kel Ewey classifications of science and myth, and also show how resources are mobilized to gain control over the definition of personhood. Possession plays a role in this process in that it may be interpreted as a struggle for the control of Tuareg identity at both symbolic and political levels. Disagreement about possession, as well as competing claims to legitimacy in the practice of healing, expose the principles to which each disputant appeals in the competition to control collective memory, to gain dominance over "the source of persuasive power in the dialogue of subculture" (Bakhtin 1960; Hebdigé 1979).

Knowledge, power, literacy, and the sacred–secular split
In examining the relationship between knowledge and healing, there is a need to analyze cultural traditions as mechanisms for maintaining socio-political and conceptual boundaries. With few exceptions (Comaroff 1981, 1985; Kenny 1986), no works have approached altered mental states by identifying systematically the main traditions or channels of knowledge, and no analysis has linked these channels to tropes and aesthetic forms in possession imagery. Among Kel Ewey, there is a source of knowledge for each healing tradition; each presents its subject, the sick or incomplete person, against a political background. Possession by Kel Essuf or *gouma-ten* spirits represents a struggle over the definition of self that has a basis in socio-political conflicts. The category of "people of solitude" expresses a paradox, a contradiction in the nature of power among Kel Ewey. "Being in the wild" or "solitude" is used to describe someone who, while not necessarily always socially marginal or deprived, is certainly of ambiguous status and in many ways contradicts idealized concepts of person. Yet, as shown, in many ways these individuals embody what is viewed as central to Tuareg cultural identity. Unravelling this paradox requires identifying the principal medium of cultural dissemination, accounting for agency in the process of cultural dissemination and for the greater prestige some forms of knowledge acquire. Among Kel Ewey, differences in perception of truth

and falsehood in knowledge legitimacy are linked to social stereotypes. Possession diagnosis fills the need for negative reference groups. While Western-based colonialism and its introduction of literacy undoubtedly play important roles in processes of knowledge transfer and in the construction of personhood, some works tend to overemphasize the West's role while downplaying that of local intellectuals (Goody 1977; Mudimbe 1986, 1988).[4] For example, among Kel Ewey, writing is identified with Islam. However, Kel Ewey use verbal instruction, musical performance, and reading in the transmission of similar types of healing knowledge, but toward different ends. The chosen medium of communication in diagnostic and healing rituals is a response to social stereotypes.

Can the sacred be transformed into the secular in Tuareg society, where these dichotomies, supposedly mutually exclusive or at least sequential, exist side by side, and where local notions of "primitive" and "advanced" thinking are applied to specific forms of knowledge and social segments? Clearly, the content of communication is of prime significance in relation to modes of thought concerning the person in sickness and health. In Tuareg society, which includes literate and non-literate knowledge specialists, political activity is channeled in this dual tradition of communication, often through particular styles of the curing of illness.

Goody (1977: 130–35) observes that although the use of written recipes may "emphasize and enshrine differentiation of a hierarchical kind, as well as permitting accumulation of modes of preparation from many localities, it has limited implications for the growth of knowledge. Such is not the case with a medical recipe. Writing gave the study of surgery power over systematic arrangement of material. It could be made the object of comment and addition."[5] Viewed in this light, Islamic scholars comprise part of what Goody calls a "restricted literacy" tradition (Goody 1977). He argues that the role of an intellectual is more prominent in a literate than in a non-literate society, for in a literate society the intellectual is transformed into a scholar, a specialist in communication rather than in production (Goody 1977: 33). Many of the differences that Horton (1967) characterized as distinctive of open and closed systems of thought can be related to different systems of communications, specifically, the presence or absence of writing (Goody 1977: 46). This broad linkage again leaves finer shades of contrast, as well as power relations, unaccounted for. In this respect, the role of Tifinagh, a particular type of Tamacheq script practiced by women that is restricted to poetry, love inscriptions, and graffiti, is ambiguous. Yet Kel Ewey Tuareg women also study Arabic and the Koran, although very few today practice maraboutism professionally.

Therefore, neither a simple dichotomy nor a unidirectional, monocausal trend stands the test of local variations. As shown, there is a whole range of attitudes within Tuareg society itself toward possession (from serious consideration of it as a health problem, to views of it as strategic and manipulative behavior, to its portrayal as theatre), which raises questions about previous methods used in anthropological generalizations about this phenomenon within a single social setting, let alone across diverse cultures. There is a need for greater insight into local paradigms of personhood surrounding the ritual process, individual case studies, and general trends. Case studies provide the individual contexts of possession, ritual embeds them in processes of communication and control, and local knowledge and power systems provide the backdrop or texture. If local options for curing reflect internal knowledge hierarchies by providing a battleground for ideas, who controls the flow of some channels and the crystallization of others?

Koranic and non-Koranic traditional knowledge systems
Among Kel Ewey, sacred and secular traditions do not displace each other; rather, they are interwoven. The roles of intellectuals encompass both perspectives, across literate and non-literate contexts. These developments have produced competing oral media and alternative "sacred" powers in knowledge form and transfer. Two social segments – Islamic scholars and blacksmiths – traditionally serve nobles in client–patron relationships: the former as lettered religious specialists in regional history, Koranic law, and medicine, and the latter as oral historians, musicians, and intermediaries for chiefs. In rural communities, Koranic scholarship includes religious, legal, and medical studies.[6] Tuareg say that the marabout practices *taneslema* (the science of the Koran) better than others (such as nobles, for example) because he is peace-loving and does not need to fight.

Traditionally, the noble warrior needed the blessings and amulets of a marabout for protection in raids and battles. Today, marabouts practice divination and counseling, and interpret Koranic law. They are sought out for their advice by local chiefs. They are also expected to be generous, for example, to redistribute their wealth. During the Sahelian drought, one prominent marabout in the Aïr region near Mount Bagzan gave away most of his wealth in stored millet. Thus in rural areas, the split between sacred and secular knowledge and between law and medicine is not so clearly defined. I noticed that rural Tuareg understood more clearly my role as a scholar/anthropologist if I described myself as *taneslem* rather than as *professeur*.

Koranic education goes beyond the primary level; higher education is pursued after students have memorized Koranic verses. This higher level includes study of the meaning of the Koranic verses, somewhat like Talmudic study in Judaism. Other religious writings are introduced, such as the Hadiths (the traditions of the Prophet). The student also learns Arabic grammar, logic, jurisprudence, theology, and commentaries on the Koran. Although many of my Kel Ewey friends in rural Aïr would be considered non-literate in French, which is the official language of Niger, and in their local language, nonetheless they read and write Arabic. Elders told me that at one time there was a Koran written in Tamacheq with Arabic letters (similar to the Ajumi in Hausa religious tracts), but that this version of the Koran disappeared long ago.

In more nomadic conditions, while men were away on raids and caravans, women in some Tuareg divisions became primary educators by telling tales that had a didactic purpose. But marabouts, rather than women, have been the more influential educators among the Kel Ewey. A power struggle between them is suggested when elders (particularly noble men and marabouts) call the stories children's tales rather than history, and accuse women and smiths of lying. In the villages of my research, many small boys who did not accompany fathers on caravans spent much of their time in Koranic schools, although in rural areas no sharp division exists between home and school, or between secular and religious education. Intellectual pursuits are thus linked to age, descent, gender, and the types of morality and upbringing identified with them. Claims to legitimacy and power are linked to age, sex, and social stratum affiliation.

Sources of knowledge

Kel Ewey of either sex say that women are afraid to touch the Koran; furthermore, much ideology opposes female sexuality to Islamic ritual: for example, menstruating women cannot touch Islamic amulets. Although women are not technically forbidden from becoming marabouts, Bilcha, a woman who had studied the Koran intensively in her childhood but who was not a practicing marabout, told me that in the past there were more women Islamic scholars than there are today. It seems that there are social structural reasons for this decline. In the past, there was greater opportunity, with former domestic servitude, for noble women to practice the arts and education. Since the abolition of slavery, however, many Kel Ewey women are today more constrained by domestic tasks such as processing food. But a number of women still receive some Koranic education, and are literate in Arabic as well as in the Tamacheq Tifinagh script. Contrary to what has been reported about women from some other Tuareg divisions (Murphy 1964, 1967; Borel 1987, 1988; Worley 1988), many Kel Ewey women tend to echo *ineslemen*, men's disdain for Tifinagh, and consider it less important than Arabic, the alphabet of the Koran. Bilcha also seemed to agree with this view, stating that "Tifinagh and Koranic studies are not the same thing; Islam is worth more. I do not know Tifinagh, but I know Koranic studies." This view contrasts sharply with the attitudes of Iwellemeden Tuareg women from Mali, with whom I was acquainted during my residence in the capital of Niger, who enthusiastically taught me some Tifinagh script.

Kel Ewey women's traditional position of privilege has been subjected to competing tensions from legal arrangements favoring men, which are the result of sedentized lifestyles, the influence of Islamic scholars, partial dependence on a money economy mediated by husbands as middlemen, and irregular returns from herding (Rasmussen 1985: 342–47). Nobles often symbolically liken blacksmiths to women in Tuareg culture: "The smith is like a cousin or a woman; you joke with him [or her]." Smiths frequently circumvent official authority roles by acting as intermediaries and go-betweens, particularly in love affairs and curing, and by exercising their right "to pronounce what other Tuareg are ashamed to pronounce." Smiths are able to do this essentially because they lack reserve (*takarakit*), the important noble cultural value.

Medicinal knowledge and practice: diagnostic situations
Traditional medicine, including Islamic ritual knowledge, focuses on curing an individual's physical or psychological ills, or on protecting the individual against social misfortune (such as theft) and against forms of sorcery (such as jealousy and love problems). At first glance, it seems that in Tuareg cultural ideology specialized Koranic healing knowledge enjoys higher status and prestige than other, non-Islamic forms, and is regarded as the standard medical treatment of choice in many rural communities. However, a closer examination reveals a more complex relationship between the two forms of healing, one that does not conform to conventional theories of binary opposition, muted voices, or religious syncretism.

Islamic scholars are skilled in diverse healing methods. They insert Koranic verses written on paper into leather or silver amulet cases, which latter are manufactured by blacksmiths. Another healing method is to write verses on to a wooden tablet with a vegetable-based ink solution, which is then washed off and given to the patient to drink. *Alestakhara* refers to a marabout divination practice that involves writing Koranic verses and numbers on paper, placing the paper underneath the head, and sleeping on it. The marabout then dreams and counsels the patient on the basis of the content of his dream. *Alkhukum* is the week-long period of seclusion with a marabout following the possessed person's *tɔnde n goumaten* ritual. Another cure consists of the marabout writing certain combinations of Surat (Koranic verse) numbers together in geometric designs in a small book for curing a given illness. According to marabouts, the Koran is filled with medical knowledge; each verse, numbered and named, contains a remedy for any illness (except those requiring the music and noise of the *tɔnde n goumaten*). It is the order and geometric pattern of numbers that is important; some illnesses and misfortunes require one pattern, others a different pattern. Most residents indicate that knowledge of these healing skills is accessible to almost anyone, because being a specialist in the field principally requires practicing Islam "better" than most others, which means leading an exemplary life. Yet they emphatically state that maraboutism is a science (*taneslema*), as opposed to other types of knowledge, such as non-Islamic divination, herbalism, and spirit possession exorcism. The science of maraboutism consists of knowing and writing the Koran, praying, fasting during Ramadan, giving alms, and respecting other people. Anyone may learn to practice the science of maraboutism. However, although some ex-slaves and smiths are full practitioners of maraboutism as a result of special training, they are referred to by the term *al faqir* rather than *eneslem*, which is a subtle distinction indicating a social origin and occupational specialization less prestigious than that of the highly respected *ineslemen* clan affiliation. In Aïr regions there are special clans that claim to be descended from the Prophet or from the Sufi mystics who brought Islam to Aïr from the Maghreb. These *icherifan,* who also claim noble descent, are more apt to be called true *ineslemen* and are considered powerful healers. This designation is expressed in a spirit possession song verse that speaks of the need for cures by "cows' milk from herds of the *icherifan* kept in gourds."

Central to the practice of Islamic ritual, therefore, is Koranic knowledge, which, theoretically, is attainable by anyone. Marabouts' sources of prestige are primarily in Koranic knowledge. However, although this knowledge of letters seems monopolized by nobles, elders, and men, with inheritance in some clans playing a small role, much of its transfer occurs through oral tradition and ritual processes, through agents who are linchpins in Tuareg society (for example, women and smiths are not excluded). Furthermore, in actual content as well as practice, the written tradition frequently overlaps with the oral and the non-Islamic traditions, contrary to local cultural ideals (and anthropological theories) of opposition between these different knowledge systems.

One important body of knowledge in Islamic ritual is *ezzeker* music, derived from Sufi mysticism. These are songs praising God and the Prophet, and include the pronouncement that there is only one God and his Prophet is Mohammed. Men perform *ezzeker* songs in mosques and sometimes enter a trance state while doing so. But this type of possession is considered to be of a very different order from the spirit possession cured by public exorcism rituals. The former is valued more positively, because it is said to result from a feeling of inadequacy from seeing the contrast between the Prophet's devotion and that of the worshipper. However, *ezzeker* possession may become destructive; friends related several cases to me concerning men who became "crazy" from this and had to be carried home forcibly from the mosque. Marabouts say that some worshippers recite these song verses many more times than a marabout prescribes, and that it is this excessive repetition that causes the worshippers to become crazy. These types of possession are defined as "illnesses of God" (*tawarna n Yallah*) rather than "illnessess of the heart and soul in solitude." Verses of one *ezzeker* song I collected appear in free translation here:

> God is one.
> If all the world dies, it is God who will remain.
> I cry out in the name of God.
> God is one.
> There is no other.
> Come praise God.
> I cry in the name of God alone.

In *ezzeker*, the name of God should be pronounced nine times. The term *ezzeker* is generic, and refers to many different kinds of songs praising God and the Prophet. The songs are often sung in canon (round) style. Some marabouts told me they considered reading the Koran to be also a type of *ezzeker*, because "everything in the Koran is from God." These songs also have certain protective or curative powers; individuals are said not to feel anything (hunger, for example, during the month-long daily fasting of Ramadan) while reciting *ezzeker* because the power of God enters the reciter through the mind. Tuareg men insert *ezzeker* imagery into a local variant on the origin myth of Adam and Eve: the bridewealth of Adam (the necessary offering before Adam could be with Eve, his bride) consisted of pronouncing the *ezzeker*.

Yet, as shown, despite their power, Koranic verses cannot cure some types of affliction; the latter require the *tʒnde n goumaten* ritual. The *tʒnde n goumaten* ceremony is unique in several ways. First of all, it is public, which, in this case, includes being surrounded by an uninvited, irreverent, licentious audience of mixed social origins. Second, it features loud music, singing, drumming, joking, and flirting among the audience. And third, the oral art of the *tande n goumaten* is conceptualized entirely differently by Tuareg. *Goumaten* songs and their accompanying drumming music are conceptually opposed to Islam and the Koran, in local references to them as well as in the secular content of their verses.

Many local residents were reluctant to transcribe texts because they said they were afraid of these songs, which "addressed spirits." Marabouts state that after listening to *goumaten* songs, it is necessary to wash, remove, and change clothing before entering a mosque. Although most *tande n goumaten* songs feature secular subjects, such as love and economics, and contain jokes and social criticism, many also refer to Islam. A major recurring theme is the opposition between the oral tradition of these songs and the science of the Koran. The following spirit possession verse provides a good example: "[It is] word of the mouth. It is not science of learning [*teghare*], so that I am struck down while reciting it before a marabout." This partly explains why drumming is usually by smiths or former slaves, or more rarely, by a woman of any social segment, but never a male noble or marabout. Yet since these possession rites are tolerated grudgingly by marabouts, provided they are performed in neighborhoods far from mosques and at times that do not coincide with Moslem holidays, the classification of *tande n goumaten* rituals, their specialists, and body of knowledge as "anti-Islamic" is problematic. Rather, it is the social processes and communication of cultural styles taking place at these rituals that makes them so controversial. Other specialisms classified as un-Islamic or anti-Islamic, such as herbalism and divination, provoke less debate. These latter are performed in private consultation between individuals.[7]

Why *tande n goumaten* is chosen as a healing method

The most important point to emerge from this discussion of the epistemology of healing is the fact that individuals choose to undergo *tande n goumaten* rituals. Their affliction is not merely passive victimization, but is an active retreat into solitude in order to assert power, which has antisocial connotations on the surface, but which also conforms to basic concepts of the person in Tuareg society. In the local epistemology of healing and personhood, each competing healing method is a paradigm which articulates the worldview of a particular interest group, thereby providing a forum for expression of self and its contradictions and conflicts. Furthermore, individuals perform through spirit possession, and particular healing styles become codes for power assertion. While individuals do not necessarily choose to become possessed, they do choose to remain in solitude and to undergo diagnosis, which often leads to a referral by a marabout to undergo the *tande n goumaten* ritual. The style of healing as art is as important as its content and its end result of personal well-being. Possession rituals are more than a curing method; they are a medium of communication.

Possession and its images thus give voice to the "silent" person, lost in desolation and loneliness. Yet different voices have varying leverage in power play. The cases of the few men who have been diagnosed with *tamazai* depression and who have undergone the *tande n goumaten* rite serve to illuminate the meaning of this voice, which is typically expressed in a dominant feminine idiom. Throughout my residence in rural Aïr, I heard of only two cases of men being treated by the *tande*. Both cases were related to me with much laughter and astonishment. They are described below.

The case of Latou and her husband, Boukary

Latou, about twenty-four years old, is a woman of servile descent who lives in a small oasis about five miles from the caravanning village where I resided in 1983 and 1991. She is of Kel Zingifan origin, and is Kel Nagarou on her mother's side. Both she and her husband, Boukary (who is currently estranged from Latou and living with his relatives in another village, though the couple is not yet divorced), have been possessed by Kel Essuf and have had a *goumaten* rite arranged for them. Their afflictions came at roughly the same time, and seemed to correspond to certain events in their married life.

Latou was first possessed when she was about twenty-one, three years before my research began, thus some time in the early 1980s. This first possession occurred after she had been married to Boukary for five years. Boukary is a former caravanner who, due to sudden illness, had been forced to stop his work and became an invalid. His illness had been the result of an infected boil, which is believed to make the flesh soft and vulnerable to other sicknesses. Relatives explained this as follows: if the blood or fat of an animal falls on the individual, a blemish forms and digs into the flesh. The remedy is branding or cauterization, or to chew the sap of the *tamat* (*Acacia flava*), and then apply the pulp to the boil. Alternatively, one can place *taboraq* (*Balaites aegyptica*) leaves on it. It is not clear whether Boukary tried these remedies; in any case, his ailment did not subside, and in fact grew worse, eventually confining him to bed. This prevented him from performing any kind of work, and caravanning in particular. Later, upon my return in 1991, I found that his illness had become even more serious; he was said to have lost his senses and become mad.

Latou at first cared for her sick husband, but later he returned to his kin in a neighboring village near Mount Bagzan, where he remained. Latou, meanwhile, was supported by her father, a caravanner, and her brothers, who were gardeners. She and Boukary were childless. Though Latou – not Boukary – continues to be possessed and to have the *tande n goumaten* rites, friends said that the first time Latou was attacked, her husband was also attacked, and that both underwent these rituals together. Significantly, Boukary did not become possessed in a mosque, nor did his cure involve Koranic verses. According to relatives, after Boukary became debilitated he "went crazy" with *tamazai*, and he and Latou subsequently separated, though they did not divorce. Other relatives who have been possessed include a female cousin, but no other men in the family.

This case is of interest because of what it illustrates about the relation between gender typification, spirit possession idiom, and personhood. Here, a young man's physical debilitation and his subsequent removal from participation in men's economic roles (caravanning and the support of his wife) are held to be directly responsible for both husband's and wife's spirits and to require this method of cure. So it appears that the few exceptional men who undergo the *tande* treatment are in some way cut off from their normal roles, as defined within masculine personhood in Kel Ewey Tuareg culture. Thus *tande n goumaten*, with their central tropes of feminine gender typifications, are the expression, rather than the cause, of *tamazai* illness and *tande* cure.

The case of Tahirou

A second negative case of male possession corroborates this interpretation. Tahirou, a blacksmith, is of Kel Nabarro origins. He is about thirty years old. He was first brought to my attention in informal gossip. One friend told me with a chuckle that Tahirou first became possessed spontaneously at the nameday celebration of the oldest daughter of a prominent resident of his village (of no relation to Tahirou), where smiths sang praise songs and grilled meat, as it is customary for smiths to do at nobles' rites of passage. At the very mention of Tahirou's name, several people began to laugh. An elderly woman, a frequent possession patient, Hawa, laughed uproariously in response to my questioning about this rare case of male possession. A distant cousin of Tahirou also jokingly called Tahirou a "slave" (*ekli*), a term used to denigrate individuals of any social status whose behavior does not conform to normal expectations among Kel Ewey.

Another instance of Tahirou's possession and *tande* cure occurred later, when Tahirou was in love with and wanted to marry a Kel Iforghas smith woman (a marriage his family opposed, due to her different origin: smiths, in particular, adhere to the ideal of marrying close within the community). A third possession attack occurred when Tahirou began negotiations to take a second co-wife, Asahara, but had problems raising and paying the bridewealth among male patrilineal kin. He finally succeeded in marrying her, but only after a long struggle.

Tahirou does not practice the craft trade of smiths in metallurgy; instead, he works in a relative's garden, and lives just outside of the village limits. According to a brother, Amo, he is admired for being generous, never refusing aid to relatives. Yet people often seem to mock him behind his back for his spirit attacks. At such times, he has overall body aches and other *tamazai* symptoms. Though his general health seems good, one of his children died at an early age. Other relatives who have been possessed include a maternal aunt and woman cousin, but no other men.

Here again, the possessed male displays traits viewed as not conforming to standard gender and class typifications in Kel Ewey Tuareg culture. Tahirou, a less than successful smith compelled to work in someone else's garden, is viewed as an effeminate man; his spirit attacks, unlike those of most men, do not respond to the treatment of marabouts, and their treatment with the *tande* rite makes the patient anomalous in terms of person definition as expressed in possession tropes. Men, for example, are not supposed to dance the head dance; and since they carry swords in everyday life, the ritual sword clutching "to cut and separate and chase away spirits" serves no purpose for them. The possession treatment, which features the playing of the *tande* drum by either women, smiths, or slaves, and which revolves around the songs learned and sung only by young women, again underlines the marginality of the possessed man. Thus it is not the spirits in themselves that connote femininity among Tuareg; rather, it is the manner of curing them, with distinctive music and dance, that is identified with traits opposed to noble and male personhood. Thus possession aesthetics are culturally defined as feminine in terms of the transfer of knowledge and idiom of expression, although there are among the possessed individuals who may experience varying degrees of "deprivation." But it is not deprivation in itself that causes possession; recourse to possession requires a trigger that, in fact, arises from paradigms of "normal" personhood. The affliction of men like Boukary and Tahirou reflects problems they have experienced in conforming to masculine gender role typifications. Yet their cure reinforces their problems because of its anomalous nature. It is viewed as defying notions of masculine and feminine personhood as these are expressed in knowledge specialisms and possession aesthetics.

Curiosity and creativity: traditional education and apprenticeships

Among Tuareg, learning a skill is linked to upbringing; women told me that in order to sing or cure well, the person must be "well raised." This conceptualization of being well raised has moral connotations, in that the conduct of parents and elders is seen to reflect purity of origins and to ensure good marriage of children. (Elderly women say that "the marriage of children depends on the conduct of parents.") So learning is bound up with ideals of descent. Part of ideal conduct is the correct reserved behavior toward parents and other respected authority figures, such as Islamic scholars and affines; and another part consists of the individual's own behavior as a parent. Paradoxically, however, much knowledge ideally is imparted without direct questioning by youth. This view is expressed in two tales I have collected below. The first tale was told by a young married noble woman with children, and concerns the fate of a youth who seeks the unusual.

The man who wanted to see the marvelous

A man said that he wanted to see something marvelous. He walked and walked, and encountered a stream of flowing oil. A woman spirit said, "Sir, aren't you astonished?" He said to her, "What is so astonishing about a stream of flowing oil that I do not already know?" He walked and walked. He encountered buttocks that were fighting. She asked him, "Sir, aren't you astonished?" He said, "What is so astonishing about buttocks that fight that I do not already know?" He walked and walked, and met eyes that were fighting. She asked, "Sir, aren't you astonished?" He told her, "What is so astonishing about eyes fighting that I do not already know?" He walked and walked, and arrived at a home. The woman spirit turned into a woman and told him, "Come here." He came, and she prepared a meal, she had many children. She picked up the stick, and he licked it. The meal was finished. She prepared another meal, and he slept. Then she sharpened her knife. The rooster cried "Yako!" She cursed it. But the rooster did not sleep. The rooster cried "Kikikiyako!" She sharpened the knife in order to cut the man's throat. The rooster crowed again. The woman put down the knife, and then she herself lay down and fell asleep.

　　The man went out. He packed his baggage and left. He went along, and he walked and walked. The female spirit awakened. There was no one there. The man traveled for a whole day. The female spirit got up and followed him. She was very tall, and stretched from sky to earth. She walked like a sand devil. Like that, like that – until she saw him throwing down his cat from his camel baggage. She swallowed the cat, and she pursued the man. The man dropped a rooster from the camel. She swallowed the rooster, and followed the man. Like that, like that – until she saw a camel's paw, and she swallowed it. The camel ran, losing paw after paw, until it had only one paw left. Then the female spirit ran and told the man, "Even if your camel has only one paw, I want to take you to that tree over there." The man and his camel ran and ran, and arrived at the tree. The female spirit pulled off the camel's last remaining paw, and ate that, and then she ate the rest of the camel. She looked up into the tree, where the man had climbed up into its top. She looked at him, and did not know what to do. Then she tore off his penis, and changed it into an axe. She began to cut down the tree. As she was chopping down the tree, the chameleon said: "Give the axe to me." She gave it to him. And when the chameleon began to cut the tree, he said to it, "Return to what you were before." So the tree became as it was before. The man then called his dogs. He called and called. He had two dogs, and as many wives. He said to his wives: "When you see the dogs, try to run, and unleash them." They told him "All right." They left, and tried to run, and one wife said, "We'll unleash them." The other said, "We must not unleash them." The two wives argued, until finally they unleashed them. The dogs ran toward the tree and when they saw the spirit woman, and they ate her. They tore her all up, and they said to the man: "Come down." He said, "I don't want to come down until you pick her up, pick up her bones from there. Then I'll come down." He said, "Now I've seen the marvelous." He divorced the wife who had argued against unleashing the dogs. The tree had to be shortened in order for him to descend.

In effect, this tale is the mirror image of the cases of the male *tande* cure discussed in the previous section, for its castration imagery suggests emasculation of the male hero who deviates from standard channels of seeking knowledge and follows the "wrong" road. Also present in this tale are the oppositions of Islamic and non-Islamic knowledge. The term here for female spirit, *djinniya*, refers to the type of spirit mentioned in the Koran, here angered at the young man. Chameleon, *tawoutte*, is considered a very wise and good animal, and in local Bagzan Kel Ewey folk etymology, the term is also used as slang for a very devout marabout (*taghaghen tawoutte*) who studies the Koran). Here, the marvelous or astonishing is implicitly understood as knowledge outside the sacred religious tradition, the seeking of which is dangerous to men.[8] Spirits are conceptualized as inhabiting remote places outside human habitation, and they are said to attack those who walk in these places unprotected by amulets and swords made by Islamic scholars and smiths, respectively. Here, the female spirit is portrayed as a kind of Siren temptress who lures, tests, and later attacks the man.

Another pervasive message in the cultural construction of healing knowledge pertains to reserve in certain types of kinship: the importance of refraining from posing questions to elderly persons or affines. Much knowledge is transferred according to who may and who may not pronounce the forbidden and shameful, such as names of husbands, fathers, and deceased ancestors (especially on the paternal side). A brief tale which I collected about a man and his mother-in-law, called The man and the ostrich, illustrates this point.

The man and the ostrich

A man married the daughter of a woman who pounded herb porridge. The man made traps to snare gazelles and moufflons. Always he would ask his mother-in-law, "Mother-in-law, how do you make the porridge?" One day, he left to set a trap, and then watched his mother-in-law fill her basket. She said, "Son-in-law, an ostrich is in your trap." They ran and ran. He said to his mother-in-law, "Climb faster, climb faster." His mother-in-law fell, and the ostrich ran.

This brief tale portrays an antisocial inversion of norms. Ideally, sons-in-law observe an avoidance relationship with affines, particularly with their mothers-in-law, before whom they cannot show their faces, eat, or drink, and whose name they cannot pronounce. It is also implicit in this avoidance relationship that a son-in-law should never ask his mother-in-law questions.

Despite the importance of literacy and Islam, and the restrictions in behavior between youths and elders and affines, much specialized knowledge, including that of the Koran, is often transmitted orally in rural areas. This transmission, however, is not supposed to occur in response to questioning, but rather through storytelling, sacred and secular songs (the boundaries between which, as we have seen, are blurred), and healing rituals employing these songs and other verbal and non-verbal media.

Another way in which knowledge is transmitted is through musical apprenticeship, which is of central relevance to possession, since much healing is accompanied by musical instruments. In the classical repertoire, each poetic rhythm, based on the author, event, or person to whom it is dedicated, is a kind of matrix from which poets (predominantly men) are obligated to be inspired to create and pattern poems and songs. These rhythms are memorized with the aid of formulas that refer to verses extracted from other poems that possess a meter similar to the desired song. Noble values of reserve and respect obligate a noble man to sing in seclusion, only in the company of listeners from his age group and with whom he has kinship joking relationships. If a man is caught in a situation of inferiority, such as singing to elders, he is vulnerable to mockery in the poetry and songs of others. Traditionally, smiths attached to noble warriors were the first to repeat their poems and songs, a privilege that they alone possessed. Today one still finds the greatest number of poets and singers among smiths, partly because smiths do not respect the rules of reserve. Because the social status of smiths permits them to circumvent the typical Kel Ewey constraints surrounding creativity, they are the principal transmitters of the repertoire.

Some marabouts have recorded melodies and rhythms in a book written in Tamacheq in the Arabic alphabet, with commentaries on their origins and the history of their creation. In epic poems, the personal creativity of the singer intervenes only rarely. It is, however, permissible to insert verses borrowed from other authors, provided that the singer respects the meter, rhyme, and scansion (hallmarks of noble warrior sung poetry) of the original poem, and at least cites a few verses from it.

Vocal and instrumental performance can only take place by executing known melodies, which are never detached from their original melodic contexts. Among Kel Ewey, I collected data on drum patterns, songs, and poetry performed specifically during the spirit possession curing rite; tales with sung refrains; and brief, half-sung, half-told lamentations often performed by women. Competence is evaluated according to aesthetic rules of vocal technique transmitted from generation to generation. Thus familiarity with the repertoire and its mode of reproduction are inseparable. Poems are memorized faithfully and reproduced by recitation. For a Tuareg singer, form counts for much more than faithfulness to the text; it is by his melodic creativity that his is recognized.

Apprenticeship to the *anzad* takes place upon female adolescence, when the girl first begins to wear the headscarf. She begins learning the *anzad* by practicing a melody called *melloloki*, which allows her to perfect the movements of the bow. Classical *anzad* melodies are first acquired by song, in solitude, and are then transcribed on to the instrument, but are accompanied always by a murmur of the throat, called "song in the soul." One friend of mine in the Kel Ewey caravanning village of my residence described how she observed more experienced players first, who then placed her hands in the correct position. She told me that due to her advancing age, she had abandoned this instrument in recent years and now devoted herself to her Islamic duties of prayer.

Apprenticeship on the *tande* drum, an instrument traditionally identified with slaves and smiths, is of a different order. Here the learning process is not hidden, for the game of *tande* is part of childhood amusements in which all smiths and former slaves participate. The different drum patterns are acquired progressively during evening festivals that feature this drum and at exorcism rites, and are easily imitated on rocks and other objects. I observed small children, playing at drumming for the possession ritual, enacting this in detail, complete with possessed patient beneath the blanket, chorus, and a drummer, who used a small toy drum. Kel Ewey regard drumming as a less serious musical apprenticeship than playing the *anzad*. The *tənde* drum can be assembled spontaneously from a mortar used to crush grain (which is identified with domestic servitude), and can be reconverted into a mortar at any time. The *tənde* is played typically in public, informal, and playful contexts. The *anzad*, by contrast, is constructed especially for playing music and is solely a musical instrument, typically played in structured situations and during formalized musical practice. Women learn possession songs from their mothers, and the singers at spirit possession rites are usually close in residence and kinship relationships; for example, wives of pairs of brothers or close cousins.

The foregoing description of the learning of music suggests that it is one of the major activities that is still consciously structured, repeated, and reproduced by individuals. Learning music seems to represent a refuge for identity, regardless of the player's social segment. Furthermore, among Tuareg it is permissible to borrow and mix learned traditions as long as they appear "noble," and as long as the noble origin of the composition is given credit. Yet persons entrusted as vehicles for transmission are not exclusively male or noble; on the contrary, smiths, slaves, and women predominate in the transfer of musical skill and thus enjoy the prerogative to change it.

As shown, knowledge specialization and decisions about its transfer are based traditionally on internal status distinctions; however, the composition or form of knowledge is separate from its transmission. Agents of composition and agents of performance are not always the same. While knowledge specialties are sometimes seen as property "belonging" to particular social strata and descent groups, performers who transfer knowledge may in fact alter its content to a significant degree. Herein resides the power of possession discourse, in its alternating modalities of sound and solitude.

PART II

ART, AGENCY, AND POWER
IN THE RITUAL SESSIONS

5

Sound, solitude, and music

The main images that recur in possession are based upon an overarching opposition between sound and solitude, and relate to the Tuareg conception and exercise of power. Among Tuareg, possession illuminates the inherently contrary and conflictual aspects of experience and action. The interaction among patients, musicians, and audience, and the reactions to the dance motions of trance and its accompanying music reveal the multiple meanings the event has for participants and non-participants. The aesthetic processes that occur during the rituals and the commentary that follows them provide new meanings in changing contexts for men and women of different ages and social strata.

The possession event draws upon different aspects of Kel Ewey social roles, especially gender, within and outside the context of trance. Possession thus informs anthropological attempts to grapple with the distinction between official and unofficial ideology, and how this comes to bear upon the choice of cultural and subcultural styles (Bakhtin 1960; Baxandall 1972; Hebdigé 1979). Tuareg possession encapsulates the contrast between the official ideology of descent, religion, and stratification, and the unofficial embodiment of illicit female sensuality in possession performance. Because it is enacted in performance, this contradiction is expressed simultaneously rather than sequentially, and evokes important themes in Kel Ewey Tuareg culture. The interweaving of aural and visual imagery in possession provides insights into the role of social conflict and power in creativity.[1]

The large number of frequent patients who are older women and adolescent girls, and who are also wives and daughters of prominent marabouts relates directly to the dance motions of trance (associated with women) and the music of the *tǝnde* drum (played by lower-caste persons). Taken together, these evoke key, contradictory themes in Tuareg culture:

109

the freedom to conduct illicit affairs outside marriage, the restrictions imposed upon men and women as they age, and jural ambiguities and constraints associated with prestigious noble descent and ownership of property. The enactment of possession allows observers to express conflicting definitions and negotiations of aesthetic form, and allows participants to redefine their personal identity. Aesthetic satisfaction is central to both cause and cure of Tuareg possession. While *goumaten* spirits may attack at any time, the music at festivals often activates them. Musical talent is not required for participation in a possession ceremony, but it is necessary for effective healing. If good drummers and singers are unavailable locally, patients undergo healing in neighboring villages and camps. Standards of performance require that the possessed individual first rise to a sitting position and perform the head dance, later collapsing to the ground "exhausted." The patient must dance in a particular manner in order to be rid of the afflicting spirits. The idea of artistic competence in the trance "style" of the patient is perceived as an important component of the cure.

Art, meaning, and social order
Responses to trance and possession ritual are based upon the manner in which possession is integrated into the wider Tuareg socio-symbolic system.[2] Music among Tuareg generally has prestige; yet there is also an undercurrent of disapproval that barely tolerates music. In popular opinion, certain instruments should be regarded with caution for they are so beautiful that they may "transport us beyond ourselves." The *anzad* and the *tande* are two such instruments. The former, a one-stringed bowed lute, is associated with heaven and the nobility. The latter, a drum struck with the hands, is constructed by stretching a goatskin across the top of a mortar, and is identified with the earth and lower social status. To marabouts, all music is suspect, and the devil is all the more involved if it is played or sung by a beautiful young woman. Musical expression, not in itself illicit, is seen nonetheless to distract people from their Islamic duties of prayer and from the noble values of reserve and dignity. Ideally, Tuareg are supposed to avoid an open display of sentiments, whether they be positive or negative. This reserve applies to the enjoyment of food, music appreciation, and especially to romantic preference. The degree to which this interdiction is practiced reflects, in large measure, social distinctions. It is not appropriate to attend a concert or listen to music in the presence of someone older than oneself, particularly if there is a close kinship tie. Significantly, the taboo is reciprocal: an older person avoids listening to music and sexual conversation in the presence of younger relatives.

There is thus a contradiction in Tuareg cultural ideology between the high artistic valuation placed on music in general and the labeling of much of it, particularly the music of the *tande*, as associated with low social status. This ambivalence is also reflected in the attitudes of the Muslim clergy who view music as evocative of unmarried love. These attitudes have a basis in social marginality. While musicians occupy no clear-cut caste, blacksmiths approach marginality by reciting genealogies, acting as go-betweens in love affairs, representing the woman in marriage negotiations, and singing praise songs. Smiths pronounce what others feel "ashamed" to utter, and also lack the dignity and reserve of nobles. Yet anyone may become a prominent musician, although different instruments and musical activities are identified with different groups. Since playing the *tande* is seen as not far removed from performing domestic labor, it is suitable for smiths, servile persons, and women.

Here it is instructive to examine more closely some features of local social differentiation. While nobles traditionally have controlled large networks of resources in varying degrees of servility and dependence, an individual's status as "free" or "slave" has never been rigidly defined. Rather, below the aristocracy there were various levels of dependants, including blacksmith clients attached to noble families, employees, tenant farmers, herders who worked on contract, and slaves. The status of each depended on their position in the larger system. Each was attached to a specific noble or noble section and had varying degrees of freedom. In addition, Tuareg assimilated outsiders, who then belonged to one of any number of servile strata.[3] Kel Ewey nobles have occupied a go-between status in this scheme, as caravan traders and relative newcomers to Aïr. Although this has conferred upon them certain commercial advantages, it has also diminished their cultural "purity" in the eyes of some other Tuareg divisions and Hausa alike: some residents of the Aïr region view the Kel Ewey as constituting but one degree in the concentric circles of Tuareg servitude. Thus it is relatively easy for Kel Ewey nobles to fall and slaves to rise in this system, and this fear is pervasive, guiding decision-making in daily matters ranging from subsistence, to the selection of a marriage partner, to criteria for artistry.

Slaves were absorbed into Tuareg society even as they were exploited economically. Thus far Scholars have emphasized the ecological origins of this pattern (Nicolaisen 1963; Keenan 1977; Baier and Lovejoy 1977). In linking this social stratification to Tuareg possession symbolism, aesthetics, and personhood, it becomes clear that this complex system has a life of its own, independent of desert ecology. Nobles attempt to cling to values and lifestyles idealized in the traditional social hierarchy. In the core area of operations (the desert), acquired outsiders were used as servants, herders, and gardeners, and belonged either to individuals, to tribal sections, or to offices. At the bottom of the status hierarchy were *iklan*, newly purchased or captured people. Some were attached directly to a master and accompanied him on travels; some were semi-sedentized; and others farmed estates in the Sahel region. Some slaves lived in their own camps, gardening for three or four months of the year and resuming transhumance after the harvest. They kept their masters' animals while they gardened and also kept the proceeds from the sale of milk. They owed masters a fixed annual payment of millet and a proportion of the increase in their own herds, and were required to give them additional millet when needed (Baier and Lovejoy 1977: 399). Slaves who were directly attached to the camps and villages of their masters were integrated into Tuareg society as fictive children, and used kinship terms to address members of the master's real family. A man could marry a female slave even though she was considered his daughter; this practice conformed to the custom of marrying classificatory daughters. If a noble married his own slave, their children took on the father's status; if he married a slave belonging to another man or woman, he could claim nobility for the children by paying a high bridewealth to the original owner. Both practices followed the injunctions of Islamic law (Nicolaisen 1957, 1963: 100–105).

Despite these kinship analogies, the economic position of slaves was very different from the economic position of real children. The slaves did most of the hard manual labor: male slaves tended herds and drew water from wells; female slaves cooked, brought firewood, and fetched water. Agricultural client peoples known as *eghawalen* performed gardening and gave a portion of their harvest to nobles. Noble men wore fine clothing and owned decorated weapons, and noble women possessed expensive jewelry. Thus conspicuous consumption by men and women of the aristocracy at one time reflected their control of productive resources: camels, weapons, and the labor of slaves and other dependants.[4] But even today, manual labor is scorned by nobles. My women friends around Mount Bagzan frequently lamented about how, formerly, slaves did all the work. These circumstances explain why the artistry and the symbolism of the *tande* acquire such resonance throughout the possession idiom.

The abolition of slavery and the scarcity of domestic slave labor have had profound consequences on the lifestyle of Kel Ewey women. Formerly, slaves who performed domestic tasks freed nobles from work, and thus enabled the women (who normally remained in villages and camps while men left on raids or trading expeditions) to pursue education, poetry, and music. Such music included singing *tande n goumaten* songs, which, it bears repeating, are learned and sung only by young women. Today most noble women, even the chief's wife, spend their days fetching water from the well, gathering and crushing grain, and weaving tent mats. While all but a few vestiges of slave labor have disappeared today in the villages and camps at the base of Mount Bagzan, there is a continuing effort on the part of many pastoralists, caravanners, and even some gardeners to remain culturally distinct from the more sedentized former slaves, popularly called Buzu in Niger. Yet such distinctions have been breaking down rapidly for some time; Kel Ewey themselves acknowledge that many smiths, gardeners, and former slaves are wealthier than nobles, herders, and caravanners.

Cultural values that assign greater prestige to those claiming noble descent persist, however, and class and gender typifications cut cross concepts of personal identity. For example, although nomadic cultural traditions confer a jural advantage upon women, this is in large measure due to leverage traditionally based on access to large livestock herds and domestic slave labor. Even independent of slave labor, forms of Tuareg inheritance protect women's property rights from male Koranic bias, female founder-ancestress myths provide strong bases for women's prestige and status, and ownership of the tent gives women economic security and jural leverage.

Nevertheless, the competing forces of sedentization, Islam, and gardening – with their greater valuing of material prosperity derived from a money economy, youthful female fertility, and the male practice of polygyny – have long created doublebinds and challenges for gender role and class identity. Songs which women perform at possession that contain such themes as slaves doing what they want and suitors who lie about wealth express these contradictions. These conflicts are also expressed by audience responses to replaying possession song recordings. Once, I played a recording of a *tande n goumaten* rite for several guests. The soloist, whom I shall call Rhaicha, was a noble woman of about forty years of age, and throughout much of her life she had enjoyed a reputation as a fine singer. Although still renowned for her vocal talent, Rhaicha usually declined invitations to sing at these ceremonies due to her advancing age. I had recorded her in a rare performance that she gave as a special personal favor.[5] Hearing her performance on tape, my guests burst out laughing and expressed some distaste for her singing. They said she was becoming "too old," and that her voice was too low and coarse for singing the *goumaten*.

Only "very young women" should sing these songs, said my guests, and their voices should sound "high" and "delicate," as such voices are associated with youthfulness.

Relevant here is the connection between possession aesthetics and reserve relationships. Many older patients are former singers or players of the *anzad*, the popular women's instrument associated with nobility, courtship, and youth. Since older women should not socialize with young men, many of whom attend festivals where they court these women's daughters, musical festivals take place at night because affines and potential affines attending these events practice strict avoidance, and are "ashamed" to encounter each other during the day. Kel Ewey kinship, like Aïr Tuareg kinship generally, is bilaterally traced, despite the emphasis on matrilineal origin in oral traditions.[6] Inheritance and other bases of property rights are complicated by kinship ambiguities.[7] Such ambiguity, however, also implies a certain flexibility. The universe of kinspeople in one's own generation consists of cross-cousins, the children of whom are known as *tegaze* or sisters' sons, and the fathers of whom are mothers' brothers. The network of marriage preferences, in ideology though not in practice, includes exactly those people who are defined as members of one's common descent group. As noted, many Kel Ewey avoid this problem by actually marrying either distantly related or unrelated persons. The issue of kinship, then, becomes primarily a reflexive problem for the ethnographer, who attempts to deduce the precise degree of cousinness, brotherness, sisterness, etc. But it is the consequences of such a system, on the level of real social action (rather than on the level of precise terminology), that is of interest here.

These ambiguities and maneuverings are played out in some aspects of the possession idiom. For example, song verses contain many different terms for female roles and ties among women. In the social setting, the most striking of these are the close ties to mother and sister, not solely from the female point of view, but also from the male point of view. The sibling tie competes with the husband–wife tie among Kel Ewey of the Bagzan region, because a number of men, even though they reside in the village of their wives, spend much of their waking existence (in work and at noonday meals) elsewhere, at the homes of their mothers. Several husbands abandoned their wives and returned to their region of patrilateral kin groups. I noticed that wives often refused to follow. This is one important problem posed for self-definition, which is articulated throughout possession imagery in tropes pertaining to labels of kinship, marriage, and friendship ties, such as orphan and the various female friendship terms in songs.

Another problem related to kinship is that individuals from outside the maternal tent are mistrusted. I noticed that a husband might often be suspected of carrying on an affair in the village of his wife, but not in his own village. Role behavior toward certain categories of kinspeople is therefore clearly specified. In this regard, Kel Ewey follow rules of behavior similar to those of other Tuareg, previously documented by Nicolaisen (1963), Murphy (1967), and Casajus (1987). The following paragraph summarizes those features directly relevant to my discussion of music.

Respect must be shown to all consanguineous relatives of ascending generations (persons known as elder brother and elder sister); and conduct toward these relatives should be like that toward ascending generations. A person must show respect toward his or her older brother, though not toward a classificatory older brother who is chronologically older. When one is with one's older brother, one does all the work on a journey, and avoids all talk of sexual matters and the use of lascivious terminology, such as *anzad* (the one-stringed bowed lute), and *tande* (the drum used at possession rituals, and at festivals and dances). These two instruments are associated with making love and with courtship outside marriage. Conversely, one should advise, aid, and protect a younger sibling of either sex. The proper decorum for a man with his sister, older or younger, is restraint. An elder sister is described as "like a mother" to her younger brother; there is neither a respectful nor a joking relationship here. A woman's behavior toward her sister ideally involves a balance between joking, sharing, and mutual aid. Cross-cousins, like parallel cousins, are joking relatives, as are all true and classificatory cousins. This type of relationship permits free talk about sexual matters, teasing, and insolence; for example, the tearing away of the cousin's veil and the snatching of belongings. Joking exists equally between the elder brother's and younger brother's children, and between the elder and younger sister's children. The relations with the first ascending generation are clearly dichotomized along the continuum of patrilaterality and matrilaterality. The father's sibling group is equated with the father as the source of authority and a potential arena of struggle; the mother's sibling group, by contrast, is the source of love and support.

I found that Tuareg joking relationships and their privileges are often extended into other domains, beyond the kinship context. As noted above, nobles, ex-slaves, and smiths also enjoy such relationships, and frequently use them to circumvent restrictions. The spirit possession ritual facilitates the superimposition of joking behavior on affinal, age, and social stratum relationships that normally would be characterized by extreme respect and reserve. Joking transforms official roles and relationships into practical ones and thus redefines personhood, although only temporarily. This is one important, albeit transitory, effect of possession imagery, and it underlines the need to examine the social face of possession in terms of its expression or style, in addition to focusing upon its causal factors.

An additional feature of kinship relevant here concerns marriage. The married couple, while constituting an important social unit at rites of passage and in postmarital domestic residence, is connected only tenuously within the realm of economics and subsistence. Husbands are often absent for much of the year, and even non-caravanners go on extended visits to kin during the rainy season in bridewealth arrangements requiring cooperative effort. Thus it is in ritual rather than in everyday contexts that certain significant kin relationships are brought more precisely into relief; their ambiguity allows them to be manipulated in class and gender conflicts. The most frequently heard kinship term is cousin (*abobaz*). The long-term purposes of consanguineous kin come more to the surface, and classificatory kin recede in significance, at rites of passage, such as weddings, namedays, and to a certain extent, at possession rites. For example, the most prominent groups of kin at a baby's nameday ceremony are a group collectively called *chidagalen*, which denotes the women on the father's side or the female affines of the mother. These persons are treated with extreme deference and respect, and are the most important guests at namedays and weddings. Normally, they do not share relaxed social relations, except if they encounter each other during evening possession rituals. To complicate matters further, due to tribal endogamy and preferred close-cousin marriage, many persons who are classified as cousins and who thus share a joking relationship are also, at specific times, affines in respect relationships. These are the tensions that are played out in the enactment of possession and in the commentary on it.

Due to their entry into reserve relationships, women singers outgrow their cultural acceptance as successful musicians, members of the *tande* chorus, and audience. They may subsequently become patients. Thereby, aesthetic competence may continue in the role of possessed person. Indeed, although many older women said that they no longer missed music and festivals, and indicated that prayer was now more important, a number of them were frequent spirit possession patients. Mana, a noble woman about sixty years old, had adolescent grandchildren. Acquaintances remarked that she appeared much older than she was because of her frequent physical ailments. She was always doctoring herself and asking others for medication, and she and her daughter often treated each other's ailments. Mana had been widowed twice and divorced once. Her former husband had remarried a woman who still resided in the same village, whom Mana often encountered at rites of passage and communal work projects. One of her possession attacks, in February 1983, occurred spontaneously, without a prearranged ritual. At noon one day during this cold, dry season, she fell into trance while listening to the tape cassette belonging to Mohammed, eldest son of the *chef de tribu* (chief of the local descent group), her cross-cousin. Other people present at the time included women and children in the chief's household, and those of the household of the chief's wife's sister, people with whom Mana shared a relaxed, joking relationship and obligations of mutual aid. The tape was a recording of a *tande n goumaten* rite that included a series of songs. As Mana performed the head dance, others periodically shouted encouragement. Her eyes were closed, and she trembled. Then she held her hand over her eyes and rested, requesting that the tape recorder be turned off because the dance was difficult. People obliged, and gave her food and water as she reclined on a mat. When I later discussed her attack with a friend, he remarked with amusement that he was not surprised that Mana had "done it again," describing her possession as a kind of lapse, comparing it to drunkenness.

Thus, while trance provides an opportunity for the performance and enjoyment of music, as well as for sociability and courtship across class lines (under cover of illness), it also evokes psychological states that are devalued in other social contexts. The statuses of older woman, affine, and noble require dignified conduct because they represent the interests of Islam, idealized "pure" prestigious descent, and (officially) class endogamy. Viewed against the socio-political and economic backdrop, these vignettes encapsulate the tension between power and symbolism in attempts to preserve personal identity under conditions of contradictory bases of power, which, not surprisingly, has deep ramifications in possession imagery. Social processes become a medium of communication and are given expression in the possession tropes that reverberate throughout the ritual, the metacommentary on it, and the aesthetics of trance. Throughout the possession idiom, then, there is a double contradiction: a cultural ideology of separateness alongside economic pressure toward homogenization, for the social segments; and a cultural ideology of equality alongside economic pressure toward asymmetry, for the sexes.

Images that Tuareg use to describe trance and curing link possession to competence and creativity, on the one hand, and to pollution and lack of control, on the other. The individual isolation of spirit affliction, associated with the wild and with solitude, leads to a lack of congruence between a concept of self and control of social personhood. The enactment of possession mediates conflicting definitions through symbolic forms that oppose the musical sound of curing and the solitude of trance. Despite the initially debilitating symptoms, for many individuals becoming possessed is indeed an appropriate expression of one's passage through the life course; the artistry of the rituals for Asalama and Mana evokes the doublebinds and ambiguities associated with these different social categories. The possession idiom comments on the way persons should be, but through a multiplicity of artistic styles that draw upon competing rather than consensual cultural paradigms. To Tuareg, aesthetically coded spirit affliction evokes dramatic and social response. The culturally constructed relationships among social categories underly the expression of sentiment and patterned modes of sound and motion during curing. The possessing spirits are representations of the person that are incompatible with the accepted definition of the self. Self-control is an important cultural value for adolescents during courtship, and also for elderly women (especially mothers-in-law), and for nobles generally. This explains the sense of a frequent joke inserted into the verses by singers: "The women who looks for men extends her neck ... supported so as not to break her back." Here, the image of possession, offered during the head dance, is associated with flirting, as is the musical drum pattern that accompanies it, which is said to imitate a "tree branch swaying in the wind."

One case in particular vividly illustrates these connections: Silimana was a woman of about seventy-five who had a number of grown children, most of whom were married. Her immediate possession symptoms were stomach aches and general body pains. Her first possession had occurred when all her children were grown, following a divorce which she had initiated in protest at her husband's negotiations to marry a second wife. The most recent attack took place the night after she had heard a possession rite held for her maternal niece. Following that ceremony, Silimana suffered sleeplessness, and relatives later arranged a ceremony for her.

However, people tended to laugh when speaking of Silimana's recurring possession attacks. They found something absurd about her association with *goumaten* spirits and possession rites. People treated Silimana with respect to her face, but in her absence they ridiculed both her person and her intermittent illness. During her own ceremony in March 1983, there was more than the usual amount of revelry among the audience. Contrary to usual practice, no one asked the patient how she was progressing. The musical performers seemed flippant and apathetic, and the songs were distinctly lacking in enthusiasm, dragged in tempo, and had little harmony. The audience commented that the songs were "dead" and some asked what was wrong with the chorus. During the pronounced revelry and horseplay, a suitor in the audience approached one of Silimana's three daughters.

The allusion to "craning one's neck" in a song verse is significant. As a woman of rather advanced age, Silimana was subject to certain behavioral restrictions. Young people in the chorus and audience felt sheepish participating in her musical ceremony, and took her curing less seriously than rites that might be held for younger women. The more advanced the patient's age, and the more potential and actual affines there are present, the more inappropriate her trance performance (and *goumaten* spirits) becomes, although it is still permissible. The possession idiom strongly evokes courtship, the unmarried love of adolescent years, and joking relationships among potential spouses, which should not be confounded with avoidance relationships among affines. A number of *tande* patients of more advanced age mentioned that their possessions began in adolescence (often during courtship, and while attending or immediately after leaving possession rituals and festivals), ceased at marriage, and reappeared again after their children had grown up (that is, after their children had reached marriageable age in adolescence). In most possession cases of extremely elderly women, Tuareg scorned the patients and considered their possession rites to be unacceptable. The music of the *tande n goumaten* evokes romantic love, free sociability, vulnerability to outside influences, and lack of personal restraint. The elderly patient, however, represents values antithetical to these states: dignity, an ideal of pure descent, and ascribed status.

Verses from the popular possession songs performed at the rites of Silimana and other women evoked these contrasts, expressing ambivalence toward marabouts and the "science" of the Koran, and lamenting the power of money, the new freedom of former slaves, and the scarcity of livestock. Ideally, Tuareg society is based upon the hierarchical order of social identity connected with descent, and the social strata are endogamous. Descent group membership is still based on *tawsit* (descent group or "tribal") affiliation, traced matrilineally among some groups and patrilineally among others. Noble descent groups, however, now hold fewer sovereign rights over the entire territory of their drum group (a political division involving ties of subordination and dependency, comprised of several *tawsiten* or descent groups), and over the camels and weapons associated with these groups. For example, tributary and servile groups were once forbidden to own weapons, and only slaves and smiths performed certain dances and played certain instruments, such as the *tande*. Koranic scholars traditionally did not raid or depart on caravans, but depended rather on the prestige of accumulated *al baraka*, or blessing power, to transfer into the generosity to their followers. Although notions of personhood based upon these traditional ideals predominate, nonetheless there are competing social strata and interests: one emerging from socio-economic practices, and one superimposed on the descent-based identity.

Yet even under the traditional system emphasizing descent, there has always been a place for courtship and unmarried love at musical festivals held during the phases of life marked by ambiguous jural status: during engagement and during the early years of marriage before bridewealth payment and groom-service have been completed. Lower-class persons and women, while constrained by the "grammar" of official ideology in religion, notions of descent, and noble and male stereotypes, nevertheless attain respect and a degree of freedom through the alternate discourse of music, poetry, and song. This ability temporarily to transcend restrictive social and gender categories resembles what other authors have referred to as an "idiom," enabling so-called "muted" groups to "reconstruct experiences in a personally meaningful way" (Crapanzano and Garrison 1977, 1980; Obeyesekere 1970, 1981, cited in Boddy 1989: 195).

However, even more divergent and nuanced processes are occurring here. Among Tuareg, there are additional opportunities besides possession for clarifying, reconstructing, and, to borrow Boddy's term, "obfuscating" experience. What, then, makes the *tande n goumaten* different from others, marked as an experience in the discordant discourse of Tuareg men and women? As in the case of *zar* possession described by Boddy (1989), the *tande n goumaten* add another layer of meaning to human relationships in which the possessed participate; each progressively resituates dimensions of personhood constituted in relations with kin, opposite sex, and members of alternative social segments. For possessed persons, human relationships continue to be revealed through their own and others' association with the spirits. Among Tuareg, however, personhood is reconstituted in contrasting ways according to different vantage points, as shown in the local critique and testimony of possession. In particular, the aesthetic overlay of possession among Tuareg extends the audience, patterns of alignment, and identifications and contrasts created by it.

Attitudes toward appropriateness and competence in possession thus illuminate the meaning of statements that love and worries cause spirit attacks, and also "make one sing better." These evaluations effectively "twist" personal definitions: to be competent in some contexts of personhood is indeed to be inappropriate; and conversely, to be incompetent in certain contexts is to be enacting the appropriate role on another level of experience. These attitudes and their outcomes in turn suggest additional, polythetic (context-dependent) chains of meaning in possession, or, as Boddy (1989: 305) and Messick (1987: 217) term it, "subordinate discourse." Rather than making local values and behaviors conspicuous by their absence in possession, and rather than overturning local values, these values are exaggerated – and manipulated – by non-possessed as well as possessed persons during the rite, in a continual debate. For example, Kel Ewey express two contradictory sentiments at once in the joking phrase "*a teha goumaten*" (she has spirits or she is in trance): simultaneous references both to possession and to the notion of being transported by beauty. This phrase refers to a person who openly expresses pleasure upon listening to beautiful songs. It also connotes being so distracted that one overlooks social convention, such as not greeting affines, elders, and marabouts, or neglecting prayer. Although *goumaten* spirits are said to be caused by spirits, Tuareg do not believe that these spirits are in the music itself. Rather, people who harbor the spirits fall into trance when they hear music at wedding dances, ceremonies for other patients, or when they listen to recorded music from the possession ritual. The contradiction is that while these contexts create a need for aesthetic expression, this is forbidden or shameful in precisely these contexts.

Local exegesis of spirit affliction and the criteria of aesthetic satisfaction correspond to the cultural expectations of behavior according to gender, class, and age. In this respect, possession constitutes a reiteration of, rather than rebellion against, more general cultural typifications of female beauty based on youthful and noble criteria: high voices and the execution of songs in a "restrained" and "delicate" fashion. It also provides a forum for airing feelings that normally must be kept under wraps. Thus in some contexts, aesthetic criteria and activity reconcile individuals to their ideal roles, for even when these roles are challenged, it is from a viewpoint defined by those in a position of power. In another respect, individuals use aesthetic activity to negotiate social rules. The enactment and evaluation of art entail a degree of maneuvering by different interest groups, albeit sometimes unconsciously and indirectly. All Tuareg admire good singers or poets, whether men or women, whether of noble or servile origins; and women, as observed, may express otherwise forbidden sentiments through song. But even this freedom is subject to strictures of an aesthetic based on noble values of restraint and reserve.

On one occasion, upon returning from an oasis of predominantly sedentized Buzu (former slaves) agriculturalists, noble residents of my caravanning village of residence bombarded me with requests to play tapes of spirit possession ceremonies I had recorded there. They said that the music of that region (*tande* music, in particular), was among the best in the Aïr, and that Buzu were "better" than other Tuareg at drumming and dancing. On the other hand, when I later sought to transcribe and translate the song texts from these tapes, my assistants remarked on how scanty the poetry was, in their view, in the songs from the oasis. In their opinion, the verses consisted mostly of vocables and expletives, rather than full words and phrases. Local explanations of this were phrased in the following terms: "Buzu [slaves] are less concerned with the words to songs [and] more concerned with the pattern of drumming, dancing, and clapping." Furthermore, though some song texts originally may have included more poetry, listeners told me that many of the oasis' contemporary singers had forgotten, or had not yet been taught, their "complete" verses. Noble residents of the caravanning villages and nomadic camps, by contrast, took pride in the poetry (*techawait*) of their song texts, and evaluated local singers on the basis of how well they remembered the words and poetry. They admired the other music, but for different reasons: for the embellishment of those songs with elaborate drumming, ululating, and clapping. Although nobles enjoyed such embellishment (and, indeed, eagerly danced to it in evening festivals), they immediately perceived it as "slave" music because they saw it as lacking in reserve and restraint. Poetry, however, was not lacking in these qualities according to their definition, and was thus associated with their own "noble" music. The loopholes in the dominant dialogue of personal competence exist at the cost of backhanded compliments.

So the possession aesthetic becomes a kind of living form (Langer 1953), and the emotive import belonging to it allows for the circumvention of structural rules in some respects, but maintains constraints and limits in other respects. For although musical talent and creativity bring social prestige, this prestige is adjusted to fit the ideology of established gender and class typifications. The criteria and standards of evaluation of style often reinforce the social rules of the audience rather than the performer, and thus perpetuate gender and class-based stereotypes, for the criteria come from the noble, male cultural values of the traditional warrior society and of Islam. The relationship between structure and action is complex. Aesthetic competence sometimes operates as part of a self-fulfilling prophecy in social power relations; while it elevates status in one way, it is self-defeating in another. Agents' strategies, the key symbolic forms they invoke in their actions, and the distribution of power in Tuareg society reveal the continuous compromises among conflicting ideals, and between ideals and conditions of existence (Bakhtin 1960; Karp and Maynard 1983: 499–500).

Aesthetic form, social intention, and personal sentiment in sound and solitude

Possession rites selectively reinforce and undermine important themes in Kel Ewey social life. They transform the predominantly solitary communications of the verbally reticent patient into a dialogue. The aesthetic dimension of possession is a kind of non-verbal "obscenity" in the language of social relations, although some of its "bite" is removed through over-analysis of it by its critics, and through efforts by participants and others to appropriate and render it respectable or at least harmless – but on a basis that contradicts its original intent. This occurs outside as well as within the local rural community, albeit in different ways. In the capital city, ethnic art fairs now include an enactment of the spirit possession ritual as a musical performance, in the absence of the possessed or a cure. Locally, as indicated, the marabout's injunction against praying after attending these rites links possession and sexual intercourse, and this association evokes the more general social freedom during possession that overturns and distorts the values of restraint and reserve. This was seen most clearly in the flirting and joking that took place during the rites that were held for Asalama and Silimana. These values are integral to the regulation of class endogamy and in-law reserve.

Participation in musical events is a kind of carnivalization of social rules *à la* Bakhtin (1960), and aesthetic form is a selective metacommentary on individual and collective constructions of social reality from different power perspectives. This behavior dramatizes the non-verbal and embodied aspects of the relationships between self and society. This relationship, with all its inversions and amplifications, "reverberates" throughout the musical, verbal, and visual interplay of the possession rite.

In the enactment of possession, aesthetic form and social context provide a polyphonic code of current social relations. The *tande* practitioners and the chorus attempt through their art to placate the spirits: on the one hand, there are direct efforts to pacify the spirits; on the other, there are specific attempts to revive the patient's soul with music. The effectiveness of the cure depends upon how well the music sounds; specifically, on its performance according to clearly articulated rules. The style of singing and drumming are as important as the subject matter of the songs and the overt function of audience actions. The drum must be loud and resonant; residents believe the distinct rattle of a silver ring, sometimes placed inside the drum, pleases the spirits. The patient holds a sword in order to ward off spirits, but also because Tuareg consider this object. often intricately decorated, to be beautiful. Many men in the audience bring cassette players to record the songs. Such tapes are highly prized, and anyone interested may listen and evaluate them later.

Among Tuareg, musical instruments are also perceived as belonging to differentiated social and cosmological categories. Friends told me that in the past, both the bowed lute and the *tande* drum were used in spirit possession rituals, but that today, at least in the Aïr region, one encounters only the drum at this rite. Both instruments are associated with festivals, rituals, courtship, eroticism, and the spirit world, and each one illuminates the meaning of the other. The music of the bowed lute or *anzad*, while largely unheard at possession today in the Aïr, is still played in other contexts and is relevant to the issues under consideration here. It is part of a more generalized symbolic opposition expressed in aesthetics, and constitutes a code in which further social differences and concepts of the person are elaborated. *Anzad* music is said to come from heaven, while that of the *tande* is associated with the earth. Neither instrument, as observed, is allowed to be named or discussed in the presence of elders and marabouts, a taboo which applies most stringently among nobles. Coming into play here is the noble value of reserve, in which smiths and former slaves are held to be deficient. Thus both instruments are alternately highlighted and suppressed in the consciousness of speakers, players, and listeners in Kel Ewey Tuareg life, depending upon context. The *anzad* is constructed with a string of hair and a sounding box made of one-half of a gourd covered with a thin membrane of skin. Traditionally, it is the instrument of the nobility, and even today it is usually played by noble women.[8] While playing the *anzad*, the musician rubs the string from time to time with the bow. The skins of these bowed lutes are often decorated with motifs painted in very bright colors, or are covered with Tifinagh inscriptions signifying the name of the owner, or verses written by admirers. Until recently, this instrument enjoyed the highest status in musical evaluation, and was used as a noble cultural "marker" to disdain influences from outside the Sahara, in the form of more recently introduced instruments, such as the *tande*. (The *tande* is related to the Hausa *ganga* and to other percussion instruments from the Sahelian regions to the south and west, and the *takamba*, a plucked string instrument, is related to the West African *kora* and other similar West African string instruments.) Many noble acquaintances in the Aïr region openly claimed to prefer the *anzad* and scorned the other instruments, although, in practice, they actually did listen to all these instruments on many occasions. Their attitude was similar to ambivalent attitudes among many persons in Western European and American society toward "classical" and "popular" music.

The *anzad* typically accompanies traditional panegyric poetry celebrating courtship and, formerly, successful raids.[9] Today, the *anzad* is the principal instrument at evening gatherings called *ahal*. The focal point of the *ahal* usually is a famous female musician, typically noble, who sits on the ground in front of her tent and plays the *anzad*, while a male vocal soloist sings lyrics consisting of love ballads and praise poetry. Among Kel Ewey of the Bagzan area, noble women were strongly discouraged from continuing to play once their children were of marriageable age and they took up *tamghart* (elderly) social status. A traditional *ahal* will include unmarried young men and women, and divorced or widowed women, but no elderly men or marabouts. Guests sit and chat, while listening to the music. Sometimes men may request their respective leaders to put embarrassing questions to the rest of the guests and impose mock penalties on those whose answers are thought lacking in tact or wit. Milk is served at the end of the *ahal*, when resources permit.

At musical performances, noble guests arrive stiffly dressed in their best formal attire. Although musical festivals are held for the purpose of sociability between the sexes, men and women must not publicly show open preference for any one person at the gathering and must maintain the appropriate reserve and decorum. All secular musical festivals take place away from the view of older persons, in particular older men and Islamic scholars. Traditionally, everyone sits in a circle, taking a place according to order of arrival, but with alternation of men and women guests. Intermittently men chant the guttural *t-hum-a-hum*, "which concerns spirits," just as they would during possession rites. In fact, women's musical performance on all such occasions is not considered complete without men's shouts and chants. Here music and free courtship intersect. Poetry during the performance has the primary purpose of winning the favor of the opposite sex through commemorating a momentous heroic deed. Though women play the bowed lute, a male soloist often sings to its accompaniment. The bowed lute itself is often the subject of praise poetry and song. In principle, it is the preferred instrument of the nobility, and nobles described it to me as beautiful and elegant. The bowed lute is yet another symbol bringing together opposites: pleasure, gender roles, illicit love, and prestigious descent.

The *tǝnde* consists of a wooden mortar, which, in non-performance contexts, is used to crush grain, usually millet and occasionally corn. Smiths or women prepare the *tande* for use as a drum by stretching the wet hide of a goat on the mortar to produce a resonant sound. By extension, the term *tande* also refers generically to the festivals during which this instrument is played, of which there are several varieties. The music of the *tande* is believed to have entered Tuareg society more recently than that of the *anzad*, and to have originated in the Tamesna region.[10] Kel Ewey told me that *tande* music is "music of the earth." Until recently, nobles did not play it; rather, they left it to subjugated groups, such as tributaries, smiths, and Buzu ex-slaves. In communities around Mount Bagzan, smiths are the most frequent *tande* players. With the exception of Muslim prayer days and funerals, when only sacred vocal music is allowed, the *tande* predominates at most public events: national state holidays such as Republic day and Independence, rites of passage such as namedays and weddings, secular dancing festivals, and the possession curing rite. In the past, *tande* festivals were also held upon nobles' collection of rent or tithe from sedentary agriculturalists. The drum appears to be connected with two forces: first, with facilitation or brokering of relationships across formalized structure, and the aggregation of disparate forces in Tuareg society in a seemingly relaxed, informal manner; and second, with the reinforcement of a structural agenda of domination and separation based on social stratum, age, and sex.

Tande performances, like *ahal* gatherings and *anzad* concerts, are considered to be excellent opportunities to get acquainted with others. But the former appear less formalized and exclusive; Kel Ewey go uninvited to most *tande* festivals, and the emphasis is on mixing social segments and kinship roles (age groups do not mix, however, because the elderly often keep their distance). At *tande* festivals following nameday and wedding rituals, and at diverse dances, I observed two recurring patterns in the Bagzan region: either women gather at the center around the drum and clap and sing, and men make a circle around them; or blacksmiths form the central circle and perform the drumming and singing. The former predominates at gardening oases; the latter predominates in semi-nomadic herding and caravanning villages. When I inquired about the reason for the latter pattern in Abardak, residents told me that "smiths have to do this, because it is work, and there are so few slaves here." Most women in the oases, they explained, were of slave or mixed origins. Reports of *tande* played by predominantly servile or tributary women in the ethnographic literature corroborate this viewpoint (Card 1981; Borel 1987). Therefore, women and nobles in semi-nomadic herding and caravanning centers still appear to regard playing the

tǝnde with ambivalence, although noble women (but never, to my obser-
vation, noble men) are beginning to perform drumming when slaves or
smiths are absent.

Thus women or smiths dominate the singing on these *tǝnde* occasions,
and men or nobles are obliged to keep a "correct" demeanor, circling
around the women in one type of *tǝnde*, and approaching smiths in a dance
and offering them sugar, tea, and coins at blacksmith performances at the
other type of *tǝnde*. These different types of *tǝnde* festivals are held most
often either in the afternoon or evening, but more rarely in the morning,
since the morning is a time of day set aside for sacred rituals connected with
Islamic prayer and sacrifice. Again, men's shouts (or, at the smith performances, noble men's dances), are considered an integral part of the
instrumentalists' performance. At one woman's *tǝnde* festival I observed,
which was held at the oasis of Auderas during a camel race, women began
the music by gathering around the wooden mortar where two light poles
were attached to the skin, one on either side. At the ends of these two poles,
two women sat facing each other and varied the tone of the drum by resting
more or less of their weight on the poles and more or less of it on their feet,
which touched the ground. The other women sat around the drum in a close
circle, one of them singing verses while others clapped their hands in time
and added their voices in chorus.[11] During this time, men from neighboring
camps and villages dressed in their best clothing, riding on their finest
camels, arrived in groups of two and three. They dismounted and
attempted to sit near the girl of their choice. Kel Ewey told me that any
woman present at that festival must quickly get up and leave if her father,
uncle, or older brother should appear. There was drumming, singing, and
general conversation for several hours. Then the men remounted their
camels, lined up, and paraded on camelback in a circle around the women.
Sometimes, there is further flirting and horseplay, as when a man might
snatch a woman's headscarf.

The camel *tǝnde* (called *tǝnde n emnes*) is usually associated with
weddings of the upper social segments. Both patterns – women singing, or
smiths drumming and singing – predominate in Aïr. But the blacksmith
tǝnde involves praise songs directed at nobles and the obligation of nobles
to give presents to smiths. In Bagzan caravanning communities, where
nobles and smiths form a majority, these smith performances usually follow
babies' namedays, weddings, and state holidays. Traditional noble ambivalence toward playing the *tǝnde* seems to have something to do with its
multifunctionalism, and its handling by non-nobles in manual labor. But,

like the *anzad*, the *tᵊnde* is present at festivals featuring mixed social segments, public display, personal attempts to impress, and desire for positive affect and group support.

From this material, it appears that musical instruments are connected with love, praise, and scorn; prestige and shame; and reward and punishment. There are also hints that musical instruments echo the concealing of one's true sentiments, and that they are linked to worldview as well as to concepts of person and social structural categories. Youths avoid mention of specific musical instruments in the presence of elders, and they also never speak of the Kel Essuf spirits. Refraining from pronouncing these names indicates respect, but also signifies an attempt to control that which is connected with a lack of control. Musical instruments, in particular the *tᵊnde*, are bound up with respect and control, but also with circumventing norms. They are usually structurally opposed to that which is sacred and Islamic. Therefore the sounds (and silences) of possession have connotations extending into social stratum, gender roles, and religion. Musical performance is, in effect, personified and animated, endowed with social, natural, and superhuman qualities defining personhood.[12]

Relevant here are Tuareg notions of cosmology in the intertwining of the spirit world and personal destiny in social life. In the local worldview, concepts of self as "normal" and self as "possessed" are not rigidly dichotomized, but rather are located on a continuum. This is most clearly seen in the overlap of Islam and indigenous beliefs and practices.[13] The continuum includes a heritage of Sufi mysticism; cultural values emphasizing modesty for both sexes; belief in spirits, the devil (*Iblis*), and the soul; and attitudes toward death.[14] A soul (*iman*) is more personalized than spirits in the Tuareg worldview: it is seen as residing within the living individual, except during sleep when it may rise and travel about. The souls of the deceased are free to roam, but usually do so in the vicinity of graves. A dead soul sometimes brings news and, in return, demands a temporary wedding with its client. Hence the theme of human-spirit marriage is linked through the soul, directly mentioned in possession songs.

Iblis is found inside the *anzad* and the *tᵊnde* instruments, both of which are associated with eroticism. *Iblis* is believed to attend nightly festivals and to walk about on Islamic holidays, and is associated with reproductive force. Possession songs never mention *Iblis* directly, but mention the human soul, and all participants state that these songs address or concern spirits. *Iblis* is more overt in the rasping guttural sound men in the audience make, *t-hum-a-hum*, said to "be about" or to "address" spirits and the devil.

Iblis is a tempter who leads humans to sin against God, usually designated by the Arabic term Allah. Kel Ewey conceptualize Allah in terms which conform closely to official Islamic dogma.

Belief in spirits is of both pre-Islamic and Islamic origin. In addition to the Arabic *djinn* (and its derivatives, *djinoun* and *eljenan*), one also hears Kel Essuf and *goumaten*, referring specifically to the people of solitude or the wild. These latter spirits are beings who remain in isolated and deserted places, and who cannot be cured by Koranic verses. The possessed person is referred to either as *gouma* or *a teha essuf*, that is, "being in solitude or the wild." Spirits are generally considered evil, but there are some "white" ones who are seen as less harmful than the "black" or "blue" Kel Essuf. When they attack adults, it is generally in the form of mental illness. In contrast to some other African peoples, Kel Ewey do not personalize these spirits individually. But there are hints that the possessing spirits have a masculine gender, for they "like" women in the way men like women in human society: for their perfume, beauty, fine clothes, etc. Many spirits are subterranean, which corresponds to the cosmology surrounding the *tande* instrument; for example, some spirits inhabit regions beneath sand dunes and are identified with smiths, working on tiny forges and playing tiny drums. The good and bad spirits are also associated with temperature: the good with coolness and water, and the bad with heat and fire. Spirits may compete for people and become jealous of individuals. Some spirits are born as humans and are later transformed into non-humans. Sometimes, humans are believed to acquire status between human and superhuman. Humans can protect against or gain control over spirits through the use of amulets and other protective measures. Some individuals believe in the existence of a guardian angel for the same purpose; marabouts, for instance, told me that each person has an angel on the right and left shoulder, who weigh the relative morality of lifetime deeds. Thus there is a duality and overlap between human and spirit, living and dead, and possessed and non-possessed worlds.

Interrelationships among visual and aural codes of possession

Thus in their visual and aural form, the aesthetic images of sound and solitude provide a channel for the experience of cultural sentiment. Central to this are visions of balance and flexibility, first encountered in the possession tropes, in conversation, decor, and song texts. Symbolic, aural, and visual features of the rite's staging are interwoven to produce positive effect. As indicated by participants in the rituals held for Asalama, Chimo, and Silimana, the drum patterns and accompanying motions of the songs emphasize the balance and flexibility of tree branches such that the songs have a soothing, relieving effect.

Emphasis is placed on the patient's personal reactions to songs. The female singers and men in the audience consider applause and encouragement, particularly the men's shouts made from the throat addressing spirits and the devil, to be an integral part of the songs. A frequent refrain intended to solicit applause is, "This song lacks supporters and so is unripe; and I am an orphan [that is, alone]." Ideally, singers are supposed to distract the patient, and to divert attention away from the body and the illness. A counterpoint exists between images of personal loneliness (orphanhood and unripeness), and the songs' effect of creating a more intimate social atmosphere, which is reinforced by the spatial organization of the rite. Singers and audience huddle closely. Though a small gap is left around the patient and the instrumentalists who sit opposite her, the general effect is of a condensed ritual space. This feature of staging contrasts with the patient's usual solitude and the everyday distance expected of affines, members of different age groups, and people of distinct social strata. The joking and flirting of the audience during all phases of the ritual, and the audience's reactions to the music during and following the ritual, stimulate the expression of social comments and personal sentiments. The staging of possession is a nexus from which different forms of experience and meaning radiate. Factors that divide, differentiate, and stratify the every day Kel Ewey social order are reflected, manipulated, and transformed in the aesthetics of the possession idiom.

6

The *tənde n goumaten* songs

Most songs performed during possession rites consist of poetic verses, recognized and referred to by local residents specifically as *goumaten* songs, although curing performances occasionally borrow songs from other genres, such as those sung at wedding dances. Thus the possession song genre is distinctive, yet flexible. However, Kel Ewey display ambivalent attitudes toward possession songs due to their association with these rites. Men, in particular, regard them with some fear and say they do not like to transcribe them "because these songs address spirits." Possession songs are learned only by women. Often, mothers teach them to their daughters, which reflects to the belief that spirits are inherited from mother to daughter, sometimes through mother's milk. Furthermore, *goumaten* songs are considered very beautiful, and even men who fear them enjoy listening to them both in live performance and on tape. When performed well, residents rank these songs on an aesthetic level of excellence with other sung poetry in local tradition.

In examining the *tənde n goumaten* songs, the primary dilemma is how to organize them most effectively for the purpose of description, explanation, and analysis, and how to represent them undistorted, as conceptualized in the local system of classification. Many, though not all, of the possession songs may be identified by their drum pattern; others may carry a title or name in common illustrating a theme or topic, or sentiment or personal name; still others have no specific title and are not identified with any of the drum pattern names from the set of five prevalent *goumaten* patterns which I encountered. Another method of classification has to do with the songs. The songs consist of sung poetry verses as well as vocables, and possessed individuals indicate non-verbally their approval or rejection of certain songs themselves. Yet the meanings of the verses and their relationship to social context are problematic for two reasons: first, there is much improvisation and poetic license on the part of soloists; and second, although residents insist that it is primarily the drumming that effects the cure by encouraging the patient to dance and to become exhausted, many texts contain praises, personal sentiments, spontaneous jokes, and general social criticism. Moreover, residents also insist that the performance of these songs is an end in itself, rather than only the means, to curing. Perhaps, then, the most useful way to discuss the possession song genre is by relating it to poetry in terms of content, form, style of delivery, rhythm, and instrumental accompaniment.

Types of Tuareg vocal performance

There exist several types of songs among Tuareg: These include: (1) men's vocal music, sung solo a cappella or in duet, with the optional accompaniment of the *anzad* (played by a woman); (2) women's vocal music, with a response chorus and with the optional accompaniment of the *tande* drum (played by a woman); and (3) religious praise singing. Epic songs, love songs, and praise songs may be performed solo, with *anzad* accompaniment, or with *tande* accompaniment. These three song types form categories according to genre, form, style of performance, social segment to which they belong, and circumstances in which they are performed.

Epic poems transmit oral history. Although war chronicles predominate in these epics, they contain frequent metaphorical digressions about lost romantic love, life in settled camps, camels, and cattle. The personal creativity of the reciter or singer is not emphasized, but it is permissible to mix poems, inserting verses borrowed from other authors. In these cases, however, it is obligatory to preserve the metric rhythm, rhyme, and scansion of the poem (and perhaps cite some verses from the original version), all of which mark its warrior and noble origins (Borel 1987: 78). Poems are traditionally inherited, and most are considered the property of various noble groups. A sung version of a poem is called *tesawit tiggat dagh ezele*, which literally means "a poem made into a song." These poems are subject to regional variation of style and mode of expression, and the poetic rhythms (*aggayan*) on which these poems are based must have scansion format.

Typically, each rhythm has a name. The names of the possession rhythms that I collected usually corresponded to events, places, persons, or states of being; only some were titled by their rhythm, and a number of songs either had no title, or the title could not be remembered. Examples of titles from my collection of approximately one hundred possession songs include:

Bilawanin binna (Unripe dates, connoting that the song is not "ripe" because it lacks supporters and participants); *Azel n Madou tan Maman* (Song of Madou composed about Maman); *Tessani* (My liver); *Taraye tetrama* (Route that leads west); *Ninechema imanin* (The sentiments of my soul, and other titles derived from "my soul"); *Assouwe* (Men's dancing well); *Atchalab tchalab* and *Dile dile* (men's dance in which pairs of men approach a chorus of women, and another men's dance characterized by swaying to and fro on the legs). The most popular and recurrent songs named for drum patterns were: *Tan daman* (Something in my soul, which connotes something rare, fleeting, and quickly concluded); *Talawankan* (a rhythm and drum pattern which, like branches of a tree, is swaying, slow, and supple, and is said by residents to convey sadness as well as strength and resilience); *Damisa* (another rhythm and drum pattern, which means leopard or tiger, and which convey length, swiftness, and duration of stamina; this song is usually sung to encourage the person to dance longer); *Idougdougan* (a very rapid rhythm and drum pattern, said to be played in order to make the patient dance very fast and collapse, and thus be cured); and *Idoukal* (Plains of In Gall, described metaphorically in folk etymology as the palm of a hand, alluding to a lover; also a very rapid drum pattern and rhythm).

Possession songs, poetry and instrumental accompaniment
Unlike most epic and praise poetry song verses, verses sung at possession rituals more often refer to the inward and the personal. In this respect, they contrast markedly with the titles and names of rhythms from bodies of songs sung elsewhere, such as those listed by ethnomusicologist Borel.[1] These latter more often refer to external conditions, events of collective history, and features of the natural environment.

Because different poems may be performed to the same rhythm, several possession songs may appear individually, either named or untitled, as well as under a few principal rhythms, drum patterns, and song titles. Significantly, in possession sessions the *tǝnde* drum provides the rhythmic accompaniment to these songs, so in the context of possession, the poetic rhythms also designate the accompanying drum patterns. In non-possession sung poetry, by contrast, the bowed lute provides the melodic accompaniment. Some residents told me that in the past the lute performed this function at possession rather than the drum. But the drum has now replaced the lute in all the local curing rites I witnessed in the Aïr region, although residents do not seem to know how, why, or when this substitution occurred.

Each Tuareg division "owns" a set number of rhythms. In informal conversation, Kel Ewey use the term "rhythme" in French translation to refer to both the rhythm of poetic verses and their accompanying drum pattern. The five principal drum patterns/poem rhythms that predominate among songs performed at Kel Ewey exorcism rituals (*tan daman, damisa, talawankan, idougdougan,* and *idukal*) also served as titles for some songs, and referred to the rhythms of their sung poetic verses. It is unclear how this merging between poetic meter and drum patterns came about. The sung poetry is very ancient, and has its origins in the noble warrior tradition; the percussion instrumental accompaniment, as observed, was introduced more recently into Tuareg culture by former servile peoples from south of the Sahara. The song titles of certain Kel Ewey possession songs seem to have been forgotten altogether, and residents referred to them by themes recurrent in their texts, or by vocables and refrains, such as *golama* (orphan) and *imanin* (my soul).

In Tuareg music, traditionally each poem and song rhythm would correspond to a set melody played on the *anzad*, and would be sung by men. It is interesting, in this regard, that literate Kel Ewey transcribers told me that they viewed current possession music as incomplete or "degenerate," explaining that in the past, possession rituals were accompanied by the *anzad.* Indeed, many residents, particularly nobles, also complained that possession singers today often forget or leave out some original words or verses. Typically, listeners judge each exorcism song according to the intactness of its original poetry. This structural fidelity was held up as the aesthetic ideal, despite the contemporary emphasis upon the drum pattern as the most effective component of the cure, and despite frequent improvisation in actual performance practice. In fact, what some (literate) listeners considered "mistakes" were actually the results of intentional improvisation by the soloists. The social ramifications of this interpretation become significant, especially in view of the unanimous agreement that drumming is the most important part of the curing process today.

Each component of the possession song – drum pattern, context and style or performance, and verse content – merits equal attention. In fact, listeners even considered the informal accompaniment of the audience to be important for the songs to be complete: men's shouts of encouragement, their *t-hum-a-hum* rasping sounds, and their *echikiskiskis* (swishing sounds made with the lips and teeth in accompaniment to the dancing, "to make it prettier"); and women's call-and-response patterns, clapping, and ululating. The images conveyed by sung verses are also valued in and of themselves, as poetry. One text I collected, belonging to the *tan daman* (something in my soul) drum pattern, is considered by residents "one of the best" in its poetry among the sung poems in possession. It is presented here in free translation:

> *Tan daman*
> Follow me in singing
> I am an orphan
> I am a child
> burned by love
> Love in the soul
> That which has left with my soul
> Like milk and water together
> like the taste of salted meat in the mouth
> It arrives in the liver and attaches itself
> like the cushion of a camel saddle
> made of bands stitched closely together
> It glides like water on a smooth rock
> It arrives in the liver, like the well-attached branches of the tent
> It infiltrates like water does the well
> Alas, my soul!
> Oh, my song partners
> Applaud and give rhythm to the song
> Clearly
> The creator who possesses me
> Refresh my liver
> which cannot be refreshed by water
> It must have milk kept
> from the milking of young cows
> from very young cows, of the Sherif [clans who claim descent from the
>   Prophet]
> kept in gourds.

This song, richly evocative with vivid imagery, was performed in October 1983 at a possession ritual in my secondary site of research, a semi-nomadic village about half a mile from my residence, for the wife of a local chief whom I shall call Halima.

Halima was frequently possessed and thus reclusive; even between spirit attacks she remained in her tent most of the time, while her teenage daughter did the cooking and housework. Her husband traveled often and, when at home, was occupied with political and business affairs. Like Asalama, Halima was often described as having a chronic case of depression by local residents. She was often physically ill as well: her general illnesses included fevers, headaches, and bloody noses. Halima was almost always resting in bed in her tent within the walled compound of her husband, the chief of a local clan in this village. Her husband conducted his business and political meetings in his own mud house, and traveled to Agadez on extended visits. Halima had been to the Agadez hospital several times, but the doctor there was unable to diagnose her illnesses. Frequently possessed by spirits, Halima did not participate in many social events and almost never visited anyone outside the immediate household. Although Halima would not speak to people or meet their eyes, she did not seem hostile or averse to visitors, greeting them enthusiastically and indicating loneliness. Her moods would shift from buoyancy to moroseness.

Halima had five living children; two others were deceased. She was of noble origins, and her mother and her husband's father were distant cousins. The immediate circumstance of Halima's first possession was her recent marriage, before the birth of her children. The symptoms were general weakness and respiratory problems. Three rituals were arranged for her by women relatives: two in March 1983, and one in October 1983. Rumor had it that Halima was bothered by the frequent absences of her husband. On my later visit in 1991, Halima continued to sustain intermittent spirit attacks, and still fell ill frequently. During the entire rainy season, she was in bed with colds and bronchial infections. Numerous children ran undisciplined around her home. As Halima was the wife of a chief, her property was jointly owned by her husband, so her rites were held under a canopy within the walls of her compound. Thus there was no need for her to leave home, in contrast to some other patients, who are escorted by close female relatives or friends to the ceremony at the home of a maternal relative, blacksmith, or *tǝnde* player. Halima lived near her maternal aunt, Silimana, the frequently possessed elderly woman encountered in the previous chapter.

The local exegesis of the song text sung for Halima is interesting because of what it suggests about possession songs generally in terms of their origin and form. Songs performed at possession are very old, despite contemporary improvisation and modification through such details as social commentary; in addition, their poetic verse rhythms and drum patterns originally were part of other genres that evolved from the traditional repertoire of sung poetry (in fact, some rhythms and patterns continue to be borrowed from other genres).

Although the *tǝnde* tradition is separate from the *anzad* tradition, some possession songs have emerged from each tradition. It is thus tempting to hypothesize, albeit with caution, that at least some *goumaten* songs may have emerged from a fusion of the noble warrior sung poetry and the non-noble, recently imported, *tǝnde* percussion music and its associated dances, of slave origin. This interpretation makes sense when combined with my previous observations concerning Tuareg music. The rhythm and melody of a given traditional sung poem were probably composed by the same author, although some of the sung poems in Aïr exorcism rituals are anonymous, their authors forgotten or unknown by many local residents, (perhaps because the songs came from adjacent regions). Originally, only *anzad* players had the right to diffuse the rhythm and melody "copyrighted" by the given noble section that owned it, and even then the modification was permitted solely in its instrumental form, without the verses. According to local residents around Mount Bagzan, possession songs do not belong to any particular group today, or perhaps the ownership has been forgotten. But the data above suggest that these songs at one time may have been part of the poetic "property" of various noble divisions.

In this sense, possession aesthetics reflect wider disputes about the "ownership" of meaning, having to do with status and prestige in traditional and changing Kel Ewey Tuareg culture. At least according to the viewpoint of the status quo, these songs have a kind of "renegade" quality. In some respects, their content, form, and performance style are associated with freedom, self-indulgence and subversion of formal institutions of descent and official religion. This rebellious quality can be interpreted as the result of two sources: (1) their former association with traditional poetry, which is why, in current possession contexts, the songs are sometimes considered by local listeners as incomplete or "impure," and divorced from the original "owners"; and (2) their secular subject matter of personal sentiments, such as love, worry, and anger – precisely the symptoms of *tamazai* – and their rumored direction at spirits. Thus the songs are perceived as artistic, but also as coopted or appropriated. Some noble acquaintances, mostly male, even described them as "anti-noble" (in the sense of being appropriated from former, noble copyrighted ownership) and "anti-Islamic" (in their profane rather than sacred subject matter, and in their object of address, that is, spirits).

When asked to identify a particular *goumaten* song, female singers and transcribers in the Aïr region as well as my Tamacheq teacher in Niamey typically responded by giving the name of the rhythm; occasionally, they would give a title independent of the rhythm, such as Song of Madou Composed about Maman, or they would say that the song was unnamed. Possession songs appear to have evolved from a mixed tradition of epic and love poems, melodies and rhythms played on the *anzad*, and *tənde* dance music.

The most important criteria for distinguishing different genres of *tənde* music – such as camel *tənde* wedding songs and *tənde* spirit possession songs – are the distinctive repertoires of struck drum patterns, although there is the occasional "crossing over" of these patterns in the performance of different genres on the same occasion. But when this occurred, listeners could readily identify the original genre. For example, a few possession song rhythms are also heard at weddings. The content and style of the songs are distinguished by subtle markers. In effect, many themes (such as romantic love, descriptive tales, or praises) recur throughout different genres of song. However, in possession songs, there was a marked preference for songs focusing upon personal sentiments, rather than on descriptions of battle exploits or epics praising heroes. Furthermore, it is the singers – above all, young women with "high" voices and "delicate" delivery or expression – who have the most important function in posses-sion singing, for these songs, like most *tənde* songs, must be performed by young women. This requirement, along with the freedom to improvise, makes *tənde n goumaten* songs fundamentally different from other sung traditions. Not only are form and content important, but the performer and consequent style of the song are important as well. In these songs, the female soloist may create and improvise both text and melody according to her choice, and may construct them without constraints (with the exception of rhythm), borrowing texts or portions of texts composed by other singers of the region. This flexibility is the key to the relationship between power and creativity in the *tənde n goumaten* songs.[2]

Let us return to the *Tan daman* song text. The soloists in this *Tan Daman* song, whom I shall call Amina, Tahibout, Hadijatou, Rhaicha, and Dabo, are neighbors of diverse social origins, and all but Rhaicha (whom we encountered earlier, at her cousin's wife's ritual) are considered young women. Dabo is a smith woman. Amina, Tahibout, and Hadijatou are sisters of noble origins, from a family of prominent Islamic scholars.

Amina, a famous singer, and her two sisters Tahibout and Hadijatou come from a household of women who are all renowned for their singing and musical talent, and who have a history of frequent possession. These women seldom go into trance during rituals at which they perform as musicians and singers; rather, their possession has occurred independently, in rituals arranged separately for them as patients. Amina, the eldest daughter, is between thirty and thirty-five years old, and is married to a government functionary, a primary school supervisor, whose salary and pension are high by local standards. Throughout her husband's career, Amina's nuclear household lived during the school year in Hausa towns to the east and south of Aïr, and would spend the rainy season (also the season of frequent weddings and festivals) in Aïr with Amina's maternal family until around 1990, when her husband retired and moved with her permanently to her parents' village. Her husband, Hamid, is an Agadezian Tuareg. The couple are more cosmopolitan than other local residents due to their travels. Her husband is literate in French and some Arabic, and receives a national newspaper in his Agadez post office box.

Amina speaks some Hausa, is used to the ways of the towns and other ethnic groups, and is self-conscious about her cultural and economic differences from others in her village and extended family. For example, she practices household hygiene (such as using soap and covering dishes) and says, ruefully, "rural people don't know cleanliness," and is generous with food and distributes medicine from Agadez. (Indeed, occasionally Amina would offer me presents of meat in secret during my visits, which elicited some embarrassment on my part.) Yet this difference creates some tension between Amina and her mother and sisters. She and Hamid are constantly badgered for food and other items, and while they usually comply with her family's requests as well as the requests of local smiths, they sometimes indicate minor annoyance. She confided to me that she preferred some smiths to others, and rolled her eyes with annoyance, "bracing" herself every time smith women attached to her family came around to her home for the presents they expect from their noble families.

Hamid initially built a mud house for Amina to live in during her visits, located to one side of her mother's compound. When Amina and Hamid returned to take up permanent residence in the village just before my most recent visit in 1991, this household had expanded to include additional buildings enclosed within an elaborate, high mud wall, perched atop a small hill. Indeed, it had become a small fortress, for the couple were among the first to install locks on their doors. By 1991, Amina had given up the traditional women's nomadic tent; an extremely unusual, but not unknown, act in the semi-sedentary villages around Mount Bagzan. Also by 1991, Amina and her husband had started a small boutique on one side of their home. Amina's herds to the south of Mount Bagzan, around Aderbissinat and Tessoua, are under the care of a former slave woman, to whom Amina gives clothing and rights of usufruct.

Amina is greatly admired for her vocal talent; but when residents listen to recordings of her voice, they say that she is "getting on in years" and that her voice, while still attractive, is "becoming older" and no longer has the "youth" and "delicacy" ideal for possession singing. Although Amina was not in trance during Halima's ritual when she sang the *Tan daman* song with the other soloists and chorus, Amina has become possessed in the past.

Amina's first possession occurred before her engagement, during adolescence, near the home of her mother. Her immediate symptoms were a sore neck and the inability to straighten up. Her most recent possession occurred about three years before this ritual, in the early years of her marriage. Generally, however, she considers herself to be in good health, like most members of her family.

Amina is one of five daughters and two sons of Tinjo and Iboua, a prominent marabout. Iboua is often away on pilgrimages to shrines and mosques, and attends conventions of marabouts in Tchirozerine and Tabelot (important Islamic study and prayer centers in Aïr). Like many among Kel Ewey *ineslemen* (Koranic scholars), Iboua is a devout Muslim. *En route* to the conventions held following Ramadan fasts, Iboua told me that he and other scholars adhered to a rule of silence. Yet at other times, Iboua and his family appear outgoing and gregarious. There appears to be no problem with the close association, within a single household, of Islamic scholarship and secular musical performance. Iboua does not appear hostile to his female relatives' musicianship, or to their intermittent possession attacks. Rather, he seems proud of their singing fame (though he does not comment openly on it), and shrugs their possession off with a chuckle.

Members of this household, who claim noble descent but are of mixed origins, are prosperous economically; the two sons work in the garden of the husband of one daughter, Hadijatou, and receive 50 percent of the harvest. Tinjo herself has four camels, fifteen goats, a donkey, and five ewes. She also controls a number of livestock jointly with her newly-married daughters, all of whom except Mina (who lives most of the year in another village about sixty miles away, with her husband who teaches there) continue to reside in her village. In 1983, two of her daughters shared her kitchen and herds during uxorilocal residence and payment of bridewealth. By 1991, only one remaining married daughter, Tahibout, the youngest and latest to marry, had not yet disengaged her herds or kitchen. Tahibout often plays the *asakalabo*, accompanying the choral and solo singing at possession rituals. She gave birth to a son before her husband's return from a trading expedition over the rainy season of 1991. She had hoped he would return for the baby's nameday, but this day came and went, and still her husband had not returned. She became depressed thereafter, remaining inside her tent, either seated or lying down asleep. On my visits, all she was able to tell me was, repeatedly, "Essuf, Susan, Essuf!" (which is the term used for the spirits of solitude or the wild). Tahibout underwent spirit possession curing rites, staged twice during my residence in 1991, in June and July.

In early August, Amina, Tinjo, and Hamid took Tahibout in an agricultural extension truck to the Agadez hospital, where she was given six penicillin shots, along with advice to eat a more varied diet. Hospital personnel had diagnosed that her symptoms were the result of infection and fever following childbirth, as well as a depressed immune system due to poor eating habits. I discussed this diagnosis with her family, and they told me that nothing so far had worked to cure her "spirits." Her secularly educated brother-in-law, Hamid, the retired functionary, insisted that her problem was malnutrition; she "only ate millet." Other members of the household, both male and female, vigorously denied this, still attributing her illness to "essuf," or solitude. Tinjo's daughters married men of contrasting socio-economic, educational, and occupational backgrounds; thus their responses and those of other family members constituted a running commentary on possession, which corresponded to their contrasting situations. After about one month, Tahibout gradually began to feel better, emerged from her tent, dressed and made up with care, and told me her spirit illness "was better." Once again, she began appearing at musical events, either singing or playing the *asakalabo*.

Tahibout's mother, Tinjo, was a popular singer in her youth, and sometimes became possessed as well. She performed at all *tande* festivals, not solely *tande n goumaten* rites. Now all her daughters perform regularly. Amina and Hadijatou are especially renowned as singers. Tinjo regards herself as elderly and as having "many in-laws," so she no longer performs these songs. Tinjo's first possession attack included symptoms of headaches, dizziness, and lack of speech for two days. She was at her mother's home, newly married, and had not yet had any children. Her most recent attack occurred about fifteen years before my residence in the region. She describes spirits as coming with long teeth and big eyes, taking her and swinging her. Generally, however, Tinjo is gregarious and demonstrative, rather than reclusive, and attends many nameday and wedding celebrations. Yet this behavior is not contradictory when it is recalled that Kel Ewey possession may sometimes be brought on by happy events, as when one responds to beautiful music. Although not all singers become possessed, many possessed women are either current or former singers and musicians; and one woman singer told me that her possession occurred on an occasion of joy, when she sang at her son's wedding.

Hadijatou, one of the middle daughters, is married with three children, and is an extremely sought-after singer. Her voice is considered among the most beautiful in the area, and she also tells folk-tales. Hadijatou sometimes taps out the drum patterns of possession songs on the mortar as she pounds millet during•daytime tasks, teaching her baby to clap in time to them. She also brings her baby along to the evening rituals, holding her in a goatskin sling on her shoulder even during singing performances. Yet by 1991, the married couple with whom I resided told me that, since Hadijatou's eldest daughter, now a teenager, had recently married, she now had many in-laws and "had to be careful about this [singing]." Hadijatou seems conscious of this new status and its concomitant reserve relationships: she now covers her mouth with a corner of her headscarf whenever she sings during afternoon (daylight) festivals. However, she has continued to sing at evening possession rites as usual.

I became very friendly with the family of Tinjo and Iboua during 1983, and I often stayed overnight in their home. I developed a particularly close friendship with Hadijatou and Amina. I consulted them about the vocables found at the beginning, middle, and end sections of Tuareg sung poetry. Hadijatou indicated that the vocables serve the purpose of relaxation and diversion. French-speaking informants referred to the vocables as "refrains for the rhythm." According to ethnomusicologist Borel (1987: 90), these sounds also appear in songs outside possession, and in fact throughout Tuareg music, and they serve to even out an otherwise odd number of meters, and to preserve time. The contraction or deletion of syllables also serves this purpose, particularly in *tande n goumaten* song verses, which makes their transcription and translation extremely difficult. Indeed, Tuareg from beyond the Bagzan region, even within Aïr, often had difficulty in this task. Some of these vocables also seem to place emphasis upon the verses following them. The length of sung poetry varies, depending upon content, improvisation, and audience encouragement. I noticed that improvisation and audience encouragement are particularly important in possession songs, and that verse content is often "bent" to accommodate these two elements, rather than vice versa. Soloists sometimes improvise for the purpose of individual commentary, such as insulting a rival, or playfully reproaching the men in the audience for "distracting" women singers.

There does not seem to be a consistent sequence of possession songs. Judging from my total recordings of over fifty possession rituals and approximately one hundred songs, the same rhythms and songs are performed at a number of different possession rituals, but may appear in different order. Alternatively, different patterns may be performed entirely. For example, songs are performed in diverse order according to individual preference, and individuals at different rituals spontaneously select songs from a flexible repertoire. As observed, soloists frequently improvise spontaneously and also "bend" (or in the local viewpoint of some literate listeners, "distort") language to accommodate rhythm and individual whim. Many verses directly address or refer to other singers, musicians, and members of audience. Occasionally, as shown earlier, there is an oblique reference to the woman in trance. Although some songs contain rich poetic verse, praise a loved one, or express critical or satirical social commentary, most appear to subordinate at least some of their content to musical and rhythmic considerations, thereby modifying what many Kel Ewey informants considered the "original" content of poetic song verses. Songs vary in length from a few verses (with many repetitions and mostly vocables) to lengthier works with richly descriptive imagery.

Conclusions

The foregoing material concerning song provides further insights into how the symbolic and aesthetic elements of possession are integrated into the socio-political system. Regardless of the order of the songs, there is a pattern pervasive throughout all spirit possession rituals. First, at the beginning of the rite, the possessed person always lies prone under a blanket. At many rituals, slower-paced songs might be performed during this period; as the songs and drumming quicken and become more elaborate, the patient rises to a sitting position and begins shaking her head from side to side, slowly at first, and then faster and more vigorously. But – and this is the second aspect of the pattern – the possessed person almost always remains seated, facing the drummer and surrounded on one side by the women's chorus and on the other by the general audience. (The sole exceptions I noticed were at Chimo's ritual in the oasis, and at a single rite in the caravanning village of my residence.) Possession songs often last from two to three hours. Alongside them, and sometimes interspersed into their verses, much joking and flirting occur, usually between chorus and audience, which provokes spontaneous, improvised responses to immediate situations and persons present, as well as more generalized commentary.

Thus the meaning of key statements such as "spirits like music and jokes and require them for a cure" can now be connected to features of these sessions, previously analyzed in isolation: (1) themes recurrent throughout the curing songs and their ritual context of performance and interaction; (2) the role of joking, laughter, and horseplay both within the ritual and outside it; (3) the ambivalent attitudes of all Muslim clergy and many noble men toward it; and (4) play and elements of inversion in the song performance in terms of anthropological theories on carnival and jokes as

145

anti-rite. (See in particular Gluckman 1965; Douglas 1975; Handelman 1979, 1990; Turner 1982; Kapferer 1983; and Bakhtin 1960; as well as more recent works on aesthetic style and social resistance by Gadamer 1975, 1986; Hebdigé 1979; Baxandall 1972; and Bristol 1985.)

As Bristol (1985) points out, the problem of meaning cannot be considered independently of the problem of authority. Possession songs are thus troubling and troublesome, in the sense that they represent something more than a system of images and transgressive rhetorical devices, and are more complex than the simplistic opposition of tradition versus subversion. A number of apparent contradictions arise in song themes and their performance. On the surface there is official disapproval from the Muslim clergy of the rites' verse content and performance atmosphere; there are men's assertions that these songs "address spirits or devils" and marabouts' injunctions against praying after these rituals without precautionary ablutions; and there is frequent opposition in verse content between Islamic study and secular *goumaten* songs as "word of the mouth." Yet clergy frequently encourage patients to undergo the curing rite. In fact, although marabouts are not present at the ritual, they indirectly participate and even encourage it by diagnosing for *goumaten* spirits, referring patients to *tande* practitioners when spirits seem to be incurable by Koranic verses and to require beautiful music, songs, and jokes. They also consult with patients during seclusion between spirit possession ceremonies. Furthermore, many songs frequently address God, as well as secular love concerns, and allude to male and female companions in specific role relationships.

Although most songs are secular in their subject matter at first glance, a closer scrutiny reveals that they interweave secular and sacred themes beneath the surface of apparent contradiction and opposition. This combination of secular and sacred raises questions about two anthropological assumptions: (1) the evolving theories in anthropology on possession that derived meaning from possession only in relation to Islam, from early views of the rituals and their spirits as a rebellion against Islam, to more recent perspectives of possession as a "foil" for Islam in Muslim communities (Kennedy 1977; Lewis 1966, 1971, 1986; Boddy 1989); and (2) standard ethnographic portrayals of Tuareg either as devout Muslims (Duveyrier 1864; Nicolas 1950; Norris 1975), or as "lax" about Islam and strongly influenced by pre-Islamic features, in particular matriliny (Nicolaisen 1961; Murphy 1964; Casajus 1987). Dominant themes in verse content and performance with joking and social commentary suggest that, while possession songs may in many respects seem to subvert official structures in Kel Ewey society, they do not completely overturn them or have meaning solely in relation to them. Thus it is more useful to include possession song style in exploring the meaning of the exposed contradictions rather than to focus solely on cause or content alone, and to relate these aspects to wider mazes of conflict surrounding the person and society. Then attention can be redirected toward cultural and symbolic aspects of possession with greater insight, and connected to broader issues in this book.

A number of scholars have opened up new perspectives on possession by focusing upon art and play in ritual performance settings of diverse cultures. Prominent among these ideas is the circular issue of maintaining or overturning structure: whether these performances reinforce structure, as Gluckman (1965) argues; or whether there are alternative interpretations of these performances, but usually as some sort of response to a prior structure (Kapferer 1983; Handelman 1990).[1] Contradictions inherent in Tuareg possession song themes and tropes suggest the issue of maintaining or overturning structure is misleading, or at least incorrectly phrased. For both functions appear to operate simultaneously in the dialogue between verse content and audience ambience. This dialogue provides a battle-ground for ideas, tugging and pulling at defining the terms of existence. Song themes and performance contexts give rise to discourse among major interest groups: between the sexes and social segments, including the Islamic clergy. The song themes, as well as non-verbal visual, aural, and kinesthetic tropes, provide a forum for debate; style becomes the window dressing for larger issues. This debate is apparent in the alternating attitudes of songs between praise and encouragement, on the one hand, and insults and lamentations, on the other. These attitudes or modes of expression connect to major themes addressed in verse content: kinship and other social roles (in particular, female kinship and social class relation-ships among women as well as between men and women); close marriage and orphanhood; references to states of being and parts of the body (including the metaphorical image of spirits mounting the possessed); and cosmological/medicinal aspects of natural vegetation (such as plants and trees). The associations of these images transcend curing in their signifi-cance, and extend into other domains in Tuareg society: namely, marriage and the wedding ritual; notions of love and the institution of courtship; and concepts of reserve and joking in certain relationships, such as those between cross-cousins, between noble and smith, between noble and former slave, and between mother-in-law and son-in-law. These emerge as crucial in the relationship of possession aesthetics to self-definition.

There is a logical fit between the themes and images of performance and the context of the songs. For example, the composition and spatial arrangement of audience and performers are crucial. There is a mixed-sex audience, and yet the chorus is invariably composed of women, and the patient is almost always female. There is a large discrepancy between the ages of audience, musicians, and chorus on the one hand, and that of some patients, on the other: all except the patients must be youthful, and, as observed, if the patient is not an adolescent engaged to marry, she is often an older woman with children of marriageable age. Among Kel Ewey, as pointed out in a song verse, elderly persons normally do not attend musical performances at night, and it follows that most of those present at the curing rite are youthful. Only the *gouma* may be an older woman, well past her childbearing years. Yet songs sometimes mock elderly patients, which brings up a paradox: both sexes may attend the *goumaten* rite, but a man should not be a patient; all ages except the elderly may attend as audience, but older women (defined, among Tuareg, as women with grown children of marriageable age) may attend only as *gouma*. The male audience, in principle, stands far from the female chorus and patient throughout, though in practice a group of young men often forms opposite the singers as the ceremony progresses.

Other features of the dress and movements of the patient also merit attention. Women do not normally carry swords; these are associated with men, as both decorative accessories and protective weapons.[2] The head-band worn by the patient resembles that worn by a young bride during seclusion in her mother's tent. Finally, the head dance of the patient stands in stark contrast to other dances, performed only by men at weddings and namedays, and sometimes on the sidelines during a *goumaten* rite or upon its conclusion.

What is particularly striking about Tuareg possession singing is that it serves as a vehicle for imposing a non-serious, ludic festival or performance frame upon a serious, curing ritual content, thereby enabling the patient to discuss and redefine very serious issues under the cover of multiple frames: illness, cure, and theatrical performance. These multiple frames of reference are necessary in order to save face. The song verse subject matter breaks down, comments upon, and then reconstitutes various gender, kinship, and class roles and relationships in Kel Ewey society. For example, frequent mention is made (in both reference and address) to ties among women and female kinship ("my girlfriends, my women companions, women of my village, female neighbors, neighbors who are also my female kin"), as well as to ties of sexual love outside marriage, which is almost always secret, illicit, forbidden, or unrequited love. The two other most prominent roles mentioned, orphan and twin, also have significance.

Throughout the songs, the phrase "I am an orphan" denotes soloist(s) complaining about the lack of singing and gestural support from chorus and audience on the surface. However, *golama* (orphan) in Tamacheq specifically means "orphaned from one's mother", hence the continuation of the theme of female kinship. Supporting the song implies much more than mere performative excellence and audience enthusiasm; it means moral support and participation in the communication code and its associated program of action.

Female ties have served, among Tuareg, to counterbalance the male bias in Islamic ritual, inheritance, and descent. By participating, performers are brought into the social sphere, thereby furthering this agenda, as well as contributing to the aesthetic goal of beautiful music. This was exemplified in the case of Chimo, the possessed adolescent girl who was comforted by song verses, but was also warned at the same time not to make a fool of herself in her problematic love preference which was opposed, significantly, by her relatives. This warning in effect prepared her psychologically for her eventual arranged marriage to someone other than her secret lover.

The term *inemela*, also frequently heard, refers to partners in a particular form of marriage, in which pairs of brothers are married to pairs of sisters. They are viewed as "twinlike." This is a marriage ideal preferred by mothers who are cousins; many women seek to arrange matrilateral parallel cousin marriage for their children because this keeps bridewealth matters simple and retains property in the family more securely. However, young people scorn men who contract such marriages, viewing them as self-serving and more likely to be loyal to their mothers and sisters, rather than to their wives. Many songs allude to this type of marriage, indirectly and under the cover of Tamacheq terms for friends in the same family, neighbors, or even twins. Significantly, local beliefs place emphasis upon pleasing twins, despite the fact that they place an economic burden upon a semi-nomadic society. Therefore, references to metaphorical as well as kinship twins obliquely articulate a problem in wider society: the divergence between individual (love) preference and economics.

In many verses, there are references to trees: *agar*, *afagag*, and *tiboraq*. An extensive spirit mythology surrounds these trees. The *agar* (*Maerua crassifolia*) is reputed to be the shelter of spirits, and Kel Ewey refuse to rest in its shadow or sleep at its base unless they have given its trunk a few axe blows to make the spirits harmless. They also believe smoke from its wood causes blindness. But its powers may be focused in a positive direction also. A person who has been bitten by a rabid animal should climb the *agar* tree, which must then be chopped down, causing the spirit to leave. The *afagag*

(*Acacia raddiana*) tree forms large, nest-like clumps that Tuareg say hide spirits, for which reason people should avoid sleeping beneath it. The *tiboraq* (*Balanites aegyptiaca*) is also believed at times to shelter spirits. Tuareg fear its ashes and smoke, but also use them as protection against spirits. Tuareg also attribute demonic powers to smiths, who manufacture ladles and axes from its wood.

These trees, all of which are associated with spirits, curing, madness, smiths, danger, and cultural marginality, are also associated with creativity. This connection is seen clearly in the smiths' transformation of these trees from natural to cultural substances. They all have certain features in common: their interiors are difficult to penetrate, and they have a tufted, hirsute appearance, suggesting dangerous powers hiding in their thickness. Song verses, drum patterns, and dance motions also associate spirits with the solitary soul of the afflicted, as well as with the wild zones outside human society. Central to this notion of affliction are the two concepts of the internal soul (*iman*) and the external and remote wild (*essuf*). Many songs begin with the phrase "my soul." Tuareg believe that the soul wanders during dreams, and that its travel to the wilderness desert during possession may result in a change in one's character. Both love and sadness reside in the soul.

The performance context of these themes enables a reframing of personal experience, without necessarily overturning wider power relationships. As shown, rather than displaying reverence toward the affliction and rite, Kel Ewey joke about it and frequent participants in it; they also joke and horse around during the ceremony. As a backdrop to songs, which marshal the structural resources of support for the patient and assert the status and power of various interest groups, the flirting and joking of the audience reconstitute these elements and provide commentary on the serious themes. During the singing there is frequent alternation between serious and non-serious frames. However, it is joking, play, and laughter that predominate. The atmosphere in the audience appears jovial, even raucous, varying from one ceremony to the next. Most people present, with the exception of the patient (who never laughs or jokes in her trance state, in marked contrast to the audience and chorus), engage in horseplay and flirting. The question here is what this contrast means; how the transformation takes place, and what exactly the relationship is between patient as "straightman" and audience and musicians as buffoon, and between both patient and audience as artists in enacting the music, songs, dancing, and supporting roles in shouts, ululating, *t-hum-a-hum*, and applause.

Women known to be frequent patients are considered to overuse the rite, and this is regarded as somewhat shameful, particularly among the nobility. This concept is tied to notions of reserve (*takarakit*) and dignity (*imojar*). The former is associated with certain kin and class roles and relationships, such as those between in-laws, among nobles, and between husband and wife; the latter is an attitude associated with the nobility. Both notions are conceptually opposed to the joking attitudes and relationships (*erawan* or *adelen*) existing between cross-cousins, nobles and smiths, nobles and former slaves, and smiths and former slaves. These relationships are further complicated by symmetry in some and asymmetry in others. The sense of *takarakit*, often translated in the literature as shame, avoidance, or respect, is in my view more accurately conveyed in English as reserve or restraint. *Erawen* is its opposite: a sort of effusive and undisciplined behavior that includes teasing, usually with a familiar attitude verging on insult. These two polarities appear to dominate many relationships in the kinship, age, and gender spheres. The concept of reserve has implications for moral conduct. To say of someone, *Wur ila takarakit* ("He doesn't have any reserve"), is among the worst of insults. In the case of children, this is often heard from adults as a form of reprimand after anti-social acts. It is also used in certain contexts by members of the upper classes to reproach individuals of lower social strata, such as blacksmiths and former servile groups, who, according to popular stereotypes, are deemed to be deficient in reserve. Throughout the possession songs, there is the assertion of power of various interest groups: nobles, warriors, female kin, maternal roles, and official marriage.

The performance context of possession allows the inversion of typical power relationships and roles: for example, affines freely mix together and joke (contrary to their usual conduct of reserve); a patient may indirectly express her love preference; and members of different social segments may flirt who normally would not marry. As shown, in Kel Ewey everyday life and during life crisis rites, there is an alternation between distance and closeness, and between the separation and mixing of these categories of persons. Members of the lower social strata organize and preside over the rite as curing practitioners and musicians, and they are judged most proficient in its aesthetic component by other Tuareg. Members of the upper social strata are frequent patients. Likewise, while the possessed person may sometimes be an older, even postmenopausal woman, only young people sing, play the curing instruments, and attend as audience. In social relationships, then, people in positions of authority are constrained by dignified, reserved behavior in everyday sociability and in sacred ritual. The elderly, the religiously devout, and the upper classes may not do certain things openly, while younger and lower-class persons preside except under the cover of illness. This restriction includes letting off steam, or enjoying emotional, sensual, or artistic expression. Anyone may attend the rite (nobles as well as persons of servile origin. affines as well as cousins, men as well as women), but such free association is usually restricted, or at any rate highly formalized, in other contexts of interaction. Men and women stated that "one reason the rite is held at night is so that persons can see their in-laws there; whereas in daytime, they would be ashamed."

Thus while possession may have a certain subversive intent, it is more than cathartic or manipulative. Of fundamental importance to understanding possession symbolism, as well as its broader context, is the flexibility and consequent reversibility of status within the local social structure, in terms of gender, as well as in kinship and social status over time. Flexibility and reversibility are present not solely within possession, but also outside it in the "normal" state of affairs, between kinspeople and different social strata. Despite clearly defined rules, roles are easily reversed and there are fuzzy pockets of ambiguity in gender, kinship, and class behavior. This gives an odd twist to possession tropes, which, in this light, appear as inversion only on the surface; they produce a doubling of consciousness, alternately inversive and hyperbolic in continual redefinition.

Relevant here are claims invoked by Kel Ewey of either sex and all social segments to define their public personhood: namely, emphasis upon Islam and pastoral nomadism. Men in particular invoke Islam to secure their distinctiveness from women, who otherwise constitute a force to be reckoned with due to their protection by traditional non-Islamic legal devices, such as tent ownership and non-Koranic inheritance. Women invoke pastoral nomadism – for example, in the form of the nomadic tent – to safeguard these devices. It is no accident that both tent-like and warrior-like imagery, and references to both Islam and spirits, permeate the symbolism of the possession repertoire. These references help preserve dominance over, and separation from, other forces that are threatening to personal social identity and resources. Women are key participants in this process of differentiation and definition.

While Tuareg society is distinctly bounded in the use of the Tamacheq language, in other social and cultural features it takes on the aspect of a series of concentric circles, of varying tributary or aristocratic status, with membership in one circle defined in terms relative to another circle. Included in these concentric circles are aggregates of dissimilar peoples, traditionally organized in client–patron relationships on the basis of descent and hereditary, endogamous, occupational specialization. These peoples have been absorbed through kinship as they have been economically exploited. The privileges of noble and smith women, have depended in effect upon the traditional subjugation of slaves of either sex. Varying degrees of servitude and dependency, rather than rigid, "either/or" definitions of status groups, have provided Tuareg with a geographical continuum of resources upon which to fall back in times of drought.

Although the southern Tuareg are primarily pastoral nomads, their economy has always straddled the frontier at the southern edge of the Sahara and Sahel, and they have invested in many forms of trade and production throughout the region. Aïr Tuareg, in particular, have relied on trade with areas centering on Hausa states. Yet this dependency is underplayed in cultural ideology; Aïr Tuareg boast, for example, that they can live on milk for an extended time, only periodically requiring grain to supplement their diet. Young women are encouraged to consume great quantities of milk when there is a sufficient amount of it, in order to promote early fertility, and also to underline the nobility and "purity" of descent that is identified with pastoral lifestyles. Income with which to purchase grain and goods is derived from the sale of animals, through the provision of services dependent upon livestock production, and through involvement in the caravan trade.

For centuries, this has produced two divergent yet mutually dependent effects: it has ensured noble privileges, under which are subsumed more general legal protection for women, such as ownership and inheritance; and at the same time it has enabled former slaves to move into various positions across ethnic and class lines, as resources shrink. Thus, for personal security it is necessary to demonstrate continually how others differ – according to kinship, class, or opposite sex. Men are in danger of becoming woman-like; cousins affine-like; nobles, smiths, and slaves, alike. Thus the possession discourse becomes, not exactly an "alternate discourse" (Boddy 1989; Moore 1990), but one reflecting blurred distinctions and creating new ones. These distinctions are not solely the result of recent diachronic change, but have been present from a period that long antedates Nigerien independence. Possession, essentially an oxymoron, is part of the effort to demarcate boundaries and establish control while seeking individual freedom, and at the same time keeping these strands separate. It is this contradictory, two-fold process that is central to expressing the local construction of personhood, and which permeates images of possession.

In this, the overarching theme of opposition between sound and solitude encapsulates the ironies and contradictions of Tuareg society. Art, power, and affliction intersect with a number of key cultural values that lead to contradictory behavioral expectations. Notions of artistic competence are closely connected with conduct that is permitted or forbidden in other contexts. Nevertheless, the interplay of aesthetic form and intention cannot be reduced to conscious manipulation nor seen as directly causal. The art of possession emerges from, and powerfully negotiates, problematic relationships of social order.

Concluding analysis

The patterning of aesthetics and symbolism in possession embodies and communicates sentiments experienced in other areas of social life. Not surprisingly, Tuareg observations and responses concerning aesthetic forms in curing spirits have analogues in human behavior: aesthetic activity (in making music, singing, and dancing) and the indigenous exegesis of tropes reflect the status of performers and participants, and instruments and styles of expression in possession are linked impressionistically and synesthetically to a multiplicity of statuses in local culture. The aesthetic and symbolic codes in possession connect the event to abstract values as well as to concrete actions. Becoming possessed, or "being in the wild" or "solitude," a core metaphor of aesthetics as well as affliction in Kel Ewey culture, is one way in which creativity is used for social ends. But the reverse is also true: individuals utilize social ends for the sake of creativity. "Being in the wild" or "solitude" is, in essence, being swept away from social convention. Therein resides the power of possession to elicit ambivalent attitudes from individuals responding to it. But the relation between possession, madness, aesthetic creativity, and the intentional practice of social power in this healing drama is complex and consists of permutations rather than simple inversions of social rules. Much of the curing process reforms and constrains the possessed, it is true, by evoking cultural typifications. But the aesthetic satisfaction of curing also supports individual creativity and expression, mitigating the state of "being in the wilderness or solitude."

The role of music and song in possession suggests that the social practice of these rituals is not solely a summation of decisions or a reflection of ideological consensus, but rather the creative ability, defined alternately as affliction and art, to comment on the human condition in ways consistent with socially structured beliefs about personal identity. Sound and motion are powerful vehicles for expressing individual conflict and transformation as well as collective ideology and emotion. The enactment of possession mediates the conflicting definition of self through symbolic forms that place the musical sound of possession in opposition to the desolation of trance.

To Kel Ewey, aesthetically coded spirit affliction evokes dramatic and social response.

The culturally constructed relationships among social categories underlie the expression of sentiment and patterned modes of sound and motion during curing. Social context illuminates the meaning of the possession idiom, but does not explain all aspects of aesthetic style and form. Rather, social context is a shifting framework for the aesthetic and symbolic play of competing viewpoints and knowledge surrounding the construction of self.

Concepts of personhood in female spirit possession cannot be treated in isolation from the overarching concerns that impinge upon gender. The enactment of possession includes some processes of appropriation of the cultural elements defining the person. For example, dress defined as "Tuareg" comes from the Central Sudan: the indigo cloth and swords used in Aïr are identified with Tuareg, and, more precisely, with noble nomadic culture, but many are actually manufactured in Hausa centers. Men and women friends in the caravanning villages and oases of my research told me that Kano, rather than Agadez, is valued as the source of "quality" consumer goods. Cultural events, such as *tande* musical festivals, including the possession rituals, are centered around a drum constructed from a mortar normally used to crush grain, of sub-Saharan origin and associated with domestic servitude.

Tande events are popular entertainment among Kel Ewey of all social segments, and, as shown, women of diverse social origins participate in the cure as patients and as musicians. But nobles insist that "slaves make good drummers, and are better at dancing." Usually, a smith or ex-slave, or, more rarely, a women of any social origin, plays the drum, which is considered central to the cure. Many Kel Ewey nobles, especially men, still feel ashamed to play this instrument, for it is the symbol of sedentary gardening, servitude, manual labor, the earth, and, by extension, subterranean spirits. The *tande* drum stands in sharp contrast to the chief's *ettebel* drum, which may never touch the ground or be touched by members of lower social segments. Yet, as seen, all Kel Ewey, except older male marabouts, eagerly attend *tande* performances, though only women are supposed to perform the head dance and sing the accompanying songs. Thus there is a contradiction between ethnic, class, and gender ideology identifying items with male, noble, nomadic cultural values, and their non-Tuareg economic base and cultural elaboration by women and members of diverse social segments. These items play prominent roles in the specific accessories of the possessed person and in the general symbolism of possession: for example, the indigo cloth for the veil, the sword, and the *tɔnde* drum; and the women's headdress and associated symbolism of head and hair during possession, especially the head dance with its more generalized code or motif of "swaying tree branch."

The person thus appears to be a kind of pivotal point or nexus of competing and sometimes contradictory forces, idealized as a continuum in local conceptualization. In this respect, a more accurate phrase to convey the state of the possessed person might be "contested person." The person as a bundle of contradictions is not the same thing as the person divided or separated into different yet complementary components. The person resides at a kind of crossroads of identity, subject to fission and fusion of conflicting spiritual and social influences, suspended between idealized status, symbol, and power base. Although possessed persons are not necessarily deprived or divided selves all the time, spirits can return at any moment.

The *tɔnde n goumaten* rituals are oxymoronic. Possession involves suffering and requires cure, but Kel Ewey consider persons in contact with superhuman forces to be fortunate and vulnerable at the same time, and regard the possession experience as having a double face, in the same way that ritual devotion may be positive or negative, or both at the same time. Local notions of the *tamazai* depression that often triggers trance, as well as the aesthetics and symbolism of spirit possession, address this transformative dimension of personhood. But the person is elaborated upon rather than changed in the tropes recurring within and outside the possession ritual: in the role of music, song, and dance; in the opposition between sound and solitude; and in ritual reversals and exaggerations. Elaboration also occurs in metacommentary about possession, in local contrasts between "illnesses of the heart and soul" and "illnesses of God." Tuareg spirit possession thus makes a contribution to the need for a cultural theory that considers signs as real, and authority or the last word as open-ended, a theory that resists the tendency to pin down possession in mechanical, unidirectional, and causal explanations.

Curing rituals are never actually concluded, because spirits can always return. This state of affairs thus becomes a discourse; participants and non-participants alike discuss it, and in so doing remove events, objects, and processes from their original context in Kel Ewey culture and society. As Handelman (1990) observes, possession builds, destroys, and resurrects. The event works through contradiction, conflict, and synthesis: through the antithesis of disorder and order, uncertainty and certainty. To change the condition of the patient, the curers toy with the premises of an ordered world. Yet, in my view, all acts are not necessarily equally consequential, and in their web of intent some are, in fact, inconsequential. Among participants and non-participants alike, possession stimulates critiques, but these critiques can differ in outcome; some of them may defer to others. In analyzing them, there are continual replacements of messages without the complete overturning of prior messages.

In spirit possession, the fate of the person, and the prospective reverberations of the various possible outcomes, become subjects for serious comment throughout and outside the rituals. What possessed persons intend as to their own predicament and destiny, and what is actually enacted, become the centerpiece of debate, in which local conceptions of boundaries between public and private aspects of gender, age, and social stratum, and between art, religion, medicine, and science, are constantly under scrutiny. Possession thus illustrates the limits of deconstruction in poststructuralist anthropological theory: the deconstruction of meaning requires the replacement of meaning. The study of possession enables us to elaborate upon the production and reproduction of the culture and anthropology of personhood in contemporary rural Niger.

Notes

Introduction

1 In this I follow Karp (1987, 1989), Karp and Maynard (1983), Kenny (1986), and Boddy (1989) in approaching altered mental states, not as debilitating syndromes, but rather as initiating a creative dialogue.

2 For a more comprehensive discussion of these different levels of analysis, but from a somewhat different theoretical and analytical perspective, see my 1986 PhD dissertation; see also Rasmussen (1987 and 1991b) for discussions of Tuareg women's ritual roles through the life course; and Rasmussen (1989) for Tuareg concepts of health and illness.

3 See, for example, Turner (1982), Handelman (1990), and Schechner (1985).

4 See, for example, Lewis (1966, 1971), Kennedy (1977), Bessmer (1983).

5 For a critical discussion of these problems, see Comaroff (1981, 1985), Boddy (1989), and Stoller (1989).

6 For critical discussions of such emphases see, for example, Lévi-Strauss (1963), Lewis (1966, 1971), Shack (1966), and Curley (1973). See also Karp (1987, 1989) and Rasmussen (1992b).

7 These aspects of possession need not be mutually exclusive, as Karp (1985) and Kenny (1985) have observed in their studies of so-called "culture-bound syndromes". See also Turner (1967, 1974, 1982) and Comaroff (1981, 1985).

8 See Rasmussen (1989: 128) for a discussion of interconnections among anomaly, mental illness, creativity, and constraining knowledge–power systems.

2. Inversion and other tropes in spirit possession rituals

1 This does not completely resolve the issue of whether there is change or reversal, or even, as more recently formulated theories have suggested, "alternate" and "multiple" voices. For despite the escape from circular arguments of "rituals of reversal," there still tend to be assumptions that there is a prior order, against which possession reacts, derives meaning, or, at the very least, is contrasted.

2 In the courting situation, however, the suitor must be gone from the compound of the girl's mother by sunrise the next day, for if he is seen by her mother his act is defined as rape. It is difficult to make conclusions regarding the consequences of rape, because of its allegedly rare occurrence in rural Tuareg communities and the

reluctance of residents to discuss it even hypothetically. Rape is considered extremely shameful to rural Tuareg men. There seem to be parallels here between the idea of the suitor obligated to be gone by sunrise and the end of the possession sequence.

3 See Derrett (1973); Borker (1978); Delaney (1988); Leach (1958); Hallpike (1979); and Drewal (1977). Delaney and Hallpike, for example, interpret the covering or cutting of hair as related to women's subordination and general submission to social control, respectively. Tuareg women are not jural minors, continue to own property after marriage, may initiate divorce, and their worth is based on more than childbearing capacity. Although Tuareg women customarily take up the headscarf upon reaching marriageable age, one sees married women without them, and such women are not, contrary to what Delaney reports about Turkish women (1988: 88), open to sexual advances.

4 In the literature, authors report that masks are depersonalizing, used in social distance and control (Drewal 1977). They convey the idea of power and yet vulnerability. The person is free from the ordinary consequences of his or her personal actions; so masking is a protection. It is like a mouthpiece, seen as an impersonal force. The Western bias sees masking and covering as disguises, but according to the African viewpoint, these types of headdress transform the wearer's identity. There is new meaning created from a coexistence of opposites.

5 Functions suggested are diverse. Duveyrier (1864) hypothesized the hygienic: protecting the eyes from sun, wind, and sand, and the mouth and nose from dehydration. But this explanation does not explain why men remain veiled when in camps or asleep or why women are unveiled. According to Arab travelers, veils mask warriors from their enemies on raids. Arabs also joke disparagingly that Tuareg men veil their faces "to hide their ugliness." Many explanations have touched upon the mouth in one way or another. Gautier (1935) observed that evil spirits enter through the mouth and there are taboos surrounding the mouth. According to Lhote (1944), it is shameful to expose the mouth before women, and these associations are accentuated among the nobility who, being conscious of their elevated social status, regard the taboo concerning the mouth as so important that the veil is never discarded before women, parents, or other respected persons. Lhote thus sees the veil as extending to all respected persons. Yet he admits this does not explain the lack of face-veil among Tuareg women.

6 For a discussion of the use of dance to express tensions between self-control and illicit love, in a different ethnographic context, see Cowan (1990).

3. "Like a tree branch swaying in the wind": the head dance

1 For a fuller discussion of this process in reggae music see Hebdigé (1979: 39–44).

2 Forge (1973: xiv) has argued that there seems little evidence of genuine universal symbols or causal "blueprints" or models in the plastic arts or in any other medium of communication. Although it is obvious that the human body, its parts, and its functions are a source of many powerful symbols in ritual as well as art in most human societies, and that this may provide a basis for cross-cultural impact, the beholder will interpret what he or she sees in terms of one's own cultural symbolism and meaning constructions, which may be very different from the creator's culture.

3 For example, the discussion of the role of dance in the ritual therapy of the Anastenaria of Greece by Danforth (1979), where dance is an expression of the anxiety and tension associated with the conflicts which may have been partially responsible for illness and provides the patient with an opportunity for motor discharge and cathartic relief.

4 Michael Baxandall, in describing fifteenth-century Italian painting, notes interrelationships among social change, quality of material, and quality of skill; he links the general shift away from splendor to social mobility and its problem of dissociating oneself from a flashy new rich (Baxandall 1972: 15).

5 A few scholars (Jean 1909: 236; Rodd 1926; Lhote 1979–80; Tschudi 1952–53; Gabus 1958) have provided some useful documentation on Tuareg art manufacture, performance, and cognitive styles in time and space, but their works tend to be descriptive, isolated from social context. Prussin (1988: 3) links technological styles which characterize nomadic and pastoral architecture to those used to fabricate iconographies.

4. Illnesses of God: personhood, knowledge, and healing

1 I collected the tale entitled "White cow" (*Tas mellet*), from a young married noble woman, daughter of a local chief, with a small child, in a semi-sedentized caravanning village near Mount Bagzan. Although its motif recurs commonly throughout Africa, and even suggests certain features of the perhaps universal "Cinderella" motif, details of its imagery show nonetheless strong Tuareg cultural elements. In particular, the economic rivalry among married sisters and related tensions between mothers, daughters, and the latter's new husbands are central here; these tensions revolve around early groom-service and bridewealth obligations and uxorilocal residence. For a fuller description, see Rasmussen (1987).

2 I collected this tale, again paraphrased here, from a noble man, a semi-sedentized gardener, in a village of diverse social segments, who practiced caravanning, gardening, and livestock herding.

3 For a full discussion of the uses and limitations of the case study method, see Crapanzano and Garrison (1977: Introduction).

4 In his analysis of traditional Western classification schemes used to describe differences between societies, Goody (1977: 12–14) observes that one common theme in differentiating between societies has to do with the contrast between myth and history. Tuareg also make this distinction: myths or folk tales (*imayen*), told predominantly by women, smiths, and children, according to Islamic "dominant discourse" are equated with "lies," and thus involve a backward look at that which is either untrue or unverifiable. In Goody's view, the distinction between *mythos* and *historia* comes into being at a time when alphabetic writing encouraged mankind to set one account of the universe or the pantheon beside another and hence perceive the contradictions that lie between them. From this, he identifies two senses in which the characterization of the "savage mind" as "pre-historical" or atemporal relates to the distinction between literate and preliterate societies. This perspective expands the problem of communication means beyond literacy. In the modern bureaucracy, separation between official duties and personal concern, through written codes of communication, were intrinsic to the development of more wide-ranging, more depersonalized, and more abstract

systems of government. At the same time, the shift from oral intercourse meant assigning less importance to face-to-face contacts, whether in the form of interview or audience, personal service or national festivals, in which renewal of ties of obedience was often as significant as religious rites (Goody 1977: 16). Goody suggests that many aspects of vague Western dichotomies between "primitive" and "advanced" thinking can be related to changes in mode of communication including, but not limited to, various forms of writing. I believe he goes beyond previous approaches by not simply describing the differences, but relating them to a third set of acts, thereby providing some kind of mechanism for differences or changes in mentality assumed to occur. Yet the problem remains: what is the anthropologist to do when she/he encounters similar hierarchies, sequences, and ethnocentric privileging of knowledge systems within a single society?

5 Whatever was put in writing received immense authority. Learning contained in manuscripts surpassed that of any one individual. So this was split into specialisms. It led to "the same split that arts displayed between composers and reciters ... For instance, the difference between physician and magician: the former acts mechanically and by books, the other is a priest, acting through his own religious feelings" (Goody 1977: 130–35).

6 Keenan (1977) and Norris (1972, 1975) have documented how Islamic education entered Tuareg regions through migrations of clans of Koranic scholars and Sufi mystics originally from Tademekket in the Maghreb. In Norris's view, lettered Islamic scholars are similar in some respects to the Murabtin or Zwaya among the Moors, though among Tuareg they do not usually correspond to a coherent class. Only in a few cases do they wield any authority, and while Tuareg nobles respect marabouts for their knowledge of the Koran and their piety, nobles in some regions consider marabouts to be semi-tributary. I found that Kel Ewey attitudes are ambivalent; on the one hand, marabouts enjoy high prestige and also exert significant political influence; on the other, they are subject to obligations to redistribute wealth and are sometimes associated with malevolent rather than beneficial powers (Rasmussen 1992b).

7 Female herbalists (*tinesmegelen*) or "medicine women" usually treat women's and children's stomach ailments. Diviners conduct a type of psychological counseling. For further discussion of these curing practices, see Rasmussen (1991b: 758–59).

8 For a discussion of problems of imposing binary oppositions in symbolism of gender and official and unofficial religion, see Stewart (1991).

5. Sound, solitude, and music

1 This model of structure recalls Giddens' (1979: 28) notion: as "the unintended outcome of the agents' bringing about of effects at the same time as it is the medium through which those effects are achieved."

2 Earlier approaches to aesthetics tend to assume that most forms of aesthetic expression represent a reinforcement of, rather than rebellion or resistance against, the viewpoint of social elites (Merriam 1962; Fraser and Cole 1972; Forge 1973; Fagg 1977). Other approaches link different aesthetic forms to more general forms of symbolic and semiotic expression (Laude 1971, 1973; Calame-Griaule 1957, 1986), designate art as self-evident (Wagner 1986), or provide a

dynamic sense of the musical, visual, and verbal interplay in performance/participation (Schieffelin 1976; Fernandez 1982, 1986; Feld 1982). These latter works make it possible to examine affective phenomena, not in terms of "tug-of-war" between the symbolic and the instrumental, or circular arguments of structure vs. overturning of it, but interpretively as transformations of meaning (Rouch 1978; Lambek 1981; Gibbal 1982; Stoller 1984; Kapferer 1979, 1983), and as a layering of visual and musical images (Schieffelin 1976; Feld 1982).

3 Throughout the nineteenth and early twentieth centuries, slavery was important to pastoralists of noble and tributary social strata. In the 1960s, Oxby reported the occurrence of domestic slave labor in rural areas (Oxby 1978). Baier and Lovejoy (1977: 399) describe how Tuareg took captives when they participated in wars between sedentary states, or during raids on sedentary peoples. Kel Ewey captives were often exchanged for those of Kel Geres to distance them from homelands. Once acquired, slaves became fully assimilated into Tuareg culture, and their status began to evolve. One way this occurred was through kinship analogies and myths emphasizing cooperation and fictive kinship between parties. For example, the Tin Hinan myth of the origin of the noble–slave or client–patron relationship and its feature of tithe, is used to validate a proportion of harvest given by sedentary oasis client populations to nomadic noble sections. Another means of assimilation has been the common practice (particularly among Kel Ewey) of intermarriage between Tuareg men and servile women. I found a few vestiges of usufruct arrangements between former *iklan* and their former masters in some areas of Aïr today.

4 See Keenan (1977) for a description of how the traditional system – noble monopoly over material resources – began to break down, well before the French colonial presence. See Baier and Lovejoy (1977: 399) and Kopytoff and Miers (1977: 46) for documentation of social and economic "loopholes" for social mobility, long present in the desert-edge socio-economic and ecological system. As slaves moved physically away from the core area and went deeper into the Sahel, they moved into a more complex social system: that of the Hausa. Here again, although they were free, they were marginal, and to establish a niche they had to adopt a quasi-ethnic corporate identity, which was defined, ironically, as that of former Tuareg slaves. In other words, their new marginality in more sedentized communities across the Saharan–Sahelian spectrum has been resolved by rooting the new identity in their former marginality in nomadic Tuareg society. This has given substance to the continuation of their clientship to the Tuareg, albeit now symbolic. Moreover, marriages across social strata, while not actively prevented, are considered antisocial; negative sanctions usually take the form of gossip behind the offender's back, or ridicule in poetry and song. These conditions all indicate how easy it is for slaves to rise, and for nobles to fall, in this type of system.

5 The favor was for her cousin, with whom she had a joking relationship; he was the husband of the possessed woman. In recent years, Rhaicha had not usually granted requests to sing at spirit possession or any other public musical event. She had no objections to my recording of her voice, however, once she agreed to give the performance.

6 A recurring issue in Tuareg ethnography has been whether or not, and the extent to which, Tuareg are matrilineal. In matriliny, theoretically, mothers and sisters

of heirs enjoy status. As Oxby (1978) points out, however, the term matriliny presents a problem in that it is used not only to designate certain institutions, but also to characterize entire societies and cultures in general. The variations among different Tuareg divisions are often ignored; thus the issue becomes which kinship links are most important, and what factors other than kinship are important in determining relationships between generations. Nicolaisen (1963), Oxby (1978), and Murphy (1967) favor bilaterality in certain aspects of Tuareg social organization. Others, in particular Casajus (1987), emphasize its matrilineal components, concentrating in particular upon the inheritance form called *elkhabus*. Tribal allegiance, in practice, is expressed through the mother. Ideally, however, political office should go from father to son, except among the Kel Geres, where traditionally it has been transferred from maternal uncle to nephew. Thus both patrilineal and matrilineal ties are important. But there are other important criteria in addition to kinship, such as wealth and personal qualities of leadership. Marriage rules favoring unions between close cousins are the ideal rather than the practice for the majority; for although Aïr Tuareg divisions express a preference for cross- and parallel-cousin marriage, in fact most are married to distantly related or unrelated persons.

7 Nicolaisen (1963) and Murphy (1967) have elaborated on this. The Kel Ewey Tuareg have a system related to that of the Hausa-speaking population of Agadez, and farther south into the Sahel (specifically, the Damagarem region between Zinder and Kano). Kel Ewey terms for brothers and sisters are never used classificatorily. All parallel cousins and cross-cousins are known as *ibobazen*, and children of all cousins are known as *tegaze*, used both for males and females. In contrast to some other Tuareg, Kel Ewey do not make any distinction between parallel- and cross-cousins. Murphy (1967) concludes that endogamy has produced multiple forms of relationship between people and has raised the potential for role conflict, constituting what he terms a "problem," resolved by amorphous features of kinship, including the dropping of collateral names on ascending generations (which made it difficult for both myself and residents to identify second-degree cousins, and nearly impossible to go beyond that), and extremely shallow genealogies, often three or four generations back. On these points, my findings are broadly in agreement with those of Murphy (1967: 167), except that I noticed a general reticence about naming elders and deceased ancestors, particularly on the paternal side; this could influence the results of genealogies as well.

8 Card (1981) and Borel (1987) report that, in some regions where these groups are found, some tributary women have taken it up. I knew one elderly former slave woman in my village of residence, also frequently possessed, who had played the *anzad* during her youth. Thus the class associations of playing this instrument are breaking down somewhat, but its music is still identified with the nobility.

9 According to Lhote (1944: 329), Tuareg women used to inflict punishment on men by refusing to play the *anzad*; so formerly, warriors were motivated to be brave in battles and raids by this music because of the fear that their wives or sweethearts would refuse to perform on this instrument for them if they lost.

10 See Card (1981) and Borel (1987).

11 For a description of the technical aspects of music of the camel *tande*, see Card's ethnomusicological study of Tuareg music: "it has a rapid tempo, and the drum

patterns [are] formed of binary and ternary subdivisions in duple meter," said to imitate the gait of a camel (Card 1981: 6).

12 These associations are further illustrated in a tale collected by Pottier (1947: 213), which speaks of "the sinister sound of the *ettebel* [the chief's drum, which, in contrast to the *tənde*, may never touch the ground] as it announces war"; and further, "Listen! Evil spirits are hidden in the wind which blows, you hear them, with the aid of cymbals [*ganga*, derived from Hausa], beat on the outdoors ... Infernal music!" In another tale collected by the same author, *anzad* music accompanies the ascent of a first-born noble son into heaven, who has been rejected by his father because he does not resemble him physically.

13 Spirits, for example, are mentioned in the Koran.

14 For more detailed description of the devil, see Nicolaisen (1961) and Rasmussen (1991b). Apart from during the *tənde n goumaten* possession ritual, certain persons are believed to have special pacts with the spirits. Their methods of contact require observing strict rules: they must keep themselves very clean, for Kel Essuf detest dirt; they must sacrifice a goat every seven days, for Kel Essuf like blood, and during this sacrifice one cannot pronounce the Muslim "Bissmillah" benediction; and they must not marry without the authorization of their spirits. Pottier (1947) has recorded a tale illustrating the existence of good water djinn, who carry out a protective curse; fire *djinn* are generally evil and destructive, yet these spirits also protect blacksmiths.

6. The *tənde n goumaten* songs

1 The names of possession songs I collected contrast with the titles of songs not sung at possession rituals, listed by ethnomusicologist Borel (1987). For example, *ener* means gazelle; *balla* denotes the surname of Bodal ag Katami, chief of the Kel Denneg between 1820 and 1840; and *shin ziggaren* refers to the battle between Iwillemeden and Kel Geres in 1871 (Borel 1987:79). They also contrast with titles of other non-possession songs I collected in Kel Ewey communities.

2 My terminology here closely parallels the sense in which "power" and "creativity" are used by Arens and Karp (1989).

Conclusions

1 These studies are valuable, however, in demonstrating that ritual and dramatic forms achieve their effects through what Karp (1985) terms "the transformation of the everyday into the extraordinary experience." There is a key to resolving this problem of tending to assume that possession and other rituals derive meaning from reaction to a prior structure. Recent poststructuralist approaches to art, play, ritual, and drama (Lambek 1981; Turner 1982; Kapferer 1983; Karp 1985, 1989; Handelman 1990) enable us to view curing rituals as systems of communication and transformation that identify and elaborate on local typifications of personhood as an expected tendency, rather than focusing on disorder in the sense of a reaction against prior structural constraints.

2 Following this line of reasoning, such masculine accessories as the sword may be viewed as part of the oxymoronic elaboration occurring throughout possession, rather than as an instance of true inversion or reversal. This perspective also opens up additional meanings of such accessories; namely, associations with the noble class, as well as with masculine gender.

References

Arens, W. and Karp, Ivan, eds. 1989. *The Creativity of Power*. Washington, D.C.: Smithsonian Institution Press.

Baier, Stephen and Lovejoy, Paul E. 1977. "The Desert-Side Economy of the Central Sudan." In *The Politics of Natural Disaster*, ed. M.H. Glantz. New York: Praeger, 144–75.

Bakhtin, Mikhael. 1960. *Rabelais and His World*. Trans. Helene Iswolsky, 1984. Bloomington: Indiana University Press.

Barth, Heinrich. 1865. *Travels and Discoveries in North and Central Africa, Being a Journal of an Expedition Undertaken under the Auspices of H.B.M.'s Government in the Years 1849–1855*, London: F. Cass.

Baxandall, Michael. 1972. *Painting and Experience in Fifteenth Century Italy*. Oxford, New York, London: Oxford University Press.

Beidelman, T. O. 1971. *The Translation of Culture*. London: Tavistock Publications Ltd.

1974. "Kaguru Names and Naming," *Journal of Anthropological Research*, 30: 281–92.

1980. "Women and Men in Two East African Societies." In *Explorations in African Systems of Thought*, ed. Charles Bird and Ivan Karp. Bloomington: Indiana University Press.

1986. *Moral Imagination in Kaguru Modes of Thought*. Bloomington: Indiana University Press.

Benjamin, Walter. 1968. *Illuminations*. Trans. Harry Zohn. New York: Harcourt, Brace, and World.

Bessmer, Fremont. 1983. *Horses, Musicians, and Gods*. South Hadley, Massachussetts: Bergen and Garvey.

Biebuyck, Daniel P. and Van den Abeele, Nelly. 1984. *The Power of Headdress: A Cross-Cultural Study of Forms and Functions*. Brussels: Tendi S.A.

Boddy, Janice. 1989. *Wombs and Alien Spirits*. Madison: University of Wisconsin Press.

Borel, Francois. 1987. "Une Tradition orale de classe chez les Touaregs du Niger," *Ethnologica Helvetica*, 11: 77–100.

1988. "Rhythmes de passage chez les Touaregs de l'Azawagh (Niger)." In *Cahiers de musiques traditionnelles (1)*. Geneva: Ateliers d'ethnomusicologie.

Borker, Ruth. 1978. "To Honor Her Head: Hats as a Symbol of Women's Position in Three Evangelical Churches in Edinburgh, Scotland." In *Women in Ritual and Symbolic Roles*, ed. Judith Hoch-Smith and Anita Spring. New York: Plenum Press, 55–72.

Bristol, Michael. 1985. *Carnival and Theatre*. New York: Methuen, Inc.

Calame-Griaule, Geneviève. 1957. *Introduction a l'étude de la musique Africaine*. Paris: Richard-Masse.

1986. *Ethnologie et langage*. Trans. Deidre Lapin, *Words of the Dogon World*. Philadelphia: Institute for the Study of Human Issues.

Card, Caroline. 1981. "Tuareg Music and Social Identity." PhD dissertation. Indiana University.

Casajus, Dominique. 1987. *La Tente dans l'Essuf*. Paris and London: Cambridge University Press.

Comaroff, Jean. 1981. "Healing and Cultural Transformation: The Tswana of Southern Africa." In *Social Science and Medicine*, 15B:3: 367–78.

1985. *Body of Power, Spirit of Resistance*. Chicago: University of Chicago Press.

Cowan, Jane. 1990. *Dance and the Body Politic in Northern Greece*. Princeton: Princeton University Press.

Crapanzano, Vincent and Garrison, Vivian. 1977. *Case Studies in Spirit Possession*. New York: John Wiley.

1980. *Tuhami: Portrait of a Moroccan*. Chicago: University of Chicago Press.

Curley, Richard T. 1973. *Elders, Shades, and Women*. Berkeley: University of California Press.

Danforth, Loring. 1979. "The Role of Dance in the Ritual Therapy of the Anastenaria." *Byzantine and Modern Greek Studies*. 5: 141–63.

Delaney, Carol. 1988. "Mortal Flow: Menstruation in Turkish Village Society." In *Blood Magic: The Anthropology of Menstruation*, ed. Thomas Buckley and Alma Gottleib. Berkeley: University of California Press, 75–94.

Derrett, J. Duncan. 1973. "Religious Hair," *Man: Journal of the Royal Anthropological Institute* 8 (2): 100–103.

Douglas, Mary. 1975. *Implicit Meanings*. London: Routledge and Kegan Paul.

Drewal, Henry. 1977. "Art and the Perception of Women in Yoruba Culture," *Cahiers d'Etudes Africaines* 68: xvii-4, 545–67.

Duveyrier, Henri. 1864. *Exploration de Sahara: Les Touareg du Nord*. Paris: Challamel, Aine.

Fagg, Bernard. 1977. *Nok Terracottas*. Lagos: Ethnographica for the National Museum.

Feld, Steven. 1982. *Sound and Sentiment: Birds, Weeping, Poetics and Song in Kaluli Expression*. Philadelphia: University of Pennsylvania Press.

Fernandez, James. 1982. *Bwiti: An Ethnography of the Religious Imagination in Africa*. Princeton: Princeton University Press.

1986. *Persuasions and Performances: The Play of Tropes in Culture*. Bloomington: Indiana University Press.

Forge, Anthony. 1973. *Primitive Art and Society*. London, New York: Oxford University Press.

Fraser, Douglas and Cole, Herbert. 1972. *African Art and Leadership*. Madison: University of Wisconsin Press.

Gabus, Jean. 1958. *Au Sahara: Arts et Symboles*. Neufchâtel: Musée de Neufchâtel.
Gadamer, Hans-Georg. 1975. *Truth and Method*. Trans. Garrett Barden and John Cumming. New York: Seabury Press.
    1986. *The Relevance of the Beautiful*. Cambridge: Cambridge University Press.
Gautier, E. F. 1935. *Sahara: The Great Desert*. Morningside Heights: Columbia University Press.
Gibbal, Jean-Marie. 1982. *Tambours d'Eau*. Paris: Le Sycomore.
Giddens, Anthony. 1979. *Central Problems in Social Theory: Action, Structure, and Contradiction in Social Analysis*. Berkeley: University of California Press.
Gluckman, Max. 1965. *Politics, Law, and Ritual in Tribal Society*. Oxford: Basil Blackwell.
Goody, Jack. 1977. *The Domestication of the Savage Mind*. London: Cambridge University Press.
Hallpike, C. R. 1979. "Social Hair." In *Reader in Comparative Religion*, ed. W. A. Lessa and E. Z. Vogt. New York: Harper and Row, 99–105.
Handelman, Don. 1979. "Is Naven Ludic?" *Social Analysis* 1 1: 177–92.
    1990. *Models and Mirrors*. Cambridge: Cambridge University Press.
Hebdigé, Dick. 1979. *Subculture: The Meaning of Style*. London: Methuen.
Horton, Robin. 1967. "African Traditional Thought and Western Science," *Africa* 37 (1): 50–71; (2): 155–87.
    1983. "Social Psychologies: African and Western." In Meyer Fortes, ed. *Oedipus and Job in West African Religion*. Cambridge: Cambridge University Press.
Jean, C. 1909. *Les Touareg du Sud-est: L'Air*. Paris: Emile Larose Librairie-Editeur.
Kapferer, Bruce. 1979. "Ritual Process and the Transformation of Context," *Social Analysis* 1: 153–76.
    1983. *A Celebration of Demons*. Bloomington: Indiana University Press.
Karp, Ivan. 1985. "Deconstructing Culture-bound Syndromes," *Social Science and Medicine* 21 (2): 221–28.
    1987. "Laughter at Marriage: Subversion in Performance." In *The Transformation of African Marriage*, ed. D. Parkin and D. Nyamweya. Manchester: Manchester University Press, 137–54.
    1989. "Power and Capacity in Rituals of Possession." In *The Creativity of Power*, eds. W. Arens and Ivan Karp. Washington, D.C.: Smithsonian Institution Press, 91–109.
Karp, Ivan and Maynard, Kent. 1983. "Reading the Nuer." *Current Anthropology* 24 (3): 481–503.
Keenan, Jeremy. 1977. *Tuareg: People of Ahaggar*. London: Allen Lane.
Kennedy, John G. 1977. "Nubian Zar Ceremonies as Psychotherapy." In *Culture, Disease, and Healing*, ed. David Landy. New York: Macmillan Publishing Company Inc., 375–85.
Kenny, Michael. 1985. "Paradise Lost: The Latah Problem Revisited." In *Culture-Bound Syndromes*, ed. Ronald C. Simons and Charles C. Hughes. Dordrecht, Holland: D. Reidel Publishing Company, 63–77.
    1986. *The Passion of Ansel Bourne: Multiple Personality in American Culture*. Washington, D.C.: Smithsonian Institution Press.
Kopytoff, Igor and Miers, Suzanne. 1977. *Slavery in Africa: Historical and Anthropological Perspectives*. Madison: University of Wisconsin Press.
Lambek, Michael. 1981. *Human Spirits: A Cultural Account of Trance in Mayotte*.

Cambridge: Cambridge University Press.

Langer, Suzanne. 1953. *Feeling and Form*. New York: Charles Scribners Sons.

Laude, Jean. 1971. *The Arts of Black Africa*. Trans. Jean Decock. Berkeley: University of California Press.

1973. *African Art of the Dogon: The Myths of the Cliff-Dwellers*. Trans. Joachim Neugroschal. New York: Brooklyn Museum in association with Viking Press.

Leach, Edmond. 1958. "Magical Hair," *Man: Journal of the Royal Anthropological Institute* 68: 147–64.

Leiris, Michael. 1934. *L'Afrique fantôme*. Paris: Gallimard.

1958. *La Possession et ses aspects théatraux chez les Ethiopiens de Gondar*. Paris: Plon.

Lévi-Strauss, Claude. 1963. *Structural Anthropology*. Trans. Claire Jacobson and Brooke Grundfest Schoepf. New York: Basic Books, Inc.

Lewis, I. M. 1966. "Spirit Possession and Deprivation Cults," *Man: Journal of the Royal Anthropological Institute* (1): 306–29.

1971. *Ecstatic Religion*. Harmondsworth: Penguin.

1986. *Religion in Context: Cults and Charisma*. Cambridge: Cambridge University Press.

Lhote, Henri. 1944. *Les Touareg du Hoggar*. Paris: Payot.

1979–80. "Le Vêtement de peau chez les Touaregs. Hypothèse de son origine," *Bulletin d'Archaéologie Marocaine* 12: 323–54.

Merriam, Alan P. 1962. *A Prologue to Study of African Arts*. Ohio: Antioch Press.

Messick, Brinkley. 1987. "Subordinate Discourse: Women, Weaving, and Gender Relations in North Africa," *American Ethnologist* 14 (2): 210–25.

Metraux, Alfred. 1959. *Voudou*. New York: Oxford University Press.

Moore, Henrietta. 1990. *Feminism and Anthropology*. Minneapolis: University of Minnesota Press.

Mudimbe, V. Y. 1986. "African Art as a Question Mark," *African Studies Review* 29 (1): 1–4.

1988. *The Invention of Africa*. Bloomington: Indiana University Press.

Murphy, Robert. 1964. "Social Distance and the Veil," *American Anthropologist* 66: 1257–74.

1967. "Tuareg Kinship." *American Anthropologist* 69: 163–70.

Needham, Rodney, ed. 1973. *Right and Left: Essays on Dual Symbolic Classifications*. Chicago: University of Chicago Press.

Nicolaisen, Johannes. 1957. "Slavery among the Tuareg of the Sahara: a Preliminary Analysis of its Structure," *Kuml*: 91–133.

1961. "L'Essai sur la religion et la magie touarègues," *Folk* 3: 113–60.

1963. *Ecology and Culture of the Pastoral Tuareg*. Copenhagen: Royal Museum.

Nicolas, Francis. 1950. *Tamesna: Les Iwillemeden de l'Ouest*. Paris: Imprimerie Nationale.

Norris, H. T. 1972. *Saharan Myth and Saga*. Oxford: Clarendon Press.

1975. *The Tuareg: Their Islamic Legacy and its Diffusion in the Sahel*. London: Aris and Phillips.

Obeyesekere, Gananath. 1970. "The Idiom of Demonic Possession: A Case Study," *Social Science and Medicine* 4: 97–111.

1981. *Medusa's Hair*. Chicago: University of Chicago Press.

Ong, Aiwa. 1987. *Spirits of Resistance and Capitalist Discipline: Factory Women in Malaysia*. Albany: State University of New York Press.

Oxby, Claire. 1978. "Sexual Division and Slavery in a Tuareg Community." PhD dissertation. London School of Economics.

Pottier, Jeanne. 1947. *Légendes Touaregs*. Paris: Nouvelles Editions Latines.

Prussin, LaBelle. 1988. "The Dynamics of Household Production and Consumption in the Nomadic Context: Studies of Stylistic Variation and Change in the Sedentarization Process," presented at a conference on architecture in Bologna, Italy. Bellogia ms., 1–32.

Rasmussen, Susan J. 1985. "Female Bases of Power in a Tuareg Caravanning Village." *Proceedings of the 11th Annual Third World Conference*, 1: 337–55.

———. 1986. "Gender and Curing in Ritual and Symbol: Women, Possession, and Ageing among the Kel Ewey Tuareg." PhD dissertation, Bloomington: Indiana University.

———. 1987. "Interpreting Androgynous Woman: Female Ageing and Personhood Among the Kel Ewey Tuareg," *Ethnology* 26 (1): 17–30.

———. 1989. "Accounting for Belief: Causation, Misfortune, and Evil in Tuareg Systems of Thought," *Man: Journal of the Royal Anthropological Institute* 24: 124–44.

———. 1990. "Ownership at Issue: Tuareg Myths of Separation and Metaphors of Manipulation," *American Journal of Semiotics* 7 (4): 83–108.

———. 1991a. "Veiled Self, Transparent Meanings: Tuareg Headdress as Social Expression," *Ethnology* 30 (2): 101–17

———. 1991b. "Lack of Pràyer: Ritual Restrictions, Social Experience, and the Anthropology of Menstruation among the Tuareg," *American Ethnologist*, 18 (4): 751–69.

———. 1992. "Reflections on Tamazai, A Tuareg Idiom of Suffering," *Culture, Medicine, and Psychiatry* 16: 337–65.

Rodd, Lord Francis Rennell. 1926. *People of the Veil*. London: Macmillan Anthropological Publications.

Rouch, Jean. 1978. "On the Vicissitudes of the Self: The Possessed Dancer, the Magician, the Sorcerer, the Filmmaker, and the Ethnographer," *Studies in the Anthropology of Visual Communication* 5 (1): 2–8.

Schechner, Richard. 1985. *Between Theatre and Anthropology*. Philadelphia: University of Pennsylvania Press.

Schieffelin, Edward L. 1976. *The Sorrow of the Lonely and the Burning of the Dancers*. New York: St. Martin's Press.

Shack, W. A. 1966. *The Gurage*. London: Oxford University Press.

Stewart, Charles. 1991. *Demons and the Devil: Moral Imagination in Modern Greek Culture*. Princeton: Princeton University Press.

Stoller, Paul. 1984. "Sound in Songhay Cultural Experience," *American Ethnologist* 11 (3): 559–70.

———. 1989. *Fusion of the Worlds: An Ethnography of Possession among the Songhay of Niger*. Chicago: University of Chicago Press.

Tschudi, Yolande. 1952–53. "Quelques Aspects de la Psychologie des Touaregs," *Bulletin de la Société Neuchateloise de Géographie*, tome Ll, fasc. 4: 135–46.

Turner, Victor. 1967. *The Drums of Affliction*. Ithaca: Cornell University Press.

———. 1974. *Dramas, Fields, and Metaphors*. Ithaca: Cornell University Press.

1982. *From Ritual to Theatre: The Human Seriousness of Play*. New York: Performing Arts Journal Publications.

Wagner, Roy. 1986. *Symbols that Stand for Themselves*. Chicago: University of Chicago Press.

Weber, Max. 1958. *The Protestant Ethic and the Spirit of Capitalism*. Trans. Talcott Parsons. New York: Charles Scribners Sons.

Weinsheimer, Joel. 1985. *Gadamer's Hermeneutics: A Reading of* Truth and Method. New Haven: Yale University Press.

Worley, Barbara. 1988. "Bed Posts and Broad Swords: Tuareg Women's Work Parties and the Dialectics of Sexual Conflict." In *Dialectics and Gender: Anthropological Approaches*, ed. Richard Randolph, David M. Schneider, and May N. Diaz. Boulder, Colorado: Westview Press, 273–88.

Index

174   *Index*

history 88–94, 160n–161n
Horton, Robin 90, 92
household 8, 15, 77
  dynamics over time 2, 18, 32, 81
  fission and fusion 52, 79–80, 114
  (see also *eghiwan*; residence)
hyperbole 20–21, 31–33, 37, 152

Iblis 128
ibobazen (*see also* cousins) 163n
Iboua 140, 142
Ibrahim Ihossey ix
idiom 7, 29, 121, 130
idougdougan 133–134
iklan 112, 162n
illnesses vii, 2, 9, 27, 37, 78–83, 95
  mental 1, 11, 84–85, 86–89, 97, 99–100
  physical 13–14, 53, 56, 87, 135
incense 19, 31–32, 34, 49–50
ineslemen 95–97, 140
inheritance 48, 78–80, 114, 152, 163n
insanity 1, 18, 100, 150, 158n
intelligentsia 92–99
intention 6, 154
inversion (*see also* reversal) 20–21, 25, 29–
  35, 57, 145, 152
Islam 8, 98, 102–103, 128, 152
  among Tuareg 146, 161n
  in relation to spirit possession 40, 86,
  146–147, 158n
Islamic 7, 128–129
  attitudes toward possession 5, 11, 26, 98,
  123, 145
  scholars 3, 13–14, 138
  scholarship 88–89
  (see also *ineslemen*; marabouts)
Iwillemeden 26

Jean, C. 160n
jewelry 14–15, 28, 75, 123
  role in Tuareg culture 41, 49, 61, 72, 76,
  112
Johnson, John ix
jokes 28, 46, 132, 145–146
  in Kel Ewey culture 37
  role in possession rituals 5, 16, 32–33,
  123
  (*see also* ludic; play)
joking 33, 47, 53, 63, 115, 117
Judaism 94

Kano 28, 155, 163n
Kapferer, Bruce 31, 146–147, 162n, 164n
Karp, Ivan ix, 158n, 164n
Keenan, Jeremy 42, 111, 161n
Kel Denneg 164n
Kel Eghaser 26–27

Kel Essuf (see also *djinn*; *goumaten*; people
  of solitude or wild; spirits) 2, 129, 164n
Kel Ewey iii, v, 2–3
  history 126, 136–137, 162n
  political organization 119–120
  Tuareg confederation 26
Kel Geres 163n, 164n
Kel Igurmaden 9, 13–14
Kel Nagarou 26–27
Kel Zingifan 99
Kendall, Martha ix
Kennedy, John G. 146
Kenny, Michael 8, 91, 158n
kinship 36, 113–114
  among Kel Ewey Tuareg 48
  and descent 49
  and inheritance 48, 79–80, 114, 152
  and marriage 3, 6, 13–14, 32–34
  and social change 45, 119–120
  and social organization 114–117
knowledge vii, 87–90
  and letigimacy 92
  specialists 93–98
  transfer of 102–106
Kopytoff, Igor 162n
koura 29
Koran 11, 85, 161n
  and healing 85–88
  and literacy 88–98
  and possession rituals 85, 119
  and spirits 11–12, 102–103
  and Talmudic study 94
  men and women in relation to 11, 85
  study of 88–98
  verses from 12, 50
Kraemer, Chris Mullen ix

labor, manual 69, 106, 126–127
Lambek, Michael 164n
Langer, Suzanne 59, 122
Latou 99–100
Laude, Jean 161n
Leach, Edmund 159n
leather 63, 70–72
  and smiths 13, 70
  in gender symbolism 68–69
Leiris, Michel 7
LeVine, Robert ix
Lévi-Strauss, Claude 158n
Lewis, I. M. 40, 86, 158n
Lhote, Henri 159n–160n, 163n
life cycle 53–55
  and changing jural position 48–56, 71
  and vulnerability to spirits 50–53
  phases in 51–52
liminal 51
literacy 91–98, 104, 160n–161n

Cambridge Studies in Social and Cultural Anthropology

Editors: ERNEST GELLNER, JACK GOODY, STEPHEN GUDEMAN, MICHAEL HERZFELD, JONATHAN PARRY

* available in paperback